PALESTINE ONLINE

TRANSNATIONALISM, THE INTERNET AND THE CONSTRUCTION OF IDENTITY

MIRIYAM AOURAGH

I.B. TAURIS
LONDON · NEW YORK

New paperback edition published in 2012 by I.B.Tauris & Co Ltd
6 Salem Road, London W2 4BU
175 Fifth Avenue, New York NY 10010
www.ibtauris.com

Distributed in the United States and Canada Exclusively by Palgrave Macmillan
175 Fifth Avenue, New York NY 10010

First published in hardback in 2011 by I.B.Tauris & Co Ltd

ISBN: 978 1 78076 241 8

A full CIP record for this book is available from the British Library
A full CIP record is available from the Library of Congress

Library of Congress Catalog Card Number: available

Printed and bound by CPI Group (UK) Ltd, Croydon, CR0 4YY

from camera-ready copy edited and supplied by the author

FSC
www.fsc.org
MIX
Paper from responsible sources
FSC® C013604

Miriyam Aouragh is a Rubicon Research Fellow at the Oxford Internet Institute, University of Oxford. She holds a PhD from the University of Amsterdam.

For those Palestinians who, against all odds, continue the struggle.

For Bachir Aouragh who inspired me to question the evident.

CONTENTS

LIST OF ILLUSTRATIONS

LIST OF TABLES

LIST OF ABBREVIATIONS

ABP	Across Borders Project
ADSL	Asymmetric Digital Subscriber Line
APCs	Armoured Personnel Carriers
Arcpa	Arab Resource Centre for Popular Arts
BZU	Birzeit University
CC	Camp Committee
CMC	Computer Mediated Communities
DoP	Declaration of Principles
DPA	Department of Palestinian Affairs
DSP	Digital Solidarity Project
IC	Internet Cafe
ICANN	Internet Corporation for Assigned Names and Numbers
ICT	Internet Communication Technology
IDF	Israeli Defence Force
Int@j	Information Technology Association of Jordan
ISM	International Solidarity Movement
ISOC-P	Internet Society-Palestine Chapter
ISP	Internet Service Provider
IT	Internet Technology
ITSIG	IT Specialist Interest Group
JD	Jordanian Dinar
JITCC	Jordan Information Technology Community Centres Project
JT	Jordan Telecom
LL	Lebanese Lira
OPT	Occupied Palestinian Territories
Oslo	Oslo Peace Process

P@ISP	Palestine @ Information Society Project
Palnet	Palestine Internet Company
PalTel	Palestine Telecommunications Company
PCBS	Palestinian Central Bureau of Statistics
PLO	Palestinian Liberation Organisation
PM	Palestine Monitor
PMC	Palestine Media Centre
PNA	Palestinian National Authority
Reach	Regulatory Framework; Enabling Environment Infrastructure; Advancement Programs; Capital & Finance; Human Resource
UNRWA	United Nations Relief and Work Agency
UPS	Uninterrupted power supply
URL	Uniform Resource Locator
VoIP	Voice over Internet Protocol
WBGZ	West Bank and Gaza
WWW	World Wide Web

NOTE ON TRANSLITERATION

The simplified transliteration system recommended by the International Journal of Middle East Studies is used here. When Arabic terms or names are quoted the '*ayn* is marked by a single open quotation mark and the *hamza*' by a single closed quotation mark. Where there is no single common way for transliterating the names of places into English, such as those of the refugee camps, I have chosen the Levantine (Palestinian) pronunciation. The definite article *al* is applied where this is commonly used in colloquial Arabic.

ACKNOWLEDGMENTS

I am grateful to the many colleagues who helped me through the labyrinthine process of completing my research and writing this book. I wish to extend special thanks to my friends and intellectual sparring partners Nazima Kadir, Marina de Regt, Vazira Zamindar, Anouk de Koning, Andrew Gebhardt, Irfan Ahmad, Malini Sur, Sarah Bracke, Mayida Zaal, Nadia Fadil, Sonja van Wichelen and Marc de Leeuw. I am grateful to Ruya for his unceasing work on the maps and graphs, to Shiar for helping with Arab transliteration, to Mohamad Yekta for his support with the photo material and to Feyzi Ismail and Peter Barnes for editing the manuscript. I am also greatly indebted to Mohammed Waked, Seda Altug and Shifra Kisch for their unconditional support on all these fronts during our time in Amsterdam. The camaraderie of you all was the oasis in an often dry and occasionally hostile academia.

My ideas for this research were formed during talks with Lenie Brouwer; her encouragement laid the foundation of my academic future. The project then really kicked off at the ASSR, with whose generous funding I was able to pursue my ideas. Annelies Moors, Peter van der Veer and Birgit Meyer offered important feedback. Gerd Baumann, Peter Geschiere, Thijl Sunier, Marcel van der Linde and Thomas Blom Hansen made the University of Amsterdam a place where I felt at ease. I am grateful that I.B.Tauris believed in my work and offered me the opportunity to turn the research into a book, and my special thanks to Nicola Denny for having provided such patient and helpful liaison during the final stages of the book.

Throughout the research I often delved into activism, which, given the developments at the time – the al-Aqsa Intifada, the aftermath of 9/11, and the 2006 war on Lebanon – was simply inevitable. Moreover, the rise and death of Pim Fortuyn, the backlash over the murder of Theo van Gogh, and the electoral triumph of Wilders, brought enormous change to the Netherlands. Intensive political engagement was only possible due to the support of my supervisor, Annelies Moors: in her I was blessed, especially in her understanding that at times one has to take a step back to take two steps forward. The organised activism was not a leisure activity – at times it was quite harsh, particularly in a context in which speaking out against the oppression of Palestinians can be linked to anti-Semitism, and when anti-racism is dubbed self-victimisation. In these frantic times, the academic world has been reluctant to take sides. Over the years, many of my fellow activists in these protests taught me that however important it is to study the world, in the way that characterises academia so well, it is also important to (try to) change it. The International Socialists Tendency/IST in Europe and the Middle East in particular provided me with overall political stamina; and, following Gramsci, 'with the pessimism of the intellect and the optimism of the will', I pay tribute to and salute all comrades.

The research about the political implications of the internet continued at University of Oxford; I particularly wish to thank the Oxford Internet Institute and The Middle East Centre, St Antony's College where I completed the final draft of this book. My critical understanding was furthermore greatly improved by valuable feedback from Sam Bahour, Rosemary Sayigh, Elia Zureik, Mike Dahan and Mike Thelwall. I would also like to mention Nancy Lindisfarne and Jonathan Neale, two wonderful academics who welcomed me to Oxford in the warmest and most supportive way, and whose values and activism I greatly respect.

The most important contribution to this book is the multi-sited and grounded ethnography, which would not have been possible without the special support of people in Palestine, Jordan and Lebanon. I thank Fadile Rubaian and Yazan Qurashi in Jordan for their friendship and support. Lebanon would not have been the same without the loving care of my 'families' in the camps, especially Kholoud from Bourj Al Barajne, Dalal and Maryam from Shatila, and Ashraf and Sanaa' Abu Khurj from Nahr al-Bared. I am grateful to Rosemary Sayigh for hosting me in Beirut, and for our many wonderful conversations. I also thank Amal Khoury, Samira and Abu Rabi' Salah, Bissan Tay, Zainab Ghosn and Mansour Aziz. Palestine left the deepest imprint, and is marked by extraordinary experiences. One evening, for instance, my dear friend Rama Ma'ri was preparing to paint our living room 'to make it brighter', when that same evening an Israeli F-16 shook us back to reality. I also thank Karma Abu-Sharif, Rani Shahwan, Reem Fadda,

Naama Farjoun, Trees Kosterman and Ali Zbidat. I especially wish to mention Mohammed Maragha and Hazem Al-Namla, who stood by me all the way – from sharing curfew breakfasts to our political engagement – and along the way teaching me more about Palestinian politics than many of the books I had read.

Neither writing nor political activism is merely a pragmatic exercise; these challenging activities depend on the support of friends and family. I thank Catelijne Houten, Edith van den Akker, Viola Martha, Bart Griffioen, Nordin Dahhan, Hanaa el-Mchrafi, Mirjam Shatanawi, Maurice Crul, Frans Lelie and Abu Zaitun. Despite our many ups and downs, my family were an important pillar. My gratitude goes to Alia Ben-Chaib, Karim and Sara, Hakima and Mo, Farah and Mohammed 'Arbi, Fatima and Nordin, and, natuurlijk, Mohammed Ali. One person connects us all. He was a gastarbeider who struggled to provide us with a better life, including the opportunity to study; but above all he was the best father in the world. There are no words to express my gratitude for your sacrifice. If only you were still here to hear this in person. Gone, but never forgotten.

TIMELINE OF THE INTERNET IN PALESTINE

1996 Telecom investors receive monopoly licence;
Several Palestinian ISPs (PalTel, Palestine Online) start to offer internet connection;
First internet cafes experiment charging 10–15 NIS per hour;
Palestine applies for .ps domain name at ICANN.

1997 Palestinian Telecom sector begin to operate and launch PalTel;
First Palestinian website (Birzeit University);
First Online radio programme from Palestine (OutLoad at BZU).

1999 Arabic Interface websites start (*Maktoob*);
Internet cafes increase, prices drop to 7–8 NIS per hour;
Total (home plus internet cafe access) penetration rate estimate : 3 per cent.

Final phase peace negotiations (Camp David: Arafat, Clinton, Barak);

2000 mIRC chat programme becomes popular in internet cafes;
Arab emailing increases;
Amman-Net website offers radia programmes via Jordan to Palestinian frequency.

Second Intifada breaks out September 29: Bush elected, 9/11, Sharon elected;

2001 Use web-cam and microphone during chat sessions;
ICANN appointed .ps domain name to Palestine.
Internet cafe price-war in the cities, prices drop further to 4 NIS per hour;
Total internet penetration rate estimate: 6 per cent.

2002 Successful Palestinian pubic relations campaigns and websites (Electronic Intifada, Palestine Monitor);
Hamas' Palestine-Info develops into prominent website.

Re-occupation West Bank, closure Gaza; extreme isolation Palestinian territories;

2004 PalTel Introduces 4-digit internet connection servies, bypassing ISPs;
RSS-feeds outdo classic hyperlink reference;
Total internet penetration rate estimate: 20 per cent.

2005 Google enables Arab search tools;
(R)evolution of Palestinian websites; from Homepages to Blogs;
Hamas' Palestine-info grows in popularity, among first with RSS feed;
PalTel home internet connection at 11 per cent.

Hamas wins elections, international boycott, Gaza siege, War against Lebanon;

2007 YouTube and other multimedia video/music programmes popular/used in Arab World;
PalTel penetration rate of home internet connection grows to 18 per cent;
Intensive debates amongst Palestinian political movements via online forums;
Internet activists in Lebanon and Palestine, upsurge bloggers;
Total internet penetration rate estimate: 30 per cent.

War on Gaza Dec 2008; Deteriorating Economy; Deficient infrastructures;

2009 Dual-governments (Fatah-led WB, Hamas-led Gaza), two Ministries of IT;
Google search in Arabic via google.ps and ICANN permits country code '.falasteen';
Rates for Household internet reach 35 per cent; for Mobile phone 50 per cent;
Palestine emerges as one of the region's fastest Social Media adopters.

1

VIRTUAL REALITY FROM BELOW

> They can stop us at checkpoints and borders, but not on the internet.
>
> *Sharif Kanaana, Birzeit–Palestine, 1999.*

On a hot summer afternoon in 1999, Sharif Kanaana and I met in his office at Birzeit University, and reminisced about a previous discussion we had had about the internet. As I brought the subject up again he said: 'The internet is the voice of the voiceless. Palestinians can now share their diaspora experiences through websites and chat rooms.' His striking words summarised my recent experiences. When discussing the impact of the internet[1] with Kanaana and others, the topic seemed euphoric, evoking a sense of excitement: the internet was revolutionary. In the years since then new technological possibilities have indeed revolutionised many aspects of Palestinian communication. Despite some of the obvious cautions – such as ascribing technologic determinist or utopian features to the internet – many enumerate the benefits of the internet for Palestinians. It could help defy the repression of everyday life in Palestine by overcoming the limitations of checkpoints and occupation and thus generate feelings of 'mobility' and 'political autonomy'. Although subsequent assessments of the political and economic potential of the internet have been much more cautious, these effects have led to a crystallisation of the virtual qualities of the internet into new political constructions.

The great enthusiasm for the online possibilities which the internet offers Palestinians reveals essential facts about offline limitations. They remind one that Palestinians do not enjoy political independence, and suggest that 'virtual' spaces provide alternatives to inaccessible offline places. They allude, in other words, to the absence of the independent territory; free access to the very infrastructures necessary for free debate, free mobility, and free democratic decision-making. The conversation with Kanaana in the late 1990s took place at a time when the promises of the Oslo Peace Process (hereafter 'Oslo') were proving increasingly nebulous. Palestinian society was shifting – people were increasingly agitated by a life that was getting worse instead of better, and Oslo had become almost synonymous with despair. Initially, a political implosion was not considered a real possibility, but it gradually felt as though a spark could cause an inferno.

Soon enough this prediction became reality. Only 18 months after that summer chat with Kanaana, what came to be known as the al-Aqsa Intifada dominated Palestinian society. Stone throwing, street clashes, assassinations and F-16 attacks could be seen on television all over the world. Meanwhile, the mainstream Western media propagated a picture of an Israel prepared to make historic offers while Arafat turned his back on the negotiations and incited his people to revolt (Dor 2004). For many viewers it seemed as if a period of 'relative calm' and 'peaceful' negotiations had been unexpectedly interrupted by Palestinian aggression. These oversimplified portrayals could never grasp the complex reality on the ground.

For Palestinians, Oslo did not become a meaningful force for change. The Declaration of Principles (DoP), signed in Washington in 1993 by Arafat and Rabin to seal the Oslo agreement, promised some form of autonomy. But the core issues – refugees, Jerusalem, economic and military self-determination – were not addressed. When Israel was confronted with its promises it refused to abide by even the minimum demands of the agreement.[2] The final spark leading to the uprising was caused by Sharon's provocative visit to the al-Aqsa site.[3]

Meanwhile, in response to immobility and occupation, the internet began to be used. This chapter begins by outlining the confrontations with, and discoveries of, a number of important paradoxes, while studying the implications of the internet among Palestinians. What the multi-sited ethnographies make clear is that Palestine, as one nation, effectively exists in multiple states; it also propagates the narratives of discontent, contrasting the false portrayals. The second part of the chapter discusses the theory and practice involved in tracing the electronic revolution in a Palestinian context. The chapter closes with the challenge of bridging online and offline methodology and the dilemmas involved in practising anthropology 'from below'.

Research under occupation

Just after I had returned from pilot fieldwork in Palestine, on 11 September 2001, a new page in modern Middle Eastern history was turned. Hysteria, fear and disbelief dominated the world, and violence reached new heights a year after the Palestinian Intifada broke out. Over and over again, television screens showed the images of aircraft penetrating the World Trade Centre buildings. Excessive calls and text messages to and from Palestine blocked the mobile network several times. Finally able to connect, conversations that followed echoed the shock; one friend said: 'This is not what we needed. You will see. They will make us pay for this.' In the meantime, news channels showed images of Palestinians cheering, suggesting that people were celebrating the 9/11 attacks. Many similar media items appeared to have been taken out of context and some even fabricated (Langlois 2005). Nevertheless, pro-Israeli spin-doctors found new opportunities: 9/11 would offer the pretext for more repression and stigmatisation of Palestinians.

The subsequent 'War on Terror' allowed for the branding of many political groups in the Middle East as 'terrorist', and soon other governments also used this pretext to blacklist dissident organisations. The fear on the ground was that 9/11 would give the newly elected Israeli Prime Minister, Ariel Sharon, *carte blanche* to crush the Intifada; and this soon became reality. Israel's crackdown on the Palestinian uprising was characterised by levels of violence and blockading not seen before. For many, the peace process has been declared dead ever since. While media attention shifted to New York, Washington, Afghanistan and then Iraq, the collective punishment of Palestinians continued, but often unnoticed. The fusion of the Bush and Sharon doctrines in the years after 2001 represented the systematic destruction of Palestinian livelihoods, albeit with less media coverage. Hence, returning to Palestine to conduct fieldwork in 2002 in the post-9/11 context, I found this new stage of the Intifada marked by closures and curfews.

Curfews have a particularly paralysing effect on society. When Israel applies a military curfew it is targeted at people and institutions, often coming without warning and with enormous consequences. Businesses, government offices, schools, hospitals and pharmacies – all are closed or inaccessible. The total isolation of towns and cities was accomplished by checkpoints and by Israeli jeeps, tanks and armoured personnel carriers (APCs) on the streets, blocking alternative entries and exists. When a curfew is imposed at midday (via loudspeakers instructing everyone to return home), the city soon turns into a ghost town, and families are hardly able to stockpile daily necessities.[4]

This effective house arrest was part of a 'collective punishment' that all residents had to undergo. There was in fact no choice but to accept reality: meetings were often called off and interviews rearranged. It was sometimes possible for us to get supplies from a small neighbouring shop; but to be forced to stay at home caused a sense of claustrophobia and isolation, the only alternative being to watch the news or to call friends to talk about the respective situations. When the curfew was lifted I applied for a home internet connection at a local internet service provider (ISP). Being connected via the internet made an immense difference. If a military attack took place during a curfew, thus visits and sometimes even phone contact is impossible, we surfed the net for the latest news, sent emails, or contacted friends to find out who were amongst the targeted.

Whereas fieldwork illustrated to me the utility and meaning of access to media and communication tools, it also raised new questions. The importance of direct internet access for Palestinians compels us to understand the everyday implications of popular terms such as 'network societies', 'virtual reality' or 'online communities', as embedded in different territorial, historical and political contexts. Multi-site research in specific territorial situations required a mapping of the Palestinian context that takes into account specific local differences.

Rethinking objectives, discovering contradictions

Virtual Palestinian communities lie at a complex intersection between capitalism, technological development, the politics of representation and different modes of governmentality. Not only does internet use reconfigure and strengthen internal Palestinian communications, it also reconstructs these relations *vis-à-vis* global audiences. The internet therefore affects Palestinian self-identity, and the way it is related to and shaped by transnational forces. It is a mediating space through which the Palestinian nation is globally 'imagined' and shaped. This global platform, this 'Palestine Online', gathers together Palestinians from different local and diasporic places.[5] Communities that were traditionally separated by national boundaries and/or travel restrictions have now found new modes of connection via internet interaction. The everyday experiences sketched above fine-tuned the general objective of this research into an examination of different types of imagined Palestinian communities, exploring how they are reconstructed through the internet and examining its role in the creation of transnational links between such communities. The different areas of study central to this research are interrelated in complex ways.

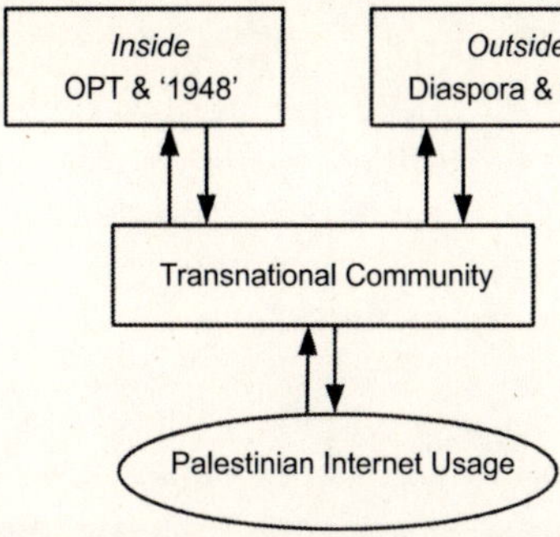

Fig. 1 Schematic diagram of the dialectic relations of the argument.

The research objective was formulated after having been faced with important contradictions between much of the utopian and deterministic euphoria concerning the internet and the everyday contestations of Palestinian life under occupation. Unravelling both online and offline relations in the different fieldwork sites showed both the limits and the potential of internet technology. Locating the research questions within their historical, political and economic contexts indicated several tensions. The first concerns the overrated idea of mobility, as the recurrent myth of globalisation. The world is in constant movement because of migration processes and free-flowing capitalism, and it is generally assumed that transnationalism presupposes more mobility. Fieldwork demonstrates something quite different: the context of the Palestinian diaspora points to immobility and to forced mobility. In other words, place not only matters – it is crucial. Narratives of exile, deportations and occupation in the coming chapters reflect these contradictions. Moreover, problems attempting to cross the border from Jordan into Palestine and being denied entry several times disputes notions of transnational mobility.

Observations and discussions in Palestine and Lebanon led to numerous examples of the immobility and exile with which people were confronted. During an interview in 2002, Samira, from Shatila camp in Beirut, expressed what many felt:

> People want to, but don't believe they can, go back to Palestine. But we should believe it, because if you cut off the hope of returning to Palestine you're nobody: a person without a homeland is like a person without roots.

The internet helped to bridge distances and overcome a sense of isolation. Zena, a 23-year-old student from Bethlehem in Palestine, was one of the lucky few with an internet connection in her home at a time when it was most needed. During an interview in Ramallah in 2001 she gave the following explanation:

> The first two weeks of the Intifada I used to chat extensively. It was very difficult to go to work because they shot people at the checkpoint; I was scared to go out. The meaning of place and time changed a lot; I'm from Bethlehem, which is not far from Ramallah. I used to visit my family every weekend. Now if I want to know how they are or need to assure them I'm OK, I send them an e-mail. When they attacked and reoccupied Bethlehem, I checked many websites and news sources on the net for information and pictures.

The second main tension that was brought to the fore by the fieldwork was the concept of a new, alternative, virtual (i.e. placeless) space. The virtual traversals to and from offline Palestinian cities and villages are often about being in space in search of a place – i.e. strengthening rather than replacing, the strong ideal of an independent territorial state. This apparent tension between space and place is very clear in the diaspora, where most Palestinians are exiled refugees and have never seen their homeland. Palestinian territory is a major feature of everyday social and political life and is commonly mentioned. During an interview in 2003, 16-year-old Shahid from Beirut tried to explain the strong urge he felt to be connected with the land and the people of Palestine: 'When you're cold, you need gloves and when you're sick, medicine, but meeting a Palestinian from Palestine is like meeting your other half, the missing piece of the puzzle.'

This relation between offline and online reality is fundamentally important. Face-to-face contact becomes a fantasy for those who only have the alternative of virtual communication. Dali, from Shatila camp in Beirut, explained during an interview in 2003 how isolation and immobility re-constitute the relevance of place and physical contact:

> You feel like drifting away as if no one's around you in the internet cafe. The only aim is to talk with him [Dali's online friend in Palestine]. But I want to see him, I feel something is missing. I shouldn't make the mistake of talking about love, but just politics and Palestine because it's impossible to meet anyway. It's hard.

Thus the alternative of merely virtual connection with Palestine also has a downside. These tensions – mobility vs immobility and space vs place – are deciphered in Chapters Three and Four, and the everyday, face-to-face implications in Chapter Six.

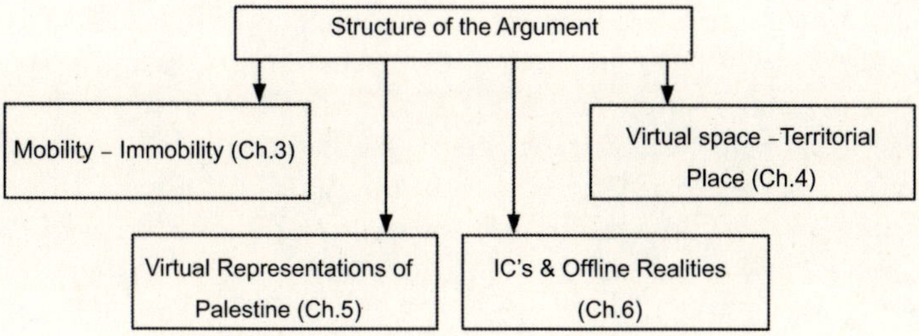

Fig. 2 'Tensions' exemplified by the research.

Delving into the impact of ICT in the various territorial settings of the research showed that localities differed enormously. Overall, refugee camps in Palestine share similarities with but differ from refugee camps in the diaspora. In Palestine itself, the refugees are not 'exiled' – they are not territorial outsiders. Even if they are located in separate sites (such as the Ama'ri or Dheishe camps), they are connected through more or less fluid boundaries. This became more difficult when checkpoints were implemented, dividing the territory into closed, controllable units. Particularly at the time that access to and from Nablus and Jenin was becoming increasingly problematic, and the wall severely restricting movement by cutting into east Jerusalem and blocking Qalqilia.

As for Gaza, it was basically cut into three parts by military borders, with catastrophic results. Gaza is much smaller than the West Bank, comprising only one-sixth of the occupied areas, but it is inhabited by one-third of the OPT population. With more than one million people, of whom a large majority are refugees, in approximately two square kilometres, it has one of the highest population densities in the world. Whereas Gaza is more impoverished, and effectively sealed off like an open-air prison, tanks and soldiers cannot go in or out at will. The Israeli army has used the dense geography as a pretext for massive air attacks on Gaza, culminating in June 2006 and December 2008.[6]

The specific location of a camp can result in more casualties. Many protests take place near camps that lie at the entrance of cities and towns. Young people clash with the army by throwing stones and rolling burning car tyres, aimed at jeeps and tanks entering the built-up areas. Many children and teenagers from the nearby camps join in these activities. Besides higher casualties, this has also meant that people in the camps often fall victim to acts of retaliation from the Israeli army.

In this context, the services of the United Nations Relief and Work Agency (UNRWA) mean the difference between survival and collapse for most camp dwellers; but UNRWA is poorly resourced and barely able to deal with current realities in Palestinian refugee camps – basic services have decreased while need in the camps has grown. Funded by the United Nations, UNRWA has been compromised by the UN's increasing loss of independence.[7] It is therefore more difficult to be a refugee in a host country than in Palestine. As mentioned, when surrounding towns are relatively accessible it means less segregation between Palestinians from camps and the cities and towns. This is clearly more the case in Palestine than in Lebanon or Jordan. What this comes down to is that the Palestinian nation is hosted in different states and thus faces different challenges. These debates call for taking a step back to question the often-mentioned idea of the 'Palestinian nation'.

One nation, multiple states

It is important to include in the analyses the differences inside the Occupied Territories as mentioned above. There are also differences between those 'inside', in the occupied territories and Israel, and 'outside', in the diaspora. The colonialist segregation and military occupation in Palestine, the particular experience of the PLO during Black September in Jordan, the Israeli invasions and civil war in Lebanon in the 1980s, and the overcrowded and poorly maintained refugee camps (and social discrimination) all represent important markers of difference within the Palestinian nation.

Geographical separations are manifest on several levels: Palestine vs diaspora; camp vs non-camp; central vs remote settings. The distance between the (capital) cities and the camps potentially strengthens the segregation or sense of isolation. Al-Bekaa camp in north-eastern Jordan or the Nahr al-Bared camp in northern Lebanon, for instance, are greatly isolated by distance and by military checkpoints.[8] When a camp is located in a capital city such as Amman or Beirut, especially when working-class suburbs have expanded to incorporate it, it becomes part of a city's social and political life. While a camp in Beirut or Amman could be visited while still leaving time for other activities the same day, a visit to Bourj al-Shamali in the south or Nahr al-Bared in the north of Lebanon was a far more difficult undertaking. Long taxi journeys from the nearest city (Tripoli or Sour, respectively) were necessary, via separate roads that at times included military posts; these everyday political realities shape our understanding of (the making of) nation states. The different impacts of internet communication technology (ICT) access and its use between countries in the diaspora and within a country may vary considerably.

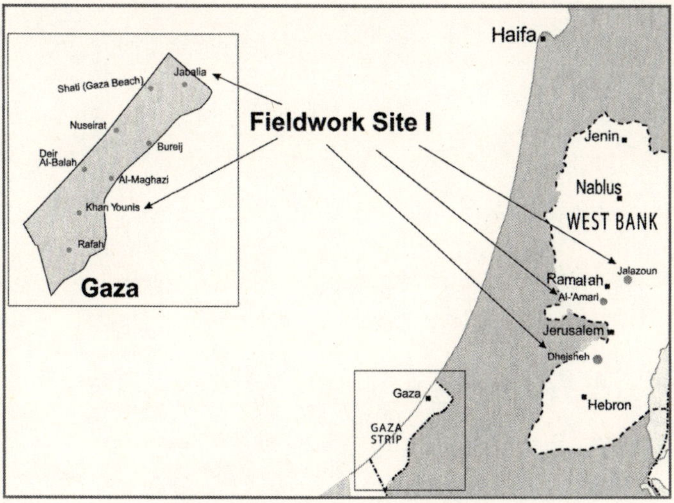

Fig. 3 Fieldwork site I – Palestine

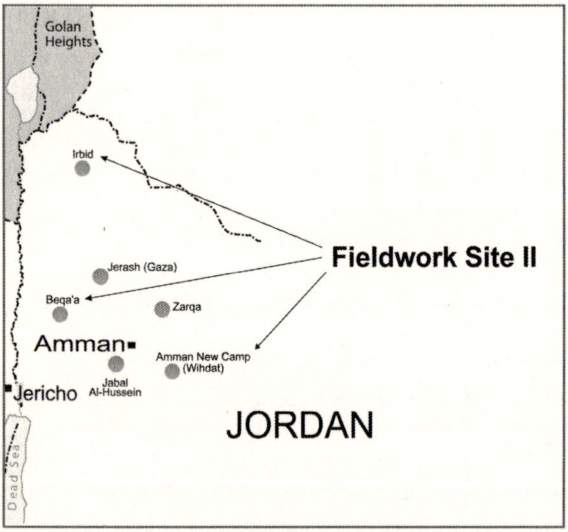

Fig. 4 Fieldwork site II – Jordan

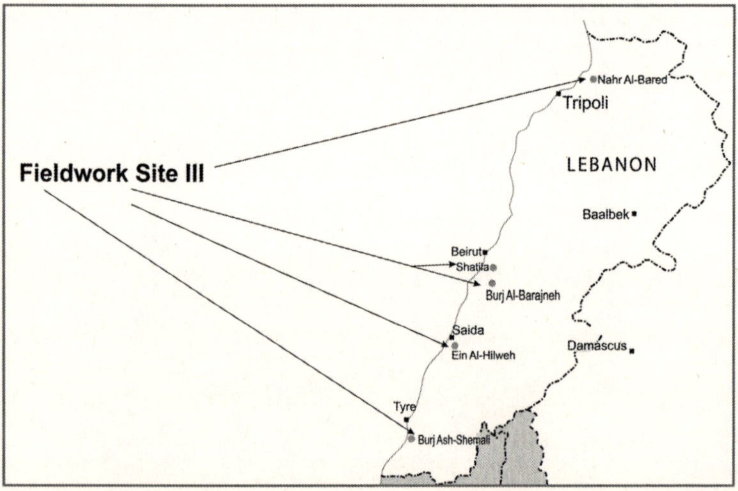

Fig. 5 Fieldwork site III – Lebanon

Nation states are undoubtedly affected by the impact of long-distance social networks, global corporate capitalism, international social movements and diasporic communities. ICT itself is shaped by the transformation from political economy to transnational systems. But the concept of transnationalism is ambiguous, representing both emancipating and hegemonic dispositions. Smith and Guarnizo in *Transnationalism from Below* explain how transnational processes can be studied through the prism of the local, national and global. Transnationalism is characterised by the intersection of migratory processes, global capitalism and technological revolution (1998: 17–24). This 'intersectionality' of the concept of transnationalism confirms that transnational identity does not imply more mobility for all. As Eagleton notes, the problem is that 'the rich have mobility while the poor have locality', and 'the poor have locality' only 'until the rich get their hands on it' (2004: 22).

This analysis partly echoes the debate concerning shifts from modern, i.e. 'outdated' nation states, to postmodern communities. The argument, infused by the contributions of Giddens (Vertovec 1999), claims a shift from 'modern' nationalism to 'postmodern' transnationalism, leading to the loss of national sovereignty and nation-state power. Appadurai observes that communication through electronic media has led to the formation of 'communities of sentiment' (1996: 8). Furthermore, the nation is also considered in competition with the state.

However, mobility or transnationalism has not led to the irrelevance of the state, nor to a decrease in the value of national identity. While acknowledging the importance of continuously adapting a notion such as the nation state, to treat it as an outdated concept is to throw the baby out with the bath-water, by giving in to the postmodern view that the state is a redundant concept. Are (emotional) power and (political) sovereignty of nation-states as such decreasing? The (direct) wars in Iraq and Afghanistan abroad, and the (indirect) attacks on civil liberties at home, illustrate how states exercise their power in the name of the nation. This tendency further contributes to the politics of coercion: 9/11 led not only to more policing of citizens, but also to a further increase in nationalism and Islamophobia (Fekete 2006, 2009).

The failure to mould nations into a single nationalist state does not mean that states stopped monopolising the required vehicles. Baumann argues that the military, the education system and the media are merged in the nation-state ideology. They continue to animate the imagined ideals, mobilised through expressions of ethnic superiority and national canons. State policies derived from the nation-state logic certainly exist, as Baumann argues:

> Populism, xenophobia and radical exclusion sealed this wholesale abandonment of political, civic, and civil values in the face of globalization. At present, the state is again being peddled, by losers and demagogues, as one nation, as if the state were an ethno-national organism; the nation is peddled as one culture, as if citizenship were a matter of culture; and culture is reduced to birth or descent (2007: 9).

Though the state is far from dead – protagonists of capitalist globalisation need the nation state to manage the international market –culturally homogenous nation states exist only in textbooks, in manuals for the military and in the media (ibid: 5). These processes stir common understandings of the relation between the nation, the state and identity, and question whether there can be other understandings of nation-making.

Xenophobia is a reminder of the oppressive, top-down reality of the nation-state. This does not mean that notions of the nation or statehood are useless. Diasporic and oppressed communities ascribe (strong) meaning to nationally-inspired frameworks, because beside the top-down character of the nation state there also exist bottom-up processes of state-building inspired by progressive national identification. National identity is particularly strong in non-state 'contested' groups (Eriksen 1993). As one of the largest and longest-lasting stateless communities in the world, Palestinians in particular hold strongly to their national identity. They and other exiled, 'imagined' communities function as 'proto-nations'. These 'new' mediations are also supported by certain imagining of geographical values, for instance experienced during territorial traversal by colonial administrators in the Americas, the carriers of modern nation-states, and novels and newspapers further shape the national identities (Anderson 1991). Though very rich and crucial references, such European colonial histories also represent a dominant impact on the understanding of national imaginations and nation-state building. How can we examine national identity in alternative ways, i.e. different from the birth of modern capitalist nation states to help reformulate 'imagined community' from a colonial context? This can be achieved by looking at examples of state-building based on anti-slavery and anti-colonial motives or of national identity associated with anti-colonial struggles.

C.L.R. James' narrative (1980) of the San Domingo revolution is a historical masterpiece and one of the most inspiring of such accounts when Toussaint L'Ouverture and his combatants broke the chains of colonial slavery and brought an end to an improbable chapter in colonial history. But James's study also shows that the Haitian revolution established one of the first independent nation states in modern times. Although close in time to the French and American revolutions, Haiti is rarely referred to in the literature dealing with the birth of (imagined) nation states. In fact, of the three, this was the only revolution that enforced the principle of unconditionally affirming the inalienable rights of all humans (Hallward 2004). Rather than nationalism motivated by colour, descent or competition, here membership was based on a history shared by oppression and resistance. This dynamic completely redefines the concepts of nation and state, showing a unique, inspiring, alternative framework:

> The odds [the Haitian revolution] had to overcome are evidence of the magnitude of the interests that were involved. The transformation of slaves ... into a people able to organise themselves and defeat the most powerful European nations of their day, is one of the great epics of revolutionary struggle and achievement (James 1980: iix).

Merely two years after the French revolution, the San Domingo revolution in 1791 lasted 12 years, until the defeat of Bonaparte's expedition in 1803 resulted in the establishment of 'the first Negro State of Haiti' (ibid: ix).

History forms a crucial backdrop to this research also because the challenge of multi-sited research is to understand the local and historical differences. The importance of the internet in Palestine is clearest when the historical background of the diaspora is addressed.

Narratives of discontent

The partitioning of India and Pakistan in 1947, apartheid in South Africa after 1948 and the occupation of Palestine in the same year are related, because they illustrate a post-WWII time frame of territorial fragmentation as a central component of colonial rule. Geographical partition and imperialism also inspired new articulations of 'nation' and 'community'. This context redefined the relationship between national identity, the (colonial) nation state, and a shared, imagined, collective narrative. The case of Palestine is particularly difficult: facing occupation and exile at the same time, Palestine can best be described as a nation without a state.

This succession of events caused major changes in the self-consciousness of the Palestinians (Khalidi 1997: 159). Self- and group-identity is shaped by people's histories, not least as victims of oppression and/or as participants in resistance. Even though it was prohibited to express Palestinian identity in whatever form, whether local or national, manifest or latent, such claims to a national identity did not disappear; on the contrary, they were preserved and politicised, particularly in the refugee camps and occupied cities. One of the clearest illustrations of the indomitable claims of identity are the incessant references to belonging to a certain village or house, even though it might have been destroyed or taken over by Israeli families. Fourth-generation refugee-camp children perceive themselves as being from Jaffa or Haifa, making the local attachments regardless of time and space. Understanding the concept of collective identity, whether online or offline, demands study of the history of the Palestinian people. Grasping the relevance of the internet, as a social-political alternative that fuels these sentiments, therefore relies on pointing out historical roots. To know the needs of the present and to remember the losses of the past, the impact of Zionism must be heard. In fact, according to Edward Said, understanding Zionism is crucial: without it the current human and political crises cannot be comprehended:

> [T]he question of Zionism is the touchstone of contemporary political judgement. A lot of people who are happy to attack Apartheid or U.S. intervention in Central America are not prepared to talk about Zionism and what it has done to the Palestinians. To be the victim of a victim does present quite unusual difficulties. For if you are trying to deal with the classic victim of all time – the Jews and his or her movement – then to portray yourself as the victim of the Jew is a comedy worthy of one of your own novels ... [I]f you say anything at all, as an Arab from a Muslim culture, you are seen to be joining classical European or Western anti-Semitism. It has become absolutely necessary, therefore, to concentrate on the particular history and context of Zionism in discussing what it represents for the Palestinians (1994: 121).

Although data is available through UNRWA, and the consequences have been further analysed (cf. Sayigh 1979, Zureik 1994, Takkenberg 1998), the number of Palestinians that were forced to leave and become stateless is subject to a recurrent debate. Predisposed chronologies, in general, overlook the fact that the birth of Israel was conceived on a land already inhabited by a people. The first part of this section counters this hegemonic narrative; such narratives are dominant and these, unsurprisingly, coincide with ideological frameworks which also shape the mass media. The second part of this section reviews how false political agreements and false media portrayals feed on one another.

In defence of history

The making of the Israeli state was based on Zionist nationalist ideology. In 1897, Theodor Herzl adopted Zangwill's famous dictum: 'The problem of Zionism is one of means of transport: there are a people without a land and a land without a people.' Long after Herzl, such notions recurred. Israeli Prime Minister Golda Meir stated in a Sunday Times interview on 15 June 1969:

> There were no such thing as Palestinians. When were there an independent Palestinian people with a Palestinian state? It was either southern Syria before the First World War, and then it was a Palestine including Jordan. It was not as though there were a Palestinian people in Palestine considering itself as a Palestinian people and we came and threw them out and took their country away from them. They did not exist.[9]

Such colonial views were repeated over and again and became tolerated in much Western history. Shohat (1989) demonstrates how Zionism in practice meant the overall exclusion of Palestinians from land, employment and politics.

After the British colonial army succeeded in crushing the first general Palestinian uprising of 1936, the UK's Peel Commission of 1937 suggested partitioning Palestine between a Jewish and an Arab state, while retaining a British Mandate area. Palestinians inevitably rejected this, and more revolts broke out (Takkenberg 1998: 9). These 'diplomatic' partition schemes were followed by UN Resolution 181 in 1947. The partition plan granted Jews in Palestine sovereignty over 56 per cent of the territory, at a time when they owned less than 7 per cent of the land and constituted less than one-third of the population: it thereby violated the most important UN principle – self-determination.

Most Palestinians were left to fend for themselves. Between August and the end of 1948 the majority fled. People from the north of Palestine fled northwards to Syria and Lebanon, those from Beersheba and some from Jaffa southwards into the Gaza Strip, and those from Ramleh and Jerusalem and others from Jaffa towards the West Bank and Jordan (Takkenberg 1998: 14). Apart from administrative resolutions granting Palestinians the right to self-determination and a return to their homeland, neither the UN nor any other international institution pressured Israel to bear responsibility and to abide by the conventions that offered justice to the Palestinians. Meanwhile Palestinian attempts to return were prevented by violence, giving Israel the chance to establish irreversible facts on the ground. This continued until the Palestinian refugee issue had become a *de facto* reality, and it was too late to be reversed – the politics of the *fait accompli*. Palestinians were simply banned from returning to their homes.

Palestinians had to flee to allow for the foundation of a new nation state, based not on citizenship but on the claimed superiority of one ethnicity and religion over another. While a new nation was being built, Palestine fell apart, becoming largely a nation of displaced refugees. The reasons Palestinians fled their villages in 1948 were largely covered up and denied for decades. But since the 1980s, Israeli historians have 'rewritten' this history from an unusually critical perspective. Morris was one of the first Israeli historians, in his Birth of the Palestinian Refugee Problem (1988), to chronicle in detail the terror and ethnic cleansing that drove three-quarters of the Palestinian population from their homes in 1948. As the myth that they fled under the orders of Arab leaders has now also been refuted by Israeli scholars, this has become a more common framework. Pappé (1988, 2006) illustrates incessantly that the primary causes were armed attacks on Palestinian villages, the latter's very weak military capacity compared to the British-backed Zionist armed forces, and lacking Arab unity in the then recently carved-up Middle East. The Zionist movement, and later the state of Israel, forced on the Palestinians a double migration: first, through a massive displacement out of their territory, and secondly through the arrival of large groups of settlers to replace the Palestinians (Safieh 1997: 6). In 1967, after inflicting a major military defeat on Egypt, Syria and Jordan, Israel occupied the West Bank, East Jerusalem and what remained of Gaza. Today, many decades later, three million

Palestinians live in the occupied West Bank and Gaza, more than one million Palestinians live within the (pre-1948) borders of Israel, and a majority of the remaining four-and-a-half million exiled Palestinians are scattered around refugee camps throughout the Arab world. The UN was forced to guarantee basic care for Palestinian refugees under UN General Assembly Resolution 302 of 8 December 1949. Its objective, carried out by UNRWA, was to prevent starvation and conditions of distress, mainly in order to maintain political stability.

Much of Palestinian life was determined by a military occupation which took increasingly violent forms. Kimmerling (1993) described Israeli policies towards Palestinians as one of the 'stick' and the 'carrot', but in the 1980s military rule became a stick far more than a carrot. In 1985 the 'Iron Fist' policy was introduced by then-Prime Minister Yitzhak Rabin, with the aim of breaking Palestinian national aspirations: resistance was to be discouraged by any means necessary, for instance by 'bone-breaking' methods.[10] But the Palestinian population was changing as well: it was no longer the passive or traumatised generation of 1948. Teachers, trade unions, women's movements, student unions, self-governing community projects and a variety of political parties had become rooted in society. The social structure of such grassroots movements played a crucial role in the formation of broad-based resistance (Hiltermann 1992). This happened against the backdrop of the PLO's defeat in 1982, which resulted in a relocation of the political centre from Beirut to the OPT.

From the 1970s onwards, West-Bankers and Gazans began to demonstrate in solidarity with Palestinians inside the 1948 borders, also known as 'Israeli Arabs'. Palestinians adopted the common hymn *Biladi, Biladi* ['my country, my country'] and a literature of resistance flourished (Kimmerling 1993: 254). Higher-education institutions such as Birzeit University, where left-nationalist students led the councils, were deeply involved in the Intifada. Student activism helped bridge divisions between rural and urban Palestinians, and prevented Israeli efforts to purchase land from farmers (ibid: 255). The outbreak of the Intifada on 9 December 1987 was a major turning-point in Palestinians' collective consciousness; and for the first time their perceptions of the conflict with Israel received a hearing by Western public opinion. For many around the world the First Intifada was an eye-opener, in that it helped to characterise Palestinians as an oppressed people.

Due to the collapse of the Soviet bloc and the start of the 'new world order', initiated by the US war against Iraq in 1991, Palestinians were forced into negotiations and agreements. Their struggle shifted from the streets to Hilton hotels. The 1991 meetings in Madrid and the official negotiations in Oslo, brokered by the US, aimed to present a solution to the Middle East conflict. All this gave Arafat an air of credibility: he was accepted as a negotiating partner, and given a measure of authority. Yet since the Palestinian territories remained colonised, and the existing Palestinian political leadership could only operate on a symbolic or very local level, this authority was soon politically insignificant, while the political and economic situation steadily deteriorated. The peace process caused broad resentment because it was based on false promises; these, and the resentment they caused, were portrayed in equally one-sided ways.

False promises, false portrayals

The period between the start of the First and Second Intifadas (1987–91 and 2000–04 respectively) is crucial, as it marks major transformations in the structures of national liberation. Hassan describes how the PLO, in the years between 1982 (the expulsion from Lebanon) and 1993 (as the PNA) abandoned 'the politics of resistance' and embraced the 'politics of appeasement'. The major problem was that its shift in strategy was predominantly defined by US interests (2003: 1) with the result that Israel retained its control of Palestinian territory (albeit under a Palestinian flag), and completely ignored the right of return for refugees. Arafat was pulled into a full and final settlement, but since Oslo did not fundamentally change anything, this had serious consequences. In fact, according to Perry Anderson:

> After eight years, the IDF remains in complete control of 60 per cent of the West Bank, and 'joint' control of another 27 per cent; a network of Israeli-only roads built on confiscated land divides and encircles the residual enclaves under Palestinian authority; the number of Jewish settlers, who monopolise 80 per cent of all water in the occupied territories, has virtually doubled; the per capita income of Palestinians fell by one quarter in the first five years after the Accords (2001b: 18).

Offering Arafat partial and symbolic independence meant abandoning any pretence of a return to the pre-1967 borders. The pressure continued as US President Clinton sought a settlement before the end of his term. The myth of a historic agreement during the Camp David meeting in July 2000 was sold by using misleading words such as 'generous' and by referring to '90 per cent of the land': misleading because it actually meant 90 per cent of only 22 per cent of historic Palestine, i.e. of the West Bank and Gaza, themselves divided by Israeli by-pass roads or settlements. Palestinians were, in other words, offered a non-viable Bantu state if they gave up their rights as refugees and their (symbolic) claims to Jerusalem. Popular opposition to what was seen as 'surrender' meant that Arafat was trapped. The illusion of a 'just peace' in the context of Oslo had vanished: Palestinians refused the dictates (Anderson 2001b: 19). Meanwhile the US exchanged its president for George W. Bush, and Sharon made a provocative visit to the al-Haram al-Sharif (the holy al-Aqsa site) in Jerusalem. Taking these events into account, the eruption of a popular uprising was hardly surprising. On 29 September 2000, immediately after Sharon's intercession and as a new generation stepped forward, the Intifada exploded in the streets, refugee camps and university campuses.

The different forms of resistance comprised a myriad of factions. Young stone-throwers in the clashes mostly hailed from among the poor and from refugee camps, while militant groups formed around the youth movements of political parties. The Intifada was made up of NGOs, secularists, Islamists and a growing number of international activists, such as the International Solidarity Movement (ISM), and soon it became a global struggle. Massive protests occurred in the Maghreb and Machrek: three million Moroccans flooded the streets of Rabat, Cairo had its own 'Tahrir Intifada', and there were even demonstrations in the usually apolitical Gulf states. Outbursts of anger were seen across Asia too, and solidarity with Palestinians emerged in the US and Europe and were adopted by the growing anti-war movements. Edward Said succinctly captured the shift in political activism:

> A turning point in the Arab history has been reached and for this the Intifada is a significant marker. For not only is it an anti-colonial rebellion of the kinds that we have seen periodically in Setif, Sharpville, Soweto and elsewhere, it is another example of the general discontent with the post Cold War order displayed in events of Seattle and Prague (2001: 30).[11]

However, unlike 1987 this Intifada took shape in a radically different context – that of a post-Cold War, post-Oslo and soon to be post-9/11 Middle East. Unemployment rocketed, and studying or working abroad became nearly impossible. With the drastic changes in the global balance of forces, with the PLO politically almost castrated, and Bush's War on Terror as the new imperial framework, the uprising was met with a response that was bloodier than ever. These changes are also important in understanding the differences between the First and Second Intifada. In 1987, the Intifada introduced a unique style of rebellion, combining characteristics of a non-violent movement with that of a national liberation struggle. Civil disobedience was an overall strategy by which various committees could challenge the Israeli colonial administration. Underground school systems and medical teams were set up, Israeli products were boycotted, and there were many cases of tax rebellions and strikes (Hiltermann 1992); the strategy also meant that large numbers of people participated. During the First Intifada, Palestinian resistance had been organised through direct (albeit underground) grassroots resistance. This proved to be no guarantee of avoiding ruthless oppression – killing, torture and prolonged detention – which had a damaging effect. The regional impact of the 1991 Gulf War weakened Palestinian morale even further.

The return of the PLO leadership to Palestine after Oslo also had significant consequences for grassroots campaigns and peoples' participation. Top-down centralisation limited the space for popular resistance from below (Andoni 2001). The Oslo interim agreement created a different environment, into which the Second Intifada was born. The PNA's partial control over some territorial areas and the fact of its monopoly of armed forces created a divide-and-rule situation on-the-ground. The militarisation of selective factions not only stalled a mass movement, it also allowed Israel to use its full military arsenal, and the presence of PNA armed security forces essentially allowed Israel to portray the conflict as a war 'between states'. The consequences were far worse than even the most violent reactions to earlier uprisings. The use of F-16s, the bombardment of civilian areas, with tanks shelling towns, the use of cluster bombs and of illegal chemicals such as white phosphorous, worsened the type of injuries and led to high casualty tolls.

In these highly contested political contexts the effects of new media and communication over the internet are more crucial. This requires a deconstruction of the underlying dominant frameworks linking theory about ICT, globalisation and mass media with the practice of occupation, exile and capitalism.

Theory *and* practice

> How could it be that this shrinking, splitting and boxing is related in any way whatsoever to the West dropping bombs on this or that part of the developing world? ... Could there be a connection between such a marginal aspect of our experience in the media and the structures of the media themselves? And is there anything linking all this to the forms and content of the media and the meanings they generate? (Wayne 2003: 1)

The logic of global capitalism reshaped our communication styles (Featherstone 1995; Kellner 1998). The potential of the internet soon became a central feature of the globalisation 'discourse', and intersected with the 'new world order' paradigm. The magic of globalisation narratives represented utopian idealisations that were often out of touch with reality. For Fukuyama (1992) and Friedman (1999), globalisation marked the triumph of capitalism and the market economy. Huntington (1996) even went so far as to stress a definitive 'clash of civilisations' between the civil West and the uncivil rest. This peculiar view arose from a preceding utopian idiom: the magic of 'postmodernism'. The discourses on globalisation and the new world order were accompanied by exciting stories about the internet creating gender equality, increasing economic development and even alleviating poverty. Via globalisation, the impact of new technologies thus merged with theoretical postmodern articulations of life in 'virtual reality'.

According to Baudrillard (1994), for instance, as technology enters every aspect of life, social environments occur like a 'simulation'; to take this further they create a society of 'post-human' species. The implosion of technologies was even seen as replacing political economy (Kellner 2002: 287). These and other accompanying texts were not only often dystopian, they were also highly philosophical. Besides the problem of clarity, postmodern theorists, for Eagleton:

> reject totalities, universal values, grand historical narratives, solid foundations to human existence, and the possibility of objective knowledge. Postmodernity is sceptical of truth, unity and progress, opposes what it sees as elitism in culture, tends towards cultural

> relativism, and celebrates pluralism, discontinuity and heterogeneity (2004: 13).

The appropriation of terminology from different academic fields and from literary and science-fiction genres has led to the widespread use of jargon, resulting in a variety of terms used simultaneously (Wilson and Peterson 2002: 452). Contrary to abstract metaphysical narratives (often using different terminology for the same ideas) grounded assessment of globalisation as the cause and effect of a restructured capitalism and technologic developments, avoids over-pessimistic or over-optimistic claims.

According to Carey (2005: 446), much of the initial, first-generation literature on the internet lacked a historical perspective with which to compare it with other media's and technologies. In what can be called the 'second-generation' analyses of the implications of the internet, many have toned down the earlier alarmist or dreamy analyses. Empirical studies show that virtual spaces and communication are not mysterious or frightening, such as Wellman and Haythornthwaite's The Internet in Everyday Life (2002) and Nunes' (2006) Cyberspaces of Everyday Life (2006). Dahhan (2003) argues that Palestinians find themselves between a rock and a hard place: discrimination of Palestinians in the Jewish state of Israel is echoed in the framework of 'computer-mediated communities' (CMCs) and ICTs.

In his influential *Information Age trilogy* (1996–98) and *Internet Galaxy* (2001) Castells' argues that societies rely on the interface between the global and the local, and that there is a relation between the virtual space of flows and the territorial space of places. Thus the emergence of network societies stems from the combined effect of technological development, economic globalisation and cultural transnationalism. Although Castells emphasises the dialectic relation, his contribution did inspire new notions of post-state networked communities.

Rather than the postmodern perception of nation states being replaced by 'non' or 'post' state networks, nations are still and more than ever entangled in political, social and economic power – global capitalism and its transnational enterprises are extremely well protected by states. Thus new technologies are not autonomous forces that themselves generate new societies, but are part of a global restructuring of capitalism not necessarily distinct from previous modes of social organisation (Kellner 2002: 289).[12] In fact, the nation-state as an outdated concept is nonsensical in the particular case of Palestine.

What often lacks is a conceptual understanding that integrates a political-economy view (for instance that the internet is a powerful capitalist commodity) as well as acknowledging the internet's value and contribution to grassroots social capital. Whereas the internet emphasises the interrelationship between society and the public sphere, the important question becomes how access to it transforms the (global) public sphere. The first part of this section takes up the critical assessment of the evolution of electronic media, which directly relates to the important queries posed by Wayne in the quotation at the head of this section, where he relates the shrinking, splitting and boxing of end credits in the film and television sector to international political economy. The purpose is to link politics with the new media, and in due course to elucidate the progressive as well as oppressive characteristics of 'globalisation'. Furthermore, such a link would explain how traditional media overlap with but differ from the electronic media with regard to national/collective identity and belonging, and how the electronic media function within broader politico-economic contexts, as the second part of this section shows.

Tracing and framing the electronic revolution

Rather than coming from nowhere, the internet is constituted by power relations and is historically and socially constructed (Franklin 2004). How does it generate new national, religious or political expressions and shape new collective imaginations, and how does it create the possibilities for (individual) grassroots access to the media? These questions account for the transnational context in researching a nation such as Palestine. Understanding how the media represent and transform society means placing them in a historical framework. A rich body of work critically analysing the emancipating or hegemonising potential of technology and the media dates back to the German Frankfurt School in the 1940s and the British cultural studies in the 1960s and 1970s and much of the early work in feminist and postcolonial studies, particularly those influenced by critical Marxist analyses. Groundbreaking contributions by Raymond Williams and later by Stuart Hall had a defining impact.[13] McLuhan's equally groundbreaking work showed the symbiotic relationship between a particular medium and the message, expressed in the phrase he coined 'the medium is the message', and in the distinction between the so-called 'hot' and 'cold' media when reconstituting various media forms. Hot media, such as print, have low levels of participation but a high level of information content. Conversely, cold media, such as the telephone, have strong participation levels but weaker information intensity.

The internet is a special product of the development of the 'electronic revolution', and reconstitutes the meaning of place, space, time and the public sphere. The mass media are dialectically related to the public sphere – a juxtaposition that has been deconstructed incessantly by Habermas (1989). The critical public sphere declined as electronic media became a field of consumption, promoting competition rather than content. Unlike the hot face-to-face media, symbolised by an ideal of the salon or coffee-house, the new development of cold media (television, radio) excluded the possibility of talking back or taking part. This process, in time, transformed communication from collectivised to individualised relations: people were turned into, and regarded as, a receiving public. Interaction between the public and the private was transformed; the public was privatised and the private commercialised. This transformation related to broader shifts of modernity. As Stevenson has argued: 'The transition to electronic communication can be connected with a change in the experiential nature of modernity' (1995: 119). The aim is to connect this larger shift, and the development of the internet, to the question of national communities.

Anderson's *Imagined Communities* (1983, 1991) offers a framework which connects the media, nation state and identity. National communities are, at least partly, imagined. Furthermore, a nation is characterised by notions of 'sovereignty' and 'limitedness', suggesting territorial boundaries and self-determination. Mass media and mass communication are important, in that when they transmit shared symbols, they shape a sense of national community. The rise of modern capitalist states would have been unthinkable without the centralisation of technology and media infrastructure that ensued from the homogenisation of newspapers and the creation of (radio and television) broadcasting corporations. Thus, looking through the prism of the media, nations are ideologically constructed entities rather than evident or ideologically neutral. In particular, as Malik (1996) shows, race and racism have manifestly played a role in the construction of national communities.

While the landmark works of Habermas and Anderson initially concerned 'traditional' media and communication, alterations in the latter's infrastructure have created space for bottom-up engagement and participative elements and have widened public and private spheres. Watching television or reading a newspaper comprises a single activity, while the internet embraces a variety of activities and multiple ways of acquiring information. Besides such mere acquisition, the rapid technological developments have influenced the ways people exchange and disseminate information.

The internet comprises different forms of engagement: one can read, write, look at pictures, watch films, listen to music and live radio programmes, talk with others, use a webcam to see each other while talking, download archive material, and so on. The internet can undermine the state's monopoly of the media, and the combination of new ways of acquiring and disseminating information have made it possible to form counter-imaginations. Later developments of user-generated possibilities (Web 2.0) decreased the gap even more. In summary, the main argument here is that mass media and communication strengthen national awareness among those in distant places, fuel a sense of community and make it possible to experience the nation's territorial contours. In his later work Anderson (2001a) came to view the internet as an important addition to the impact of media on the shaping of national communities.

Building further on the previous critique of the first-generation internet analyses, rather than an entirely distinctive technology, the internet is best understood as a 'basket' containing newspapers, radio and television. However, it is more than the sum of its parts: separately these media are largely devoid of the interactive and grassroots features of the internet. During an interview in Jordan in December 2002 Daoud Kuttab talked about the websites Amman-Net and Palestine-News and gave a good illustration of the overlapping characteristics of the internet:

> Private radio stations aren't allowed in the Arab world. This is [the internet's] power: a radio station that's doing something completely illegal in a legal way, a private radio using the internet to circumvent the laws ... we're able to reach those without internet through satellite and radio stations in Palestine, also received in Jordan because of the short distance. Radio stations in Palestine download our programmes and broadcast them on FM, for instance Radio Bethlehem 2000, Radio Nablus and Radio Amwaz, in Ramallah ... The coverage in Jordan is important because of its large Palestinian population. But perhaps Amman-Net is not of much interest for those inside Palestine because it's mostly a local Jordanian station. Amin-Net and Palestine-

> News are much more applicable with daily coverage from inside Palestine. These sites get most hits on our main website.

Kuttab's account shows how the internet is distinguished by its multi-functional nature: it includes different media forms, and even offers the possibility of crafting one's own medium.[14] The idea that internet media is completely different to newspapers or television thus exaggerates the differences and in turn downplays the structural forces that make up the internet. When the internet can be conceptualised as a basket it implies that developments in media and communication structures are part of preceding and future processes.

Kuttab's example also shows how new mass media facilitate the re-imagination and re-constitution of links between communities, and the emergence of new cross-border arenas of debate. Bringing Habermas and Anderson together, it can be argued that with greater diversification of media structures, citizens have become attached to a (mediated) 'global' public sphere and transnational imagined community. New forms of communication led to a kind of long-distance nationalism. Yet one of the outcomes of defining the impact of internet technology, given the globalisation paradigm mentioned before, is that the nation state is no longer a privileged space for the imagination of identity. The notion of long-distance nationalism is very similar to transnationalism. An important difference is that Benedict Anderson does not share the postmodern interpretation that disregards the dynamic of traditional nationalism and the place of nationalism. Appadurai (1997) outlined a transformation from national communities to 'communities of sentiments', and relates this to an assumed process of 'de-territorialisation'. It is important to consider the underlying arguments because they reappear.

A related critique is the Habermasian perception that the public sphere has shifted from democratic and rational to commercial elites. According to the rightful critique, the public sphere was in essence decidedly privileged – cf. the debates in Calhoun (1992) – and this relates to the internet as well. However, technological globalisation has another impact on the notion of public space: the growth of independent media. Warner's (2002) conceptualisation of 'counter-publics', (I will return to this later) helps deconstruct this change in terms of counter-hegemonic resistance. Most importantly it means that the public sphere expanded with new interpreters and interpretations.

Yet, taking this argument too far leads to the internet being treated as an autonomous space, transcending the reality of place and power. This transformation easily assumes the fading of the nation state's importance. The previous section shows that the state is far from dead, nor is it out of date. Moreover, instead, a sovereign and bounded state remains the framework yearned for by many a national community. In fact, when in practice its people are scattered among other states it is a priveleged space. Also central to the post-nation analysis is the idea that a new form of capitalism has emerged, and thus that accepted notions in political economy are out of date.

For Castells (2001) the idea of a – partly self-governing – network society also assumes a global elite dominating the lives of those confined to the local. This dynamic reinforces the structural domination of the online 'space of flows' over the offline 'space of places'. Hardt and Negri (2000, 2005) take off from a similar reconstitution but in a different direction, depicting a heterogeneous multitude, i.e. a (classless) networked local that is faced with a placeless global transnational empire. The idea is that by using the (open-source) internet, social movements develop alternative voices to resist the expansion of the ruling classes. Hardt and Negri advocate horizontal grassroots movements, but in their do-it-yourself autonomism the reality of what feminist scholar Jo Freeman called the 'tyranny of structurelesness' is not clarified.[15] Central or vertical structures of organisations actually become more elitist when redefined as horizontal: horizontal bodies lack the structures (elected positions and in turn visible decision-making/breaking) for accountability, and thus can be less democratic.

The often-quoted Zapatistas' and their use of the internet in their struggle against the oppression of indigenous Indians in Mexico is another source of their inspiration. But the Zapatistas are actually a contradictory allegory, casting doubt on the political relevance of the online over the offline – they were not internet activists playing guerrillas, but guerrillas who deployed the internet as part of their predominantly offline resistance. Fighting for self-determination and territorial autonomy is a far cry from space-less and border-less fantasies; in fact, territory is even a necessity or condition for virtual mobility. Unless we view the alternative and space-less world as devoid of local realities, the analysis of the new media's impact rarely articulates how the internet has materially changed political power and capitalism. Terranova (2004) argues that rather than being disconnected from a particular place, for virtual reality we need a grounded, 'real' infrastructure. This is also an important reason why the Middle East demands its own framework for understanding the implications of the internet.

Particularly since the 1990s, neo-liberal policies have coincided with profound changes in media access, especially through the introduction of satellite television such as MBC and *Al Jazeera* (Miladi 2003). A comprehensive framework for the internet in the Middle East is one that includes the relationships between the mass media, the nation-state, identity and community. Unravelling people's situated experiences with the media enables one to trace how mediated messages shape people's lives, though studying these audiences 'neither as resistant heroes to be celebrated, nor as stupid victims to be pitied' (Abu-Lughod et al 2002: 13). Furthermore, when examining how the process creates new dimensions of modern identity, these experiences themselves are mediated (Armbrust 2000). Media consumers in the Middle East have also become producers. There the internet in particular has contributed to specific ways of 'becoming a public', of creating collectivities (Eickelman and Salvatore 2003). In one of the most state-controlled regions this is no trivial development: and there has been a parallel increase in the number of journalists jailed.[16] Propelled by commercial and corporate motives, mass-media projects and their new infrastructures contribute to circumventing centralised and censored state media. Online newspapers illustrate the relation between reconstructions of collective identity and the internet: yet, the internet increased possibilities for transnational communication and thereby widened 'homeland' public spheres whereby 'some ideas of the public can be intensely local; others can be transregional and transnational' (Eickelman 2001).

Another important part of a comprehensive analysis of the internet in the Middle East is to consider, besides imperialism, the class dynamics as will be outlined further in Chapter Two. While most users of the internet in the early phase of its development belonged to the elite, this situation underwent a sea-change with the mushrooming of internet cafes. Internet penetration statistics between 2000 and 2005 show that the Middle East is among the fastest-growing regions.[17] In Palestine, Birzeit University (BZU) was the engine of this change, mobilising society to embrace the internet. In 1998 and 1999 student campaigners and volunteers at the University's Computer Centre mounted an 'Internet Festival', aiming to enthuse people and at the same time enhance their internet skills, for instance through workshops on e-mail and the use of search-engines. Students were involved in a project ('Outload') which combined radio with new internet possibilities. They aired interviews, music and discussions about local issues, which could be listened to around the world via the BZU website. These startling developments confirmed the virtues of the internet.

Looking at the internet in concrete Palestinian contexts demonstrated its gains, but also its limitations. It is tempting to overstate the meaning of cyberspace – but it can only be viewed in relation to offline, face-to-face forms of communication. The space-less instrument of the internet is, in the Palestinian case, obviously used to address issues of place or territory; for example in the repeated call for a Palestinian state, also mediated online, which will be discussed in the following chapters. The relation between the internet and everyday life, and the social implications of the former, cannot be fully understood without research that considers the broader impact of colonialism and capitalism. This is also an appeal to join offline and online methodologies.

Online-offline methodology

> Far from truncating description, it [ethnography] has its own search engine in the form of a Question ... It pulls one in the situation of not necessarily wanting to tell in advance (Strathern 2000: 59).

Strathern reminds the reader in this passage that ethnography throws up the unplanned and unpredictable. Furthermore, in order to avoid essentialising the subject of study it is important to pull together the online/offline community on the one hand, and online/offline ethnography on the other. It is not surprising that the critiques of earlier internet studies (mentioned above) engaged with anthropological-inspired methodologies. Empirical and ethnographic studies have been at the forefront of overcoming some of the useless false dichotomies. This final section is an assessment of the value of the internet as a new tool for research and as itself a new space. Looking at cyberspace from below demands research from the same perspective. The research on which this book is based took place in the context of extreme destabilisation and conflict. The unplanned and unpredictable effect on the timing and methodology of the experience greatly influenced the research.

During fieldwork everyday life was crippled by curfews and closures, by 'retaliatory attacks' and by strict border controls that prevented the entry of international activists, researchers and media professionals.

In the period from the outbreak of the popular uprising at the end of 2000 up to January 2003 more than 2,000 Palestinians had been killed and 21,000 injured. Three years later, in the midst of the fieldwork, the death toll rose to 4,000 and 31,000 respectively.[18] Overall, the death toll among Palestinians was at least ten times that of the Israelis; the situation was *de facto* and *de jure* agonising. Palestinian society was politicised, with many supporting the resistance.[19] The 9/11 attacks had paralysed the grassroots dynamics of the Intifada, while the US invasion and occupation of Iraq profoundly affected the balance of power in the Middle East. But as time went on, Palestinians were increasingly trapped between supporting the right to self-determination and resistance, on the one hand, and scepticism about the effectiveness of the uprising, on the other. Meeting people in the refugee camps in Lebanon and Jordan in this particular period provided important insights into the impact of the Intifada on Palestinians in exile.

The fieldwork covered three phases: Palestine, in 2001–02, Jordan, in 2003 and Lebanon, in 2003–04 (Figures 3, 4 and 5). The first phase provided insights into the world of web design, internet productions and telecoms policies, through interviews with representatives of ICT companies, institutions and projects and with academics in the field of ICT, and through observing and participating in activities in internet cafes, universities and community centres. When Israeli officials refused me entry to Palestine during my second visit, research focused on Wehdat, al-Bekaa and Irbid refugee camps in Jordan, including interviews with internet users there. Similar activities formed the basis of the research in Lebanon. Here the focus was on Palestinian refugee camps in and around Beirut, Tripoli, Sour and Saida, studying people's everyday engagement with the internet. Furthermore, in the light of the experiences outlined above, the role of the researcher herself needs to be reviewed; this will form the closing part of this chapter.

Anthropology from below

It can be argued that cyberspace facilitates the erosion of national sentiments and supports transnational identities in disembodied worlds, or that it is an autonomous space unconnected with place or physical reality. The scope of research on the internet is already immense, and covers a wide range of disciplines; it is therefore futile to assess the overlapping studies in their totality. The aim here is to treat the internet as a tool and a space at the same time, using classic ethnographic and new (virtual) research instruments. This redefinition of the methodological basis of research also raises questions about the ethical considerations involved, most importantly where the research respondents are not protected by (national) research regulations. Eynon et al (2008) summarise developments regarding the search for new ethical guidelines for internet research. This debate is ongoing, since the discipline of internet research is still young and dealing with new methodological and conceptual challenges. It is nevertheless important to set out a broad ethical framework because online methodological techniques are often de-contextualised, for instance online discourse analysis. Throughout the, often indirect, relation with respondents, researchers are also confronted with different confidentiality and anonymity choices or constraints (ibid: 24). These concerns are important here because internet studies and methodologies have implications for the study of identity and communities online as well (ibid: 30). The issue of de-contextualisation is particularly crucial because virtual spaces are also shaped by continual references to particular places. Many websites feature flags or links to official or (informational) political sites, which indicate that the internet does not weaken national identity but rather strengthens it. The internet is of course also a communication tool offering an alternative meeting space for members of communities. But for Palestinians to enter this 'free' space, they have first to join this space via computers and cables placed in houses or internet cafes, located in cities or refugee camps in occupied land. Meanwhile, new technologies and traditional means of dissemination still need each other, such as when e-mail messages are printed out and distributed to recipients, reaching people who do not have access to a computer.

When normative approaches overlap with conceptions of the internet, with good or bad behaviour being ascribed to its users by over-generalising from online analysis, simplistic or essentialist arguments may be the result. This can be found in hyped-up research that does not seem to correspond to complex realities. Reading for instance *Internet & Jihad* in the Netherlands (Benschop 2006) leads one to believe that online macho behaviour reflects the offline, actual radicalisation. Especially when connected to communities already under a magnifying glass, these puffed-up predictions can contribute to stigmatisation.[20]

Can the internet not be seen as part of ethnographic 'sites', and online spaces studied through active participation in chat rooms or mailing-list discussions in chorus with the everyday offline place? This way cyberspace is viewed as part of the conventional public spheres which take face-to-face interaction, its implications and its effects, into account. It is easy to fall into abstract discourses and subscribe to science-fiction arguments that human beings are on the way to becoming cyborgs or androids (Stockl 2003: 72). New realities are created when space and time overlap, but we cannot take a snapshot of online space as we do with offline space, nor expect it to fulfil a sense of belonging in the same way. This is an echo of Wellman's (1997) argument that relationships between people who never see, smell or hear each other, can be productive, supportive or intimate. This does not imply that the internet has no effect on self-representation and the ways identities are constructed; on the contrary, it helps in making public what was previously personal, and creates new links between individual and community. On-the-ground and ethnographic examination tracks people's activities and narratives 'as they cross domains and thereby create heterogeneous social worlds' (Strathern 2000: 59).

Communities are imagined and experienced as virtual but are often still actualised in interpersonal relationships (ibid: 60). However, anthropology did not play a central role in the study of the mass media, nor in the initial framings of the internet. Nevertheless, over time anthropology did develop an interest in the nexus between culture, science and technology, and thereby enriched the relevant disciplines. Ethnographic methodology with an interest in national identities enables cross-cultural, embedded and multi-sited research (Wilson and Peterson 2002: 450). The internet can also learn from visual anthropology, and vice versa; this is a vantage point already shared with communication studies via existing interdisciplinary links (ibid: 454).

The increasing mobility of people, ideas and products has challenged fieldwork methodologies and how we view cyberspace as a social phenomenon. Internet research is characterised by conditions where time and space collapse; online 'space sites' are for instance constituted by (hyper) linkages between websites (Hine 2000: 61). The websites and online representations in question are born in different offline contexts. Marcus (1995) suggests examining and working from different time-space situations and from multi-sited fields. In the context of the internet, location is both an online and offline phenomenon; 'multi-sited' here thus refers to online and offline sites. A multi-sited ethnography on the internet deconstructs social phenomena related to transnational communities on the ground and in cyberspace.

Research on Palestine, however, means that conducting fieldwork is more difficult, and the harsh offline conditions sometimes make online research techniques attractive alternatives. However, with more and more conflicts infesting the field of academic research, the possible consequence is a failure to capture complex, and at first invisible, offline realities, and a shift to armchair anthropology. What does this say about the internet as a tool? Miller and Mather (1998) argue that to know how people construct new identities on the internet entails asking users what they experience or what their preferences are, and moving beyond content analysis. Researchers need to go beyond the online text of, for example, a newsgroup posting or a webpage, as Hine (2000) suggests. Researchers need to include the producer of the text in their stories if they seek to comprehend the context that shapes it. This inevitably requires long-term engagement with the field and its informants when studying the role of the internet in constructing collective national identities or in reconstituting diasporas.

In other words, we need to resort to an ethnography that is based on the juxtaposition of qualitative and quantitative issues. Miller and Slater (2000) address this dilemma when they show that the internet does not produce its own conventions and its own society; the way in which people express themselves is only partly influenced by the internet. The availability of online technologies enhances our research methodologies, but does not replace the need for offline interviews and observation. Brouwer's (2004) work on the use of the internet by young ethnic minorities in the Netherlands shows how qualitative methods such as participant observation, informal meetings and structured interviews are crucial. This approach not only emphasises informants' views, i.e. represents 'anthropology from below', it also provides new questions. Stockl calls this form of ethnography 'immersion'; it takes the form of building relationships through the writing and reading of emails, and reflecting on them. Here 'the field is constantly present in the ethnographer's mind.' This is a reversal of the 'ethnographer-in-the-field to the field-in-the-ethnographer' (2003: 74). Thus the most important point for a critical anthropology about the implications of the internet is combining such offline research methodology with its online equivalent, and setting up multi-sited fieldwork. This combined approach made it possible, in the present case, to show how Palestinians represent and empower themselves.

Such 'anthropology from below' enables the researcher to engage with the context in a humanist manner, and to create organic links. Sometimes political contexts challenge our analyses and methods by force. The continuing possibility of safely acquiring data, information, access and knowledge, which fortifies our expertise, is impossible without the cooperation and sacrifice of those on the ground, and this emphasises a vision of equal relations between researchers and their respondents. To give back means taking sides.

Organic intellectuals

> For the Palestinian catastrophe is not just something of the past. It continues into the present in every house demolished by an Israeli bulldozer, with every firing from an Apache helicopter, with every stillbirth at a military checkpoint, with every village divided from its fields by the 'separation wall' and with every Palestinian who still longs to return to a home that is no more (Abu-Lughod 2007: 103).

The context of Palestine is marked by military violence. During the first period of fieldwork, in 2001–02, half the time was spent under curfew. Throughout that period Ramallah was separated by military checkpoints from Birzeit and Jerusalem, and therefore effectively also from the rest of the West Bank. Checkpoints were often closed, preventing anyone from going in or out. As most respondents had regular jobs or classes, interview appointments after office or school hours were difficult to obtain,[21] and conducting interviews during full-curfew days was impossible. Visiting other Palestinian cities, particularly Gaza, was a complex matter. Nablus, Hebron and Jenin became impossible because it was for me physically too difficult to use bypass routes via hills and mountains.[22] As a woman there were sometimes barriers to conducting research, such as joining street activism, visiting unsavoury internet cafes or going to remote camps in the evening. The Israeli authorities are particularly obstructive towards Arab researchers who want to work in the OPT; for me, the worst example of this was being refused permission to enter Palestine to conduct fieldwork.

Police surveillance in Jordanian refugee camps meant that interviewing Palestinians there was only allowed after obtaining permission from the government; this was a laborious red-tape process, and often ultimately a useless one. As the issue of Palestinian refugees is politically sensitive in Jordan, some interviewees were overly cautious during interviews, which thus took up more time. In short, fieldwork meant being confronted with barriers, both large and small. Doing research among Palestinians, however, also offers incredible opportunities in the form of incessant hospitality, tireless support and selfless helpfulness. Also, it matters that researchers are not simply interested in finishing their own work, especially where scepticism towards foreign researchers or journalists is not without cause and has a long history (Mitchell 2003, Rohde 2007, González 2008).

There is plenty to read about the history and politics of Palestine, but as Abu Lughod's moving account shows, there is a difference between hearing stories about Palestine from her father and actually being there:

> It is difficult to be held up by arrogant soldiers with reflective sunglasses and burnished muscles who wilfully delay you. It is different to go to an airport in an Arab taxi ... humiliating you with their power to make you sit silent though you know you are perfectly innocent ... But they [stories] can't capture this particular reality, with its growling Hebrew arrogantly proclaiming ownership, with its guns and soldiers everywhere you turn (2007: 102).

Indeed, being delayed, humiliated, interrogated, in fear and disconnected from friends sometimes resulted in a lack of motivation. It was difficult to cope with the presence of an aggressive army, with exhausting treatment at checkpoints, with disappointment over cancelled or delayed meetings and with confronting news that contacts had been arrested, injured or even killed.

The 2008 Antipode special issue *Practising Public Scholarship: Experiences and Possibilities Beyond the Academy*[23] is an important reminder that a widespread rethinking has occurred in the social sciences and humanities in the last few decades; this has also allowed for political critique of the representation and reality of knowledge, and simultaneously opened up space for political engagement. But taking sides comes with a price: sometimes researchers from Arab or Muslim backgrounds are particularly 'suspect'.[24] And even using the terms 'Palestinians' or 'Palestine' can be controversial.[25] But it has never been truer that complacency and deliberate silence come down to complicity. The ethics of taking sides in anthropology is itself a subjective notion, linked to (contested) values of research. This is a consequence of the clash between engaging as both an activist and an academic, or what Neale describes as the paradox of writing as activists and as academics: as wanting to rant and having to remain silent (cited in Armbruster and Lærke 2008).

The anthropologist James Ferguson (1990) asks what possibilities there are for offering our engagement or expertise as contributions towards emancipation and empowerment. The Gramscian concept of the 'organic intellectual' articulates how academic and political lives can be entangled. One of the basic ways for the academic to become engaged is through political participation in one's own society (Ferguson 1990: 281). Existing hegemonic forces can be challenged via NGOs, unions, political parties, universities and the media. This is even truer for those who work in states whose political system supports Israeli occupation, because:

> [t]he anthropologist who has seen 'his village' exterminated by death squads for instance, has both a special perspective and a distinctive political role to play in debates over aid to the 'Contras' or support for El Salvador. Likewise, the field researcher who knows the Palestinians as real, flesh and blood human beings, and not only as shadowy figures brandishing machine guns, is in a position to combat the deceptions and misinformation that are put forward to justify the denial of Palestinian self-determination (ibid: 286).

This research coincided with a period and part of the world where war increasingly dominates the lives of ordinary people. There are no guarantees that critical academia is going to have practical relevance, but: 'We must remember that we never know what little act will tip the scale,' as Rabbi Ascherman notes.[26]

Outline

The goal of this chapter was to organise some of the puzzling ideas concerning the role of the internet in Palestine and their – sometimes contradictory – terrains of contestation. The following chapters will focus on the creation of transnational linkages and on the shaping of Palestinians' collective imaginations. Chapter Two will introduce the theoretical and historical contexts underlying these contestations, and so contextualise the tension between mobility and immobility and between territorial place and virtual space. It will also assess the history, relevance and impact of internet technology.

Chapter Three picks up on the first of these tensions – that between mobility and immobility – and studies how Palestinian immobility relates to new virtual realities and offline/online practices. It is an account of the first internet initiatives set up locally to overcome such immobility. By contextualising the everyday realities for refugees in Jordan and Lebanon it becomes clear that the internet is embedded in exile and forced migration.

Chapter Four examines the second tension, the relationship between virtual space and territorial place, through an engagement with debates about the nation state and collective identity. It recalls the first initiatives set up to form a Palestinian virtual space. The creation of such a space colludes with territorial place because the internet is embedded in occupation and the absence of sovereignty. It questions the impact of the al-Nakba in shaping a national (imagined) community online, and looks at how the Intifada markedly boosted the internet. The chapter ends by reconstructing the beginnings of the 'Across Borders Project' in Palestine and Lebanon. The ABP brings Chapters Three and Four together: Palestinians could cross borders online and to that extent overcome their immobility.

Cyberspace motivated the creation of a Palestine Online in order partly to compensate for the lack of Palestine as territorial place. Chapter Five unravels the relationship between national identity and internet developments by looking at virtual representations through a study of Palestinian websites. The two tensions call for a grounded examination of the everyday implications, such as face-to-face dynamics. This offline, everyday face of internet technologies is examined in Chapter Six.

2

TECHNO-POLITICAL INFRASTRUCTURES

> People were stuck at home, they were bored and frustrated. The internet also became the only source of accurate news, and of chatting. This is very important because people were in need of these means of communication to express themselves.
>
> *Abu Marzouk, Gaza–Palestine, 2002.*

Technological and political developments have fed into one another, as Abu Marzouk, Director of Palestine Internet Services, explains here during an interview in Gaza. Two crucial and timely developments are taken into account in this study: regional instability, occupation and war on the one hand and an explosion of ICT ventures such as mobile network technologies and digital media on the other. This process in turn led to a fusion of place and time. The availability of the internet as a new mass medium excited many Palestinians, and we need only to surf the internet to get a sense of this fusion, through the overwhelming number of Palestinian online forums, mailing lists and websites. The everyday context has shaped the online content: the motivation most often heard for many of the internet projects was resentment at the pro-Israeli/anti-Palestinian coverage in the mainstream media.

The introduction of the internet meant new patterns in the evolution of the media and in community participation in the Middle East. In Palestine, Palestine Telecom (PalTel) was a successful company even in the first phase of the Intifada (2001–02). In addition to its monopoly status, and with the PNA infusing the telecom sector with business opportunities, socio-political factors also made a crucial contribution to the rise in internet usage among Palestinians. Due to the forced immobility, closures and curfews the Palestinian community relied more heavily on ICT, such as mobile telephones and email, to stay informed about the Intifada. Meanwhile, the international community was tapping into Palestinian sources for 'alternative', i.e. locally produced, information. *Haaretz* journalist Rubinstein (2002) guessed right: '[P] erhaps because of the roadblocks and transportation difficulties, people are using the telephone more'.[1] Palestinians regard Western media as biased. By communicating their message and revealing their everyday conditions to the outside world, they began to have a voice and face.

9/11 was like a magnifying glass: the fusion of technology and politics challenged the necessity and potential of ICT. The two major ways of interpreting the internet can be summarised as a top-down mode that emanates from corporate marketing strategies, and as an alternative mode emerging from the activities of diasporic groups (Franklin 2001). It is this last way that is emphasised here: the internet as a space for building solidarity and as a tool for empowerment.

This chapter offers a set of frameworks with which to understand the two points of departure, about unravelling the 'tension' raised by virtual mobility and virtual space. The first section will start with an examination of the two tensions before elaborating on them in the subsequent chapters. Despite the empowering characteristics of the internet and because of my focus on grassroots usage, the disempowering (neoliberal) materiality of technology still exists, and must be taken into account. For instance the term 'democratisation' is often used when in fact the process in question is one of (economic) liberalisation. The second section of this chapter therefore sketches the history of ICT in the Palestinian context, and situates the internet within an offline, embedded perspective.

Framing tensions

The two tensions introduced in the previous chapter have shaped the theoretical and thematic frameworks for this study. Rather than reiterating the theoretical debates, the key concepts are mostly referred to from a grounded approach, in other words unpacked from the social reality of technology. The first tension – the issue of mobility – relates to the offline realities of diaspora and exile: Palestinian immobility. The second tension covers the virtual-space/territorial-place dichotomy, viewed as representing the relations between the nation state, transnational identity and virtual communities.

It is important here to remember that experiences of forced mobility have been shaped by particular historic and political contexts, which have had uneven consequences. Collective national identity does not do away with class, citizenship or gender differences. Palestinians had to deal with different crises and were forced to settle in different places and conditions. As the political, economic and social contexts differed, the local experiences of Palestinians have also differed. Hence they represent different diasporic groups – stateless refugees, political exiles or successful expatriates. A number of Palestinians living in the West (i.e. holding in most cases dual-nationality) decided to return after Oslo to help build their country. Many of these 'returnees' were ICT specialists, their presence was crucial: it meant the crafting of the political and technological backbone of the internet in Palestine as will be discussed later.

Meanwhile, the Intifada led to many online debates about Palestinian politics and identity, and this interactivity not only challenged the separations between Palestinians as refugees, nationals or returnees, it also galvanised critical discussions about the political developments that were taking place and the role of the national leadership. Oslo failed in many ways because the Israeli colonial occupation continued with its full structural control over Palestinian life. The relative autonomy since the mid-1990s ended abruptly with the reoccupation of PNA areas, starting in 2001. One deeply felt frustration, affecting all sections of the diaspora indiscriminately, is the lack of mobility. In fact Palestinian mobility is best described as 'forced mobility': migration as a consequence of displacement.

Virtual mobility, real immobility

Mobility covers a wide range of meanings, from the mobility of ideas and ideologies to that of consumer commodities. The concept of mobility, and its opposite, immobility, enables macro and micro-level analyses: from studies on global industrial transformations and forced migration, to issues concerning local public transportation, ethnic segregation and accessibility. It has been argued that with globalisation these issues have become increasingly important, and henceforth have led to a 'mobility turn' in the social sciences (Hannam et al 2006: 2). Moreover, this (re)discovery of mobility as a conceptual paradigm, one that crosses a variety of disciplines, necessitates new theoretical approaches (ibid). The reconfiguration of mobility, alongside space and time, also meant that fundamental assertions associated with 'old' (20th-century) social sciences are questioned. The paradigm shift of mobility relates above all to territory, a notion itself reevaluated following redefinitions of the nation state and of capitalism as argued in the previous chapter. However, mobility and territory are shaped by unequal power relations in everyday life, and these unequal realities themselves are set within material capitalist frameworks (Harvey 1993).

This dialectic relation, rather than a flattening of categories about temporal and spatial patterns of society (dubbed 'networked' and 'computer-mediated' communities, where 'post' and 'horizontal' are attractive buzzwords), is the relevance of studying the impact of the internet. The approach delineated by Hannam et al helps to transcend the polarity of internet research discussed in Chapter One. They problematise 'both "sedentarist" approaches in the social sciences that treat place, stability and dwelling as a natural steady-state, and "deterritorialised" approaches that posit a new "grand narrative" of mobility, fluidity or liquidity as a pervasive condition of postmodernity or globalisation' (2006: 5). This stance is not only more scientific – as in actually grounded and empirical – but also less irresponsible. Shrouding the oppressive realities of immobility or the ugly causes of forced mobility in mysterious or abstract theories diminishes the sense of urgency.

For Palestinians, the notion of mobility refers mostly to exile. Transnational mobility started with the 1948 Nakba: one of the largest forced migrations in modern history (Pappé 2006). The term 'displaced' does not cover the extent of the trauma; though the truth about the mass expulsion has been systematically suppressed, had it taken place in the 21st century it would inevitably have been called 'ethnic cleansing'. The Nakba had already resulted in one of the most difficult refugee problems, and when in 1967 Israel occupied the remaining West Bank and Gaza (*al-naksa*), thousands more Palestinians were forced to leave their homes and villages, resulting in another flow of refugees and creating internally displaced Palestinians.

Palestine as a nation is thus dispersed, fragmented by the expulsion of more than three-quarters of its original population. The Palestinian diaspora can be divided into roughly three categories: Palestinians with 'travel documents' (mainly living in Syria, Lebanon, Egypt or Iraq); those considered 'nationals of convenience' (mostly holders of temporary Jordanian passports); and those holding Palestinian passports, i.e. PNA travel documents issued in the West Bank and Gaza (Rempel and Shiblak 2006). Granting citizenship to stateless refugees is a sensitive issue in most countries in the world, because this would mean the host state becomes responsible for providing protection and (economic) accountability. Restrictive laws for the stateless Palestinians are based on the principle of *jus sanguine* – nationality by bloodline (ibid). This thus enforces a situation whereby statelessness is passed on through generations. The exclusion of Palestinian refugees on political grounds or as part of international policy further undermines the struggle for equality.

As stated, it is problematic to talk of a single Palestinian diaspora, first because romanticising Palestinian refugees should be rejected: to essentialise a people, whether in positive or negative ways, is un-academic. Secondly, in the general discourse 'diaspora' may assume a certain voluntarism, though this does not apply to almost all exiled Palestinians who are not allowed to return to Palestine, not even for a visit. Only a small privileged minority, or those who were part of Arafat's cadres, were able to return.[2]

What is the role of the internet in this context of exile, fragmentation and immobility? This question refers to the impact of ICT on the birth of network societies and how such transformations also introduced new virtual cultures. Castells' trilogy (1996; 1997; 1998) argues that the most important characteristics of the new network community are formed by their timeless time and placeless space settings. The analyses are driven by the hypothesis of a new type of society, arising from the overlap of virtual and physical space. The public sphere seems to have adopted a real and a virtual character. Understanding the connection between the internet and the production of virtual space is thus crucial to our engagement with internet cultures (Terranova 2004).

However, transnational globalisation perceives mobility to be also a characteristic condition, and this is in due course fused with the notion of virtual mobility. The conception of a free flow of networks, people, commodities, information and ideas is indeed interrelated with mass-mediated networks, and may trespass on state structures. But conditions of immobility and confinement still dominate the lives of millions of people; in Palestine this signifies being confined to one area through closures or checkpoints, or a building or even a room through curfews. And neither can this new condition mean that the construction of national identities and of states' political economies are unrelated. The conclusion cannot be that virtual communities lead to a decrease of state structures: for members of a diasporic group the internet cannot reverse or escape the larger patterns of their social realities (Dawson 2003: 1). The social implications of the internet can only be understood when embedded in the material realities of an (exiled) community.

Far from 'dis-embedding' national identities, the technologies comprising the internet revive national sentiments and past or present dreams of becoming united again, and incite the struggles related to such dreams. This locus of interaction on the internet can be found among diasporas and exile communities such as the Trinidadians (Miller and Slater 2000), the Kurds (Eriksen 2006), the Pacific islanders (Franklin 2005), the Tamils (Enteen 2006) and the Iranians (Khosravi 2000). All share with Palestinians their sense of being dispersed or even exiled. This sense of belonging is linked to what Anderson and Kligman (1992) termed 'long-distance nationalism' which unifies fragmented communities. What most of these diaspora communities do not share with Palestinians is having been dispersed by force, let alone shut for so long in poor refugee camps and subjected to poverty and violence.

Like other nations which have lost territory and been dispersed for political reasons, and with large (both temporary and permanent) diasporas overseas, the Palestinian nation appears in many guises on the internet, and thrives in cyberspace. The presence of such online nations shows that the internet is being used to strengthen rather than weaken national identities (Eriksen 2006: 5–7). For many Palestinians too, the expression of their national identity and the aspirations to have a state are political and symbolic precisely because they are not available and they are brutally deprived of state protection. The expressions visualised are about shared oppression and resistance to it in the here and now, not simply as the past. The (active) construction of Palestinian national identity is indeed unique because of its colonial occupation and forced immobility (Schulz 1999). In fact, the assumption that humankind is naturally divided into national entities and that therefore self-determination is validated when a community can demonstrate this 'self-awareness' or national identification, needs to be reviewed (Sayigh 1997: xiii). One way to link transnationalism, virtual mobility and communities in cyberspace to the worlds of those who are immobile but nonetheless traverse and participate through the internet is the notion of 'parallel modernities' (Larkin 2002).

The Palestinian national identity is exceptional insofar as, beside the level of narrative and visual representations, the actual existence of Palestinians is embedded in colonialism and anti-colonial struggle. Their armed struggles provided a political impulse for the evolution of Palestinian national identity. Both Sayigh and Schulz agree that Palestinian nationalism is shaped by violent everyday confrontation with Zionism and the state of Israel, as well as being the product of nationalist discourses by exiled Palestinian political elites. Palestinian uprisings, from 1936 during the British Mandate to the al-Aqsa Intifada in 2000, have inevitably affected the Palestinian sense of self. It is in this historical context that Palestinian references to national identity are to be understood. This anti-colonialist nationalism can be identified in the online traversals and meetings between Palestinians. This nexus helps deconstruct how national perceptions relate to virtual community.

As argued at the outset of this section, mobility and territory are interdependent notions. Concepts of space and place offer interesting ways to contemplate the meaning of online interactions. Online space challenges the classic definition of place as a bounded physical location and necessitates new theoretical constructs that account for unbounded communities and spaces online (Zook 2006: 56). However, the notion of community implies more than mere interaction. Virtual groups can equally well fall short of being communities. Discussing diasporic cyberspace, Dawson thus asserts that online activities are only likely to generate a sense of community when the online interaction is anchored in a shared offline context; the significance of the internet lies where it extends to other parts of life (2003: 8). Hence, new technological developments should be seen as a continuation of, rather than a break from, older types of social interaction. Ideally speaking, online communities construct social bonds, but in what circumstances the online communities are built, and how Palestinians experience these online traversals without being situated in the actual territorial contexts, are crucial questions.

Virtual space – territorial place

> Perhaps cyberspace, with its capacity to externalize our innermost fantasies in all their inconsistency, opens up to the artistic practice a unique possibility to stage, to 'act out', the fantas-matic support of our existence ... that cannot ever be subjectivized (Žižek 1998:510).

Whereas space and place are central to understanding the geographies of the internet, 'space' and 'place' are also evocative terms for understanding the tensions between place as territory and state and space as imagined. Virtual space questions the relevance of the state, nation and identity, proposing that techno-capitalism influences internet-mediated identities. Is virtual space another kind of place? And does this 'new' type of space and thus new forms of interactivity imply new kinds of community?

The internet questions the territorial integrity of nations, but sometimes, as argued with reference to certain postmodern interpretations, it is even claimed that the non-territorial internet dissolves the national integrity of the respective communities, and their collective sense of identity. But people who identify with a given nation do not necessarily inhabit the same place.

Geographers have long studied the twin concepts of space and place. Adams (1997), for instance, discerns the geographically related metaphors for internet spaces as including 'electronic frontier', 'cyber space' and 'information highway'. Many of these notions, predominately in internet debates, have become synonymous with the twin concepts of offline and online. But how online is online? Cyber community, or experiencing a virtual life, of course requires ICT connectivity. Online interactivities can be sustained through mailing lists, chat rooms or instant messaging; they can be individual or group-based, visible or secret, public or anonymous, and so on. Space, place and nation-state are intertwined: binary views and either/or evaluations of place vs space or nation vs state are rarely helpful. The argument that an emerging 'post-industrial' capitalism has been characterised by the increasing power of the international market has subsequently been followed by predictions of the decline of the state. On the contrary, states and state institutions are extremely important – the monopoly of violence and the military response after 9/11 show this clearly enough (Kellner 2002: 290).

Virtual nations too are ideologically constructed spaces, shaped by particular socio-economic technological contexts within a particular reality. And online participation is not a static process, but is susceptible to the participant's motivation, class and technological access. Online experiences in virtual space, as in offline place, are inspired by political, public, private and community concerns. It was initially suggested that online communities would replace offline spaces as the loci of social interaction, and that communities would crystallise in cyberspace; classic spaces of community would disappear and be replaced by virtual communities (Rheingold 1993). Can a virtual community have ontological status, or is it less real than other forms of community? Inserting this debate in the context of Palestine, the idea of a virtual Palestinian community thus raises the immediate question of whether this online time-less and space-less society can be perceived as a substitute for the offline community. Palestinian diasporas refute the idea that the virtual state approximates to the Palestinian nation-state, because transformations from offline to online Palestine is a second-best choice, not a voluntary replacement. Palestinians' online motivation is shaped by experiences of exclusion, isolation and oppression – the need to connect online lies in their desire to meet offline. This is especially important for refugees who seek out others with similar experiences, interests and shared commitments: in this way, the Palestinian online community can evoke transnational unity.

This means that virtual and territorial communities are not seen as two sides of the same coin. Virtual contact cannot replace face-to-face contact, and Palestinians therefore often express a preference for offline, 'real' interaction within their community. Meanwhile, external events or constraints have a direct impact on virtual communities: neither space, nor place, nor time can be dispensed with. References on the internet to times which, for Palestinians, mark historic events in their history – such as 1948, 1967, 1982, 1987 and 2000 – symbolise this. Ismael Neshef, an anthropologist at Birzeit University, explained during an interview in 2002 how the structure of occupation relates to the internet in specific ways:

> Space, movement and borders are central; the first attraction of virtual reality is control of space and, overcoming these borders, the dialectical relation between virtual and on-the-ground space. Because of these realities, space is transcending but is also more than merely virtual. While it gives a sense of empowerment it doesn't give real [material] power because it's still limited by objective conditions. The idea of a counter, alternative space makes the virtual attractive for Palestinians. It's significant to remember that due to closures and curfews, space, place and time have different meanings for Palestinians.

What does this say about virtual diasporic communities? Do their online interactions represent what we mean by virtual communities? The internet is best approached as neither strictly defined nor completely open (Feenberg and Bakardjieva 2004). Internet use may alter geographical references, but the sense of identity connects us to territorial places (Zook 2006: 69). Neshef's comment explicates why virtual space is (tactically) employed.

Internet technology has created new opportunities for interaction between people and places, described by such hyperbole as 'global village', but how should they be understood in offline terms? What is perceived as positive interaction or empowering mediation depends on factors that go beyond the technological. Computer-mediated communication is not a neutral act. Differences in interactivity are shaped by technological factors, i.e. the nature and possibilities of the interface, and by social factors, i.e. user style or preference (McMillan 2002). As Wellman and Hampton argue, many studies of virtual communities have led to a neglect of some elementary social issues, such as the materiality of power and the interactive offline/online connection (1999: 649).

There is indeed an affinity between life online, 'networked individualism', and virtual community. The internet certainly supports new patterns of sociability, as Castells has shown. But it cannot be generalised as a global phenomenon. Some users have more space and choice than others, and spatial restructuring cannot escape political economy (Harvey 1993), neither in the sense of creating a super-mobility, as argued above, nor in the sense of a space- and time-less reality. The spatiality of social life involves conflict over mobility and movement of people (Hannam et al 2006: 4).

The internet needs to be situated, and thus it should be understood that the transformation of communities predated, and happened independently of, the internet. Moreover, since online communication is individualistic and sometimes a less personal form of interaction, the internet media may also pose problems for the development of diasporic communities, 'more [than] diasporic religious communities would care to support' (Dawson 2003: 1). Finally, the internet is predominately a global network, but is primarily organised and arranged at a local level. Virtual diasporic communities thus raise conceptual questions about the meaning of social networks in computer-mediated diasporas on the ground.

Fieldwork in Palestine, Jordan and Lebanon confirmed that diasporic communication is often expressed as collective interaction *vis-à-vis* national identity, and community often reflects the merging of the online and offline. Social practices are virtually mediated as well as actually experienced. Communities include some form of virtuality and online sociability; and even though this does not 'live up to the glorified and normatively laden concept of virtual community' (ibid: 38), the internet has fostered new online groups.

This brings the discussion back to the importance of real, offline experiences of isolation and immobility. The quotation from Žižek at the head of this section identifies the unique, dialectic possibilities of cyberspace. He adds that they constitute playful ways with which to challenge power structures (1998: 510). Because of these characteristics virtual mobility and online interactivity can also appeal to those who want to escape reality.

Virtual escapism

As discussed in Chapter One, the postmodern era encouraged a conception of the internet as being able to reorder power and identity: utopian, as a new force of change combating inequality, or dystopian, as a cause of alienation. In the early literature on cyberspace, individuals could take on identities in ways never before possible. *Turkle's Life on Screen* (1995) inspired visions of the internet as a self-sufficient space outside everyday realities; similarly, the (often unintended) impact of *Harraway's Cyborg Manifesto* (1991) has stimulated new theoretical constructs of the self, and the notion of hybrids – beings that are part human, part machine – altered the conception of identity. Accompanying debates resonate to the notion of escapism, carrying a dystopian connotation as if referring to an artificial situation. This is for instance found in Baudrillard's (1994) writings about simulation and fantasy in what he outlined as the new post-industrial/postmodern context. Simulation through virtual participation logically implies that it is not real. The concept of escapism can be useful in understanding the deeper effects of online traversing, whether negative or positive.

Excessive use of the internet can have pathological and addictive effects on people (Griffiths 2000; 2006). The notion of a sense of simulation in cyberspace that leads to escapism is an interesting one. But rather than taking it for granted that internet users become floating beings who are everywhere and nowhere, it is more relevant to investigate how internet escapism carries with it 'real-world' identities and characteristics. Notwithstanding the inability to experience face-to-face meetings – nor, as a result of occupation or exile, to travel – virtual escapism may also provide collective solitude and relief from a harsh reality. There also exists a valuable, goal-oriented escapism (Evans 2001: 70). Thus escapism can be negative and unhealthy, but also positive and healthy, in the sense of overcoming unpleasant practices, to compensate for immobility with a modicum of virtual mobility, to fight isolation with internet connectivity, loneliness with online love. Escapism is thus double-edged, passive and active: virtual leisure as a break from the reality of poverty and occupation, or simulating participation in the Intifada through cyber combat games.

Analogous to transcendence, escapism does not necessarily connote avoidance of the challenges of everyday life but a rise above them. Escapism is not a mutually exclusive virtue in terms of its effecting liberation or false consciousness, or of its motivation, e.g. to avoid offline relations. A dialectical approach counteracts the ineffectual dichotomy. Better put, escapism cements the conditions that caused it in the first place (ibid: 67). Virtual escapism can be a way out, but does not necessarily dominate the users who still have their agency: 'Far from enslaving us to these fantasies and turning us into desubjectivized, blind puppets, it enables us to treat them in a playful way and thus to adopt toward them a minimum of distance' (Žižek 1998: 510).

As argued above, 'context' is crucial; it also explains from what or where escape is sought (Evans 2001: 60). Escapism is not necessarily related to an inability to deal with situations in the every-day, or with people unwilling to change reality. What of the urge to participate in the Palestinian uprising and to join the resistance, but the impossibility of doing so because one is exiled? The Palestinian case allows little space for the exercise of free will: a Palestinian who wants to pray in the Al-Aqsa mosque in Jerusalem, but is faced with a high solid wall; the Palestinian who wants to walk in the green fields of Tarsheha; or the Palestinian who dreams of loving someone in Palestine yet is unable to meet face-to-face. Ultimately, contextualisation also implies looking at different local sites, the quality of electricity supplies, and the availability of building permits. This perspective adds a technological base to the main analyses. Such a techno-social framework (Lægran and Stewart 2003) is crucial because, as discussed at the outset of this chapter, occupation and exile fuse with the materiality of the internet.

The materiality of the internet

> The bust, when it came, thus proceeded from the dotcoms, via the telecom carriers, to the equipment suppliers and their component makers (Brenner 2003).

The ICT infrastructure in Palestine was created by post-Oslo (expatriate) returnees, some of whom got together to set up the Palestinian IT Specialist Interest Group (ITSIG), with the aim of discussing, facilitating and promoting the development of IT in Palestine. In the late 1990s, many in ITSIG were guided by dreams of (post-colonial) nation-building, and saw ICT as a central component of the Palestinian economy. This is not strange because at the time the hype about the internet partly overlapped with utopian ideas about virtual reality. Hence, a dialectical understanding of the potential of the internet is necessary if the latter's complex logic is to be unveiled.

Despite the 'free' and 'magic' IT, Palestinians could not set up an internet backbone that was actually autonomous. This did not prevent IT specialists from laying the ground for Palestinian internet usage, and despite many obstacles the IT sector was partly realised and thereby provided the conditions for the internet to develop. To map the setting of the Palestinian internet – and to gain a better understanding of its relevance – this section is devoted to outlining the technological transformation of the internet in Palestine. After a historical overview of IT there, a brief review of the internet in Jordan and Lebanon will be outlined. The chapter closes with a critical assessment of the internet in Palestine through local and global lenses. By scrutinising internet penetration rates, this assessment aims to illustrate how access to the internet is embedded in the context of occupation.

As argued previously, the internet and internet media are in themselves political and historical products. Moreover, the way Palestinians express, negotiate and defend their identity are set within the dominant politico-economic frameworks. The infrastructure of the Palestinian IT sector could only be partly realised because the underlying colonialist logic in Palestine dictates that ISPs must provide bandwidth and connectivity through Israeli companies. Hence, when deconstructing the materiality of the internet in Palestine critical analyses become crucial. The emancipating impact of the internet as a grassroots organising tool is a big leap forward; but this does not mean that its impact in terms of communication itself is completely new. First, grassroots internet use was preceded by previous communication developments. Emancipatory shifts started much earlier, for instance with non-elite access to public education or the availability of telephones, and represent a continuation in the evolution of communication technologies. However, the internet goes beyond the one-dimensional patters of the traditional media: it is a meta-medium (Kircher 2001: 138).

In Chapter One the medium of the internet was compared to a basket. It is profoundly diverse in terms of content, space and audience, and it also overlaps with other technology. At a touch of the keyboard one can find religious as well as pornographic websites, radio and television, and different types of communities. And interactivity happens both online (in virtual, anonymous spaces) and offline (face-to-face, in internet cafes). Furthermore, the existence of the internet is not immune to existing social implications. Paradoxically, whereas digital media industries proclaimed the 'death of distance' even this has a material basis, driven by old-fashioned geographic and physical requirements (Graham 2001: 405). Beside the simple absence of proper ICT infrastructures in some, rural or remote, areas there still exists (computer) illiteracy, poverty, language barriers or political violence that go towards defining the context. Both elements in this 'shift' call for a dialectic deconstruction of the internet.

Dialectics of the internet

> The political situation is the major component of our internet use, or as they say: 'al-haja um al-ikhtira' ('need is the mother of invention'). When companies can't go from the West Bank to Gaza, video-conferencing becomes more important; when people are stuck at home during curfew, internet connection with the outside world is important.
>
> *Sam Bahour, Ramallah–Palestine, 2002.*

There is no symmetry between technological progress and internet access, or between the internet and mobility. No medium can completely transcend (widening) economic gaps and the impact of the neoliberal Washington consensus (Terranova 2004: 41). The infrastructures underlying the internet itself expose the power relations that lie beneath it, for instance the strongly centralising and governing bodies that manage internet usage. The Internet Corporation for Assigned Names and Numbers (ICANN) is the regulatory board that can for instance modify cyberspace by deciding which Uniform Resource Locator (URL) names can be used as addresses of internet resources. These virtual-estate bodies thus resemble the power games and competition of real-estate corporations fighting legal disputes (ibid: 45). Mansell also argues that insofar as social and economic relations are not egalitarian within society today, we need to develop insights into the economy of new media to reveal a deeper understanding of the way in which power is articulated and shapes new media (2004: 97). The internet exhibits an inherent contradiction, both in its inception and its use: originally designed to assist the miltary, it subsequently entered the commercial market to become a major capitalist commodity, and while its diffusion has generated enormous profits, it has assisted in destabilising capitalist and military propaganda.

This calls for a framework that integrates grassroots methods of resisting capitalist domination within the context of top-down internet production. Initially, however, the internet was a salient topic marked by self-fulfilling prophecies. The utopian stance was that the internet would bring us a new kind of enlightenment. As Wellman notes: '[It] extolled the internet as egalitarian and globe-spanning, and ignored the way in which difference in power and status might affect interactions both offline and online' (2004: 124). While utopians marvelled at online euphoria, dystopian analyses warned of the bad social effects that virtual reality could bring with it. The dystopians ascribed a great deal of power to the internet's ability to influence behaviour. But the flames of the dotcom boom dimmed, and with it the internet came down to earth (ibid: 125); the euphoria surrounding the miracle of ICT had not lasted long. The internet did become an everyday tool of communication, and while it indeed benefits some groups more than others, it has become part of normal life. Wellman and Haythornthwaite (2002) show in their study that dystopian expectations have not been borne out – the more people use the internet, the more they see each other in person or talk over the phone.

A grounded and dialectic approach was absent in the early stages of internet research. Carey identifies three major flaws in the way the argument about the internet has evolved: inadequate grounding in the existing historical development of technology; a tendency to analyse the internet in isolation from the wider global technological context; and, most important, the fact that most of the early analyses failed to examine the internet in relation to the socio-economic circumstances of the users (2005: 445). What is needed is an 'embedded' approach – an examination of how and under what conditions, e.g. latent or manifest forms of control, different groups use (or do not use) the internet. The Palestinian case is of great importance in reflecting on these embedded endeavours, for several reasons.

The exponential growth of internet connections in Palestine, as well as in refugee camps in Lebanon and Jordan between 2001 and 2005 confirms that the internet has come to play an important role in Palestinian society. In the quotation at the head of this section, Bahour, a post-Oslo IT returnee, explains the importance of the internet. He is one of the founders of the Palestine Telecommunications Company (PalTel), a company which constructed a high-performance infrastructure – an impressive feat given the circumstances of military occupation in which it had to operate. Pointing out these handicaps still leaves the option of the internet as a space where solidarity and self-empowerment can be found. The internet facilitates the search for practical solutions to problems such as isolation, discrimination and exclusion. Its development helped to avoid borders and provided alternative ways of establishing social relations. The way the internet fuses media, protest and politics needs to be demonstrated in practice, as does how and for whom it has become a tool, and now part of everyday life.

The Palestinian case confirms that the internet lends itself to being both a non-elite tactic and a hegemonic strategy; that it is a part of offline reality constituting micro politics, as practised in local internet cafes, and related to neoliberal macro politics as practised by Microsoft or the military. If there were an 'Internet Manifesto' it should start with: 'Internet surfers make their own history, but not always in circumstances of their own choosing.' This juxtaposition captures the dual nature of the internet and highlights the invalidity of both utopian and dystopian claims.

Nevertheless, neither utopian free-market policies nor dystopian intellectual streams could prevent a destructive economic crash in the 1990s, with the IT sector experiencing the most dramatic consequences. A mere decade after the triumph of the neoliberal new world order many corporate scandals were uncovered. Brenner (2003) recalls that:

> [t]he revelation of WorldCom's fraud shook the market because it became perfectly clear that what had appeared to be one of the most successful companies in the telecom business had made no profits in either 2000 or 2001 (and not quite in 1998, 1999 either). WorldCom, as one analyst told Fortune in July 2002, 'seemed to have some kind of secret formula for producing decent margins where rivals couldn't': when this formula was understood, the last bit of air went out of the telecom bubble.

Only 37 internet companies out of 242 in an OECD sample made profits in the third quarter of 1999, two of them accounting for 60 per cent of the total. The losses among a further 168 companies amounted to an unheard-of US$12.5 billion. The bursting of the internet bubble was the catalyst for the collapse of telecom industries, the year 2000 beginning a seemingly endless cycle of disasters (ibid). Because the telecoms business accounted for a disproportionate share of capital accumulation, it had a domino effect. When the IT bubble burst, a merciless and unabashed capitalism was revealed as the reality behind the slick promotions.[3] Unravelling this part of IT helps to establish the internet in Palestine more clearly.

Bahour's reference, in the quotation at the head of this section, to the 'need' for the internet as the 'mother' of its growing usage and 'invention', summarises the introduction of the internet in Palestine. It was really brought to life by the returnees, their skills and capital enabling the IT sector to develop, and thus helping to transform telecoms in the context of occupation – i.e., a context where fax machines were illegal, applicants for a telephone line waited for years to get permission, and no local capital was available for setting up IT companies.

Reliance on Israel remained a factor even when, with the 1993 peace declaration, some civil responsibilities were transferred to the PNA; among these was the telecoms sector, which had been labelled a 'security sector' under the Israeli military's civil administration. Since 1967 international telephone lines between Palestine and most of the Arab world had been largely cut off, and as far as Palestinians inside the OPT were concerned, Israeli telecoms were always slow to service them. The military prohibited the use of telephone, fax and other electronic transmissions during the First Intifada – a period when contact with the outside world was critical. The only involvement of Palestinians in the telecoms field was through Palestinian employees doing the low-paid manual work Israelis would not do in Palestinian neighbourhoods (Parry 1997).

After Oslo, the status of telephone networks underwent important changes in the 1990s, and ICT became the fastest-growing area of the economy. The newly inaugurated PNA immediately privatised the telecoms sector. Major Palestinian investors were recruited and promised a monopoly licence; the investors negotiated this with the PNA, and it was issued, symbolically, on 15 November (Palestinian Independence Day) 1996. Two months later the sector was transferred to the private company PalTel. The PNA gained control of the telephone networks in the so-called Areas A and B.[4] A vast infrastructure network emerged, expanding the geographical penetration of the internet. Meanwhile, the evolution of computer technology meant cheaper computers, thus broadening the internet's social penetration. For the first time since the occupation of the West Bank and Gaza in 1967, the entire telecoms sector fell into the lap of the Palestinian authority. During our meeting in Ramallah in 2002, Bahour recalled the many challenges that they had to face:

> Our initial staff were recruited among people from the Palestinian diaspora. Yet the political constraints didn't allow us to do our job properly. Many Palestinians would love to come back, but immigration policy is still in Israel's hands. I've been here on a tourist visa for the last seven years. Even with all the experience from outside none of us were capable of building a totally new telecommunications system from scratch. Plan B was to bring expertise by hiring British Telecom consultants.

Certain private investors had already set up ISPs offering internet services, even before PalTel had coordinated the necessary infrastructure. While previous network linkages had to go through Israeli territory, PalTel covered the occupied Palestinian territories with a data-communications network blanket.[5] But companies such as Palestine Online and Palnet were licensed by the Israeli civil administration to provide internet connections, and so it was partly operating under occupation regulations. Thus when PalTel was given the telecom-infrastructure monopoly status by the PNA, these pre-existing ISPs were already roaming, via Israeli ISP providers such as Bezeq, to tap the internet into the OPT.

The presence of providers of differing status was confusing, but on the other hand it became clear that actually all providers, including the official and so-called independent, PalTel, were roaming through Israeli companies. In reality there was no fully Palestinian-controlled and independent technological infrastructure. Despite PalTel, and later Hadara, presenting themselves as autonomous communication services, they depend on the benevolence of Israel. The truth is that to go online the occupied had to tap from their occupier. A further look into this awkward situation revealed that its fate had already been sealed by the Oslo agreements. According to Bahour during our 2002 meetings:

> Why we signed this is a political discussion and relates to the incompetence of negotiators: politicians carried out technical negotiations. The Telecoms Section of the Oslo agreement (art. 36) was a disaster for us, but there's a lot in it for the Israelis. It's a captive market and they're benefiting from the existing structures. And it's important for security purposes: everything [on the internet] goes in and out through Israeli lines: they can monitor

> the Palestinian internet completely. It's therefore interesting why they don't cut the internet, when they easily destroy houses, cities.
>
> It takes them a few minutes to cut off the communication lines to the entire West Bank and Gaza if they want to.

This colonial control, mainly Israel's domination of the frequencies, prevents the PNA from managing its own telecoms resources. In 2003 Israeli telecom companies were still roaming illegally over Palestinian territories, and controlled over 50 per cent of the mobile-telephone market. Meanwhile they provided the same services to their Israeli users for one-third of the costs paid charged to Palestinians.[6] Thus, contrary to euphoric expectations of the internet, when actually placing it in the concrete context of Palestine the conclusion is that autonomy is limited and does not bring about independent infrastructures. Moreover, when pondering why Israel still controls Palestinian ICT, the final words of the Bahour quotation above – 'if they want to' – becomes even more significant.

The question is why Israel allowed Palestinians to connect to each other and the rest of the world in the first place. The two most common explanations during interviews with ICT professionals were political interests (the ability to monitor Palestinians) and economic self-interest (Palestinians paying for Israeli telecom services). At the time Palestinian subscribers received their bills and customer service from the Israeli company Bezeq. Sabri Saidam, the representative of the Palestinian chapter of the Internet Society (ISOC-P), also referred to the agreement itself during our meeting in Gaza in 2002:

> To be dependent on Israeli telecom was beyond the thoughts of every individual Palestinian. Sadly, we signed an unfortunate deal, though we were already dependent on the Israeli market. Given this subordination, to talk of Palestinian ICT development is in essence contradictory. It goes completely against the promises of independence; the symbolic significance of receiving a bill with an Israeli logo is clear.

Interviews with internet companies and cafes between 2001 and 2005 further showed that the situation remained extremely bleak. Damage to the Palestinian economy was immense: unemployment rates went up by 70 per cent, and 60 per cent of the population were living in poverty.[7]

The marketing of local goods was hampered by roadblocks and closures. On top of this, privatisation did not mean an improvement in service or lower costs, despite these being the free-market promises. Accordingly, any discussion of the place the internet holds in Palestinian society must be considered in the context of occupation. Many companies lost their ability to compete and due to a drop in income made their employees redundant, and those among them able to leave in search of better opportunities did so. Palestinian society was forced to develop a survival economy, and the dangerous situation forced companies to adjust on many levels. In the words of Palnet ISP manager Maan Bseiso, for instance, during an interview in 2002:

> Palestinians are perhaps the most adaptable people in the world. See how inventive taxi drivers are with closures, or how checkpoints have become places where people can hire luggage carriers and buy coffee and bread.
>
> A lot of businesses move into areas where it's easier to work. We transferred our office to the other side [near the B and C areas] in order to stay viable. People and businesses are shifting all the time. Now we have a 24-hour support department, and six technicians sleep in the offices because the curfews make it impossible to do otherwise.

Nonetheless, the ICT sector grew because, unlike other industries, it did not directly rely on mobility or geographical boundaries (Tarazi 2001). Another major impact was the Intifada itself. The ability to send out news and indispensable information immediately over the internet was an important difference between the First and Second (al-Aqsa) Intifada. Internet penetration was clearly influenced by on-the-ground realities. In the new context there was a remarkable fusion between politics and technology.

Internet penetration

Israel has built a highly competitive high-tech industry under the shadow of its military activities and defence division. Military investment consumes most government spending, while the ability to tap into investment banks on Wall Street opens a line into the US capital market (Escwa 2002). It is therefore no surprise that the Israeli ICT sector in Israel was founded primarily by former army specialists, particularly from within the intelligence services and by expatriates returning from California's Silicon Valley. Israel became an international centre for software development, hosting branches of some of the largest computer and research and development companies, like Microsoft and Intel. The Israeli market also profited from Palestinian privatisation. It is clear that the direct Palestinian ICT context is partly Israel itself – in fact Israel is among the top countries for IT development. Interestingly, access to (copied) software and technology is easy, not least because many Palestinians have friends or family living and working in Israel. The fact that the OPT is basically a copyright-free zone is another major point of interest.

PalTel's monopoly status meant that it represented the main technological backbone of the OPT. As all ISPs go through PalTel and (later) Hadara, this eventually comes down to a massive selling-on by Israeli ISPs.[8] Technological dependence on Israel had significant consequences for Palestine. For instance when the Israeli army was deployed in Gaza in September 2005 it destroyed the main telephone and cable lines between the north and the south of the Strip, and dumped rubble on the central part of the remaining line (Saidam 2006).

On the other hand, cyberspace is not as easily occupied or turned off and on, sealing Palestinians in at will, as checkpoints and military curfews do. The first significant use of the internet was extensive emailing and numerous newly built websites. At times, technological developments and military/political conflict sharpened the contradictions, leading to a direct clash between Palestinian internet companies and the Israeli military. The July 2002 attack on the main Palestinian ISP Palnet and the arrests and deportation of its staff reflected Israel's frustration. The army attempted to coerce the Palestinians into submission with such attacks and by dominating communication infrastructures. As more Palestinians went online, debates over the number of internet users also grew. Shortly after the internet was introduced, the estimated penetration rate was 3 per cent. In 2000, the Palnet made a preliminary investigation and came up with its first estimate: 26,000 households had signed up to an internet connection, meaning some 40,000 internet users.[9] Universities linking up students and employees, such as at Birzeit, al-Azhar, and the Islamic University together with several big NGOs, accounted for another 20,000 users. Finally, commercial concerns such as internet cafes and communication companies accounted for a further 60,000 clients, with the total adding up to about 120,000 users.

At the time, Palnet covered roughly 65 per cent of the ISP market. This would have brought the total number of internet users in Palestine to approximately 150,000, hence a confirmed penetration rate of at least 3 per cent.[10]

Palestinians have connected to cyberspace through internet cafes, especially at the time when only the few who could afford it had a home connection, which could only be obtained if one already had a telephone line. However small the figures, ISPs observed exponential growth: from 3 per cent in 2000 to 8 per cent by the end of 2002, while in 2004 the Palestinian Central Bureau of Statistics (PCBS) measured a total penetration rate of 35 per cent, of which home users accounted for 9.2 per cent. Then PalTel marketed a new service offering direct internet access through a special four-digit number. This new method could bypass ISPs and users would thus pay only local phone costs.[11] In other words, as evidenced by public and educational institutions, pre-paid internet cards and the mushrooming of internet cafes, the emergence of such facilities meant that the internet was transformed from a special service to a general retail product.

The fact that this was taking place in extreme circumstances makes this transformation even more extraordinary. Considering the economic catastrophe and continuous suffering under occupation, Palestinian technological evolution made a daring leap forward. Thus political instability did not subdue Palestinian interest in the internet. The price shifts in one internet cafe illustrates its growing popularity: *al-Carma*, located in Ramallah, was one of the first successful such cafes. At the start, in 1998, its customers consisted of a select group of people, but *al-Carma* had then progressively dropped its prices from an initial NIS 25 (US$5) per hour when it first opened, to NIS 12, and eventually to NIS 4 – less than US$1; and instead of 25 customers a day in 1998, by 2002 there were 200–300. Such increases, particularly in 2002, express the shift of the internet from a luxury to an educational and business necessity. Meanwhile, the way the internet is used has also changed.

Table 2 shows that, when analysing the level of usage by frequency (regular vs non-regular) at the time, 84.9 per cent of internet subscribers in the OPT used it regularly less than a month before. Yet it also shows that around 50 per cent of household members with subscription were not regular users. This could be because some members of households are already sufficiently connected to the internet at work or university, or prefer to access it with friends in internet cafes; or because some –

parents or grandparents perhaps – are computer illiterate and hence do not use the internet at all.

Following a more general illustration of ICT connectivity in 2004, Table 3 depicts a clear difference between private and public access rates. The proportion of households with internet access is much lower than the proportion owning a computer (29 per cent) or a telephone line (39 per cent). These general ICT figures are important because they imply that large sections of the population, though as yet only potential internet users, had the basic requirements for internet access.

Table 2 Percentage of internet usage per Palestinian household by period of time, 2004.[12]

Period of Time	Palestinian Territory
Less Than One Month	84.9
2 – 3 Months	76.2
4 – 6 Months	65.5
7 – 12 Months	58.9
Before One Year	52.7

Table 3 Ownership ICT Indicators in West Bank and Gaza, 2004.

Indicators	Percentage
Household Ownership of Land-line Phones	39
Internet Users from anywhere	35
Individual Ownership of Cell Phones	32
Household Ownership of Computers	29
Households with Printers	23
Households with Scanner	17
Households with Modems	13
Households with Digital Camera	12
Household Subscription to the Internet	10
Household Members with Web Sites	5

These numbers continued to grow: a survey in August 2005, for instance, showed that 13.1 per cent of homes were connected (Zureik 2005: 6–9). Research on ICT development in Palestine was mainly carried out in West Bank cities such as Nablus and Ramallah – the NGO hub and Palestine's economic centres. The earliest estimates of penetration rates suggest differences between Gaza and the West Bank. Table 4 shows that the average for basic ICT indicators in the West Bank, such as ownership of a computer or a telephone and access to the internet, is higher than in Gaza. However, a closer look also shows that the differences are minimal and that they are decreasing; they are also smaller when economic status is accounted for.

Additional fieldwork in Gaza revealed socio-political differences and similarities. The high costs of dial-up connection and of installation were problematic. Abu Marzouk, owner of Palestine Internet Services in Gaza, started offering internet connections in 1999, after returning to Palestine the previous year. When he began there was no local ISP in Gaza. Despite it being the poorest urban centre in Palestine, by 2002 Gaza had two more ISPs, offering a service of the same quality as in the West Bank. Also, despite a devastating economic situation, internet consumption in Gaza grew, with Palestine Internet Services tapping into the growing market by being the first to issue ready-to-use 'credit cards' for home connection, which could be bought in most local shops.

While the Intifada impeded the spread of the internet, the occupation obstructed ICT development generally. For instance, hardware can rarely be repaired or renewed because of Israeli restrictions on importing goods for the IT sector. According to Saidam during our meetings in 2002:

> Had we been given political tranquillity and grounds for elevation, the internet in Palestine would be rocketing sky high. Even after two years of repression, Palestinian society welcomed the internet and expressed interest in online communication, giving an international touch to their lives.

Israel was breaking international agreements under the Paris Economic Protocol: Palestinian-Israeli economic agreements have been 'incomplete contracts'.[13] One of these being that the PNA could import from Jordan. Jordan was not just attempting to become a regional ICT player: being host to the largest Palestinian diaspora the Jordanian-

Palestinian business relations are tighter than with other neighbouring countries.[14] The consequential ICT developments in both countries made it possible for Palestinian refugees to tap into the homeland. Generally it seemed that the Arab ICT market had benefited from its late and slow start, thus avoiding earlier mistakes and avoiding the impact of the dot com collapse.

Tapping home: the internet in Jordan and Lebanon

In 1995 educational institutions in Jordan were given permission by the National Information Centre to access the internet, and since 1996 local access via internet cafes has been available to Jordanians. In 1999, at the request of the newly crowned King Abdullah, the Information Technology Association of Jordan (Int@j) was set up to foster the development of an IT-based economy in Jordan. This was followed by the launch of an initiative known by the acronym Reach (Regulatory Framework; Enabling Environment & Infrastructure; Advancement Programs; Capital & Finance; Human Resources & Development). The main aim was to study the potential of the IT sector in Jordan, and a five-year plan specified action to be taken by the private sector.[15] The overall goal was to invite investors, mainly leading IT companies, to compete in the regional market. Aside from this government initiative, a new generation of educated and technically skilled graduates contributed to the relative success of the internet in Jordan.[16] It became possible to establish internet accounts and websites without official government approval or registration, and internet services were offered by several private companies, though Jordan Telecom (JT) remained the main supplier.

By the end of the 1990s public internet access was a fact. The ISP company Global One started by charging JD 6.5 per hour (one Jordanian dinar at the time was approximately US$1.40) for a private service; soon afterwards Nets became the first all-round ISP to offer unlimited internet service, for JD 110 per month, later reduced to JD 45; FirstNet then began to offer access at JD 1.75 per hour or JD 50 per month. Notwithstanding this gradual drop in prices, high telephone and internet-subscription costs kept the number of users relatively low. In 2004, the government sold shares to France Télécom; ending JT's monopoly was expected to improve IT access and quality, but France Télécom being mainly interested in market profits rather than investing in allowing broad Jordanian accessibility, the privatisations did not particularly improve local markets. However, the rapid growth of the internet in the Arab world in general, and the Jordanian government's policy in particular, led Jordan to become one of the leading Arab countries in the ICT field (Open Arab Initiative 2006: 13).

The internet had a 5 per cent penetration rate in Jordan in the initial phase. According to a Reach coordinator penetration figures from Jordan's Telecom Regulatory Commission were based on 70,000 home subscribers. When multiplying this by either 2.5 (a modest average) or four users (a more realistic average) per household the estimation came to a total of 250,000 internet users. In a population of 5.2 million this meant a penetration rate of approximately 5 per cent. Universities were the first large subscribers: in Jordan's university city of Irbid (the site of both Irbid and Yarmouk Universities), the main avenue hosted the world's largest number of internet cafes in one street.[17]

ICTs also became newly available for marginalised communities, particularly when the internet allowed a (limited) degree of access to the public and political spheres. The growth of ICT, most importantly in satellite television and the internet, provided new means of entertainment and communication. Alternative news analyses and commentary appeared on the internet, which led to an anomalous situation: while print and broadcast media were heavily regulated, Jordanians could readily obtain prohibited material from the internet.

For a society to become really infused by the internet it is not enough for such a development to be restricted to a moneyed elite making up only a small minority of the population. Int@j channelled internet penetration via its JITCC (Jordan Information Technology Community Centres) project. The aim was to motivate broader internet usage by targeting particular underprivileged communities all over the country. One of the local coordinators made a big *mansaf* (a Jordanian dish) and gathered families to tell them what the centres were for. According to a JITCC consultant, female trainers played a defining role, and the local centres were more readily accepted because of the connotation with education. During an interview in 2003 he explained:

> We've trained 30,000 Jordanians on computer courses so far. We have 75 centres by now – 20 started just four months ago. The nice thing about those centres is that you can find a nine-year-old next to a 50-year-old on a PC. Many were computer illiterate, and some illiterate, not even knowing how to write or type.

JITCC prepared a web template and a manual and trained all its local trainers to use these. As a consequence of Jordan's direct involvement in the refugee camps, they were able to apply to the new JITCC. Sami, one of the coordinators at the Reach initiative, and himself a Palestinian, assisted in setting up the project in refugee camps: 'The camps are overpopulated and suffer different problems. Some centres I visited in camps are working really well. Refugee camps are equally part of the Jordanian community – we don't make a distinction.' JITCC centres were opened in the al-Naser refugee camp and al-Hussein refugee camps, both near Amman, and the Jarash camp near Jarash city. Later in the discussion Sami also added: 'There is a difference between theory and practice – as a Palestinian I know that too.' During a fieldwork trip to one of the villages, the JITCC centre was closed and actually looked neglected: the project appeared to have been going downhill. The method is that eventually, after the official launch and a period of supervision, it is the responsibility of the community to build grassroots participation and maintain the project without JITCC help.[18]

Arabic interfaces on chat sites and web-design layout were motivating factors: language was important for Jordanian internet participation. 'If the internet is to be spread to the masses, language should be redirected,' said Sameeh Toqan during an interview in Amman in 2003. And so in 1998 the *Maktoob* website, which Toqan co-managed, was born as an experimental project. Offering Arabic email, the advantage was that the language of the interface (the layout and basic structure as it appears on screen during browsing) could be offered in Arabic. Its success became apparent when the number of users increased enormously, from 5,000 users following its inception to three million by 2003. The site grew into a complete portal with entertainment, music, communication channels and news. It could be argued that with government injections such as Reach, Inta@j and JITCC, and the groundbreaking changes caused by millions of Arabs joining *Maktoob*, the internet was indeed being spearheaded by Jordan. Yet Lebanon was also an important regional trendsetter in Arabising the internet at the earliest stage. Both countries had in common a free-market-oriented policy regarding ICT, as well as being a small country without natural resources and thus having a stronger motivation to distinguish themselves regionally as the leading ICT market.

Before it could really show its strength in Lebanon, the internet had to overcome many post-war difficulties. These were directly related to basic infrastructure having been destroyed by the Israeli invasions in the

1980s, and the subsequent civil war. After 1991 rebuilding the country was the main priority, although the situation remained unstable – for instance, a newly built power station was bombed in 1999 by Israel, and there was further destruction of vital electricity sources during the war of 2006. Although wars and invasions have exacted a toll on general development and good-quality access to electricity is still not guaranteed, Lebanon is one of the region's countries most gripped by ICT. It has the largest market for personal computers in the Levant (Palestine, Jordan, Syria, Lebanon) with 38 per cent of the 222,223 PCs shipped to the region.[19]

Despite damage to the technical infrastructure during the wars, the early 1990s saw Lebanon become one of the first Arab countries to go online, with the local daily newspapers *Al-Nahar* and *Al-Safir* leading the way. As in Jordan and Palestine, it was expatriate professionals trained abroad who set up many of the frameworks for ICT initiatives (Gonzáles 2001). The different factors in Lebanon's relative success included its neoliberal policies on ICT investment, and a long history of migration to industrialised countries that had led to a highly transnational (and beneficial) diaspora. However, one of the most important social factors was the openly free-minded and independent character of the Lebanese press, which refused to compromise despite years of war and sectarian strife: this relatively open climate influenced a positive attitude towards the internet. Lebanon's technological capacity stands out, and this has had an impact on the production of information in Arabic. At the core of this lie the combined effects of Lebanon's regional media network (both in print journalism and satellite television), with only limited censorship – the government functions with a more deeply rooted appreciation of free speech than most other Arab countries.

In mid-2003, five dominant ISPs were operating in Lebanon: Cyberia, Destination, Fiberlink Networks (Lynx), and Terranet. Other local ISPs also offered 24/7 internet connection through aerial-cable networks, though these were considered illegal since they bypassed fixed-line networks and were repeatedly closed down by the Ministry of Telecommunications. Although Lebanon initially did not have ADSL (asymmetric digital subscriber line) services, the ministry allowed ISPs to provide it in 2006 (ESCWA 2003: 7). Internet subscriptions were initially priced at US$63–73 per month – the equivalent of at least 10 per cent of an average monthly salary (ibid), but by the end of 2002 had fallen to US$18–20. In 2002, Lebanon had an 8 per cent internet penetration rate. Meanwhile, many internet cafes sprouted in the centre of Beirut and around the universities. At the time of the research, in 2003 and 2004, prices varied between LL 1500–3000 per hour (1500 Lebanese lira = US$1). But in the *sha'bi* (working-class areas like South Beirut's Dahia, Mreizhe or Haret Hreik, near the main refugee camps) the internet cafes were cheaper – LL 1000–2000 per hour. Then, as in Palestine, the introduction of the four-digit fixed rate brought down the cost of a dial-up connection.

People were introduced to the internet at school and work, through radio, billboards and even television campaigns. Weekly articles in leading newspapers focused on the internet and its impact. *The Daily Star's* 'Web Watch' section spotted and reviewed interesting websites, such as the independent online magazine amin.org mentioned above, or refugee-oriented projects such as palestineremembered.com. Meanwhile, television in Lebanon aired internet-related discussion programmes.

Interestingly, there was recurring anticipation that the internet would increase development – 'IT for D', as the saying went. Sweeping claims made about an information-technology revolution, transforming countries' traditional development paths were not based on facts. This did not seem to matter. A good example is the case of the World Summit on Information Society (WSIS). Despite this being a UN summit at which NGOs were invited to talk about development and bridging digital divides, the agenda for WSIS was set by the private sector and by powerful ICT bodies (McLaughlin and Pickard 2005). WSIS was organised by the Internet Telecom Union (ITU), serving powerful telecom conglomerates, partly because the Union wished to reassert its own position in the fight to control world-wide ICT regulation in the face of increasing competition from the US-government-created ICANN. As Costanza-Chock argues, ITU has an imperialist mindset and the WSIS summit was 'a plan in neoliberalism and conquering internet territories because cyberspace is a lawless frontier to be tamed under property rights and surveillance regimes' (2003: 2). The great paradox is that the underlying free-market logic of WSIS and the like increases economic (and thus digital) divides. 'Civil society' is often included in big ICT summits to legitimise and mask the neoliberal agenda; many grassroots initiatives were set up around the world to resist this course by WSIS (ibid: 4–5).

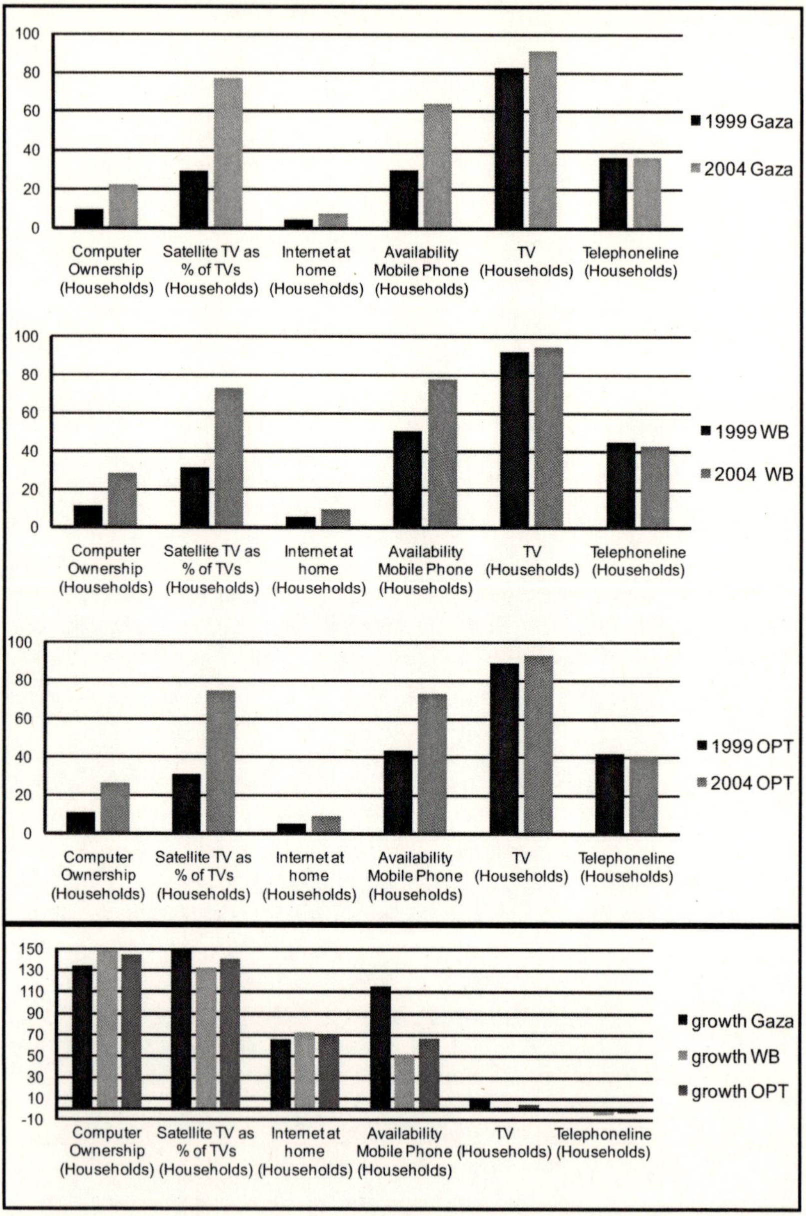

Table 4 ICT indicators & growth rates in Palestinian Households 1999-2004.[20]

Following from this critical analysis, a more pragmatic view is that the myriad of grassroots projects and PR campaigns helped tease those who would otherwise not experiment with the internet. Many then started using it through funded training and computer provision and so experience its potential. Thus for a comprehensive analysis of how the materiality of ICT has shaped the internet in Palestine it is necessary to relate Palestinian internet participation with an assessment of the politico-economic structures that characterise everyday realities. The underlying ideals of ICT development also shape the logic of internet usage in refugee camps, and raise questions about the politics of the internet.

Political economy vs. internet fairytales

A critical evaluation of the internet points to an ICT that is far from 'free' or 'neutral'. The rhetoric of development, economic prosperity and even peace is deployed to promote Palestinian ICT. Meanwhile colonial occupation and obedience to Israel is the huge elephant in the room, which obstructs justice and prosperity but which those involved in international development do not wish to mention, let alone tackle.

Tawil-Souri's incessant scrutiny of the mobilisation of the ICT mantra by funding regimes shows that this has very little to do with the development of the internet for Palestinians, but is rather about using it to de-politicise Palestinians. They are seduced by dreamlike promises of Palestine becoming a new Bangalore: 'The Bangalore of a capitalist's dreams, where everyone is happily employed behind a computer screen, and cultural, religious, gender, socioeconomic inequalities are nonexistent' (2007: 263). Western funding, and American (USAID) funding in particular, does not challenge the causes of Palestinian under-development and poverty: being unable to control the economic, political and territorial reality (ibid: 266). The deeper the conflict, the more international funding is about short-term and visible projects, for which internet projects are attractive options. It is crucial to review the Palestinian position *vis-à-vis* the internet in this context. Oddly, the complex nexus of capitalist under-development and imperialism is a disadvantage hardly touched upon when evaluating the access and penetration rates.

The internet's infrastructures in Palestine are, first, constrained by regional developments in ICT. Early evaluations of regional ICT prospects offered a depressing outlook: in addition to levels of education and economic development – the often-mentioned parameters of development – it seemed also that the state of ICT in the Arab world showed signs of developmental backwardness. The main reasons cited for problems with the development of internet technologies are restrictive media policies and a lack of acceptance of new media (Kircher 2001: 137). Kircher states that the level of technological development is not homogenous: that is, countries differ in educational standards and in their economic status (ibid: 141). It is important to make this point: the examples from Jordan, Lebanon and Palestine mentioned above show that generalising about 'the Middle East' is essentialist and unproductive. One of the reasons for hasty conclusions about obstacles to internet usage in the Middle East, is that most such obstacles were identified by reviewing the state of affairs in the 1990s, i.e. *before* the actual breakthrough.

The way Rand reports classified ICT in the Arab world – in terms of people's 'willingness' to 'develop' – is especially inadequate. Its researchers claim that one of the main barriers to a strong ICT culture is that:

> None of the region's governments, excepting Israel and Turkey, has been installed as the result of what the United States considers 'free and fair' elections. To the extent that they lack legitimacy to varying degrees, these governments maintain strong central control over most aspects of life and commerce. Besides being necessary, from the government's point of view, rule by a strong central leader or group is a cultural norm in most of these societies.[21]

The implicit assumption that all Arab/Muslim countries are much the same can be easily refuted when one compares, for instance, Syria, Saudi Arabia and Palestine. In fact, Palestine is not educationally backward and has a relatively open press compared to many other Arab countries. From the outset, Palestine participated to a relatively high degree in economic and commercial ICT development, and the PNA was clearly a motivating rather than restrictive actor. As has been described above, PalTel performed well in constructing a modern, high-performance infrastructure, especially given the difficult circumstances. Leaving this to one side, the gravest error when researching Palestine would be a failure to mention the effects of Israeli occupation and war. The Rand report fails to do this, and yet its data can easily be presented as factual, to be further replicated.

Capitalist ICT orientations have already become the hegemonic ideology, and an increasing number of Palestinian and foreign NGO projects believe that preparing Palestinians for a high-tech industry will bring employment. It does not seem to matter that Israel has already closed its doors to the (cheap) Palestinian workforce, neighbouring countries do not want Palestinian workers, and the OPT is not allowed to organise its own national economy, even if it could find a way of doing so (Tawil-Souri 2007: 271). Thus to arrive at an inclusive and comprehensive registration of internet usage by the Palestinian population is a complex task.[22] But that telecommunications became an integral part of Palestinian society, on intellectual, professional and personal levels, is clearly an achievement. As depicted in Table 3, in 2004 Palestine reached 35 per cent general connectivity in less than five years.

When scrutinising Palestinian rates of internet usage it also appears that some of the outcomes are only relatively comparable. When Palestinians gained partial control of technological infrastructure, 250,000 Palestinian households and professionals were still waiting for a telephone line. PalTel managed to eliminate these waiting lists, and this eventually allowed ISPs to provide internet connections more quickly. Within a few years more than a dozen private ISP companies in Palestine were able to optimise the infrastructure. Despite all macro-economic constraints and against all political odds, Palestinians do relatively well in terms of internet development. As Waked states:

> A desire to know how these figures compare to those of other similar countries will almost certainly arise from knowing the extent of the diffusion. The Palestinian internet diffusion rate would resonate differently if one notes, for example, that this 11.2 per cent is larger than in many other Arab countries with comparable incomes. When evaluated against Palestine's relative economic performance in the last four years – a period which saw ICT diffuse rapidly in Palestine concurrently with a pervasive economic collapse and a rapid upsurge in poverty – this relatively high diffusion level stands out even more. (2005: 10)

The political situation and the degree to which Israeli practices deter the diffusion, explained by Sam Bahour and Sabri Saidam above and analysed by Tawil-Souri and Waked here, are the most important determinants of ICT growth in Palestine. The years 1999 to 2004 –

just before and in the middle of the Second Intifada – offer important political indicators.

Although the ICT story in Palestine is still relatively young it has already passed through three distinct and important stages. Prior to 1994 ICTs were almost non-existent. From 1995 to 1999, however, the infrastructure grew rapidly, opening the door to new opportunities on which pioneering users capitalised. Since 1999 infrastructure growth has levelled off under enormous political and military pressure. The first growth trends for the OPT (144 per cent growth of computer ownership and 70 per cent of home internet connection) clearly show that access and use indicators have increased rapidly. The statistical summaries in Table 4 give a fair overview of the relative growth rates; they focus on the data of all ICTs between 1999 and 2004.[23]

Analysing the statistics further also shows that the diffusion of telephone landlines exploded after 1995, and remained constant since 1999, when it had reached 40 per cent of households. This increase opened an important door for other ICTs to grow until 2004, a door previously kept closed by Israeli forces. It is crucial to acknowledge the epistemological framework in the ways ICT development is defined. To avoid conceptual obstacles such as those created by Rand, measurements hinting at success or failure, above all, must be critically deconstructed when the group which is the subject of research lives under a military occupation that controls the technological infrastructure.

The Palestinian case cannot be reduced to simple statistical representation because, as Waked argues: 'It lies at the centre of international conflicts, now claimed by some to be conflicts of "civilizations"; it is at the crossroads of superpower interests in the Middle East; and it involves some of the most important humanitarian crises' (ibid).

Conclusion

'It is unlikely that any country in the Middle East and North Africa, including Turkey but possibly with the exception of Israel, will fully enjoy an information revolution during the next decade' (Rand 2003: xiv). Even in 2003, when ICT showed an exponential growth in Palestine, the Rand research could not predict any positive developments, nor did it specifically mention the Palestinian case. When depending on Israeli telecom providers a seven-year waiting list was normal in the OPT, and international phone connections between Palestine and the Arab world were virtually non-existent. Telecommunication became a subject of negotiation during the Oslo talks, and looking back, there were small evolutionary leaps: PalTel was the first experiment of the new PNA, while the post-Oslo returnees marked the birth of a new Palestinian ICT sector. The major (Mobile) *Jawwal* grows given its monopolist status.

This chapter argues that instead of generalising about weak ICT and Arab reluctance to develop it, ICT infrastructure should be measured relatively. Many ICT indicators are based on general conditions taken as universal, such as state sovereignty, demarcation of the nation state, and ownership/access to the infrastructure. In the case of Palestine, these conditions are simply not present, and thus the indicators on which they are based do not hold good.

This chapter started by presenting the theoretical frameworks around the two central tensions – space and mobility – which were examined with regard to national identity and coupled with virtual community. Mobility and immobility were linked to analysing what transnationalism means for the Palestinian diaspora, given the statelessness of its members. After having laid out the theoretical frameworks and contextualising the materiality of the internet, the next chapters are shaped around ethnographic studies in which the offline implications of internet participation, and of the contradiction between virtual mobility and everyday immobility and between space and place, are discussed. This contradiction has led to big and small discoveries and possibilities for dispersed and exiled communities trying to reconnect in cyberspace.

3

PALESTINIAN MOBILITY OFFLINE AND ONLINE

> Golda Meir once demanded: 'The Palestinians? Who are they? They don't exist!' But that was us streaming into Lebanon, Syria and Jordan, with tales of horror, persecution and fear, walking around in a daze, confronting one another with a set of baffling facts, but willing to wait for a few weeks, even months to return to our towns, homes, offices and businesses.
>
> *Fawas Turki, 1974.*

The importance of a Palestine mediated online relates to the vast discrepancy between a collective longing for justice and the lived experience of injustice. This sense of injustice is further deepened by a prolonged rejection, over the course of some 60 years, of the right to self-determination, and made even worse by a *denial* of the 1948 exodus, or simply by the *acceptance* of Israel as a historical fact without reference to the sacrifice of Palestine. Novelist Fawas Turki refutes Golda Meir's famous mantra and the whitewashing of the events of 1948 with personal tales, bearing historical evidence of Palestinian dispossession. As discussed in Chapter One, the paradoxical problem is the immobility caused by a history of forced mobility, leaving the majority of Palestinians homeless, colonised or displaced. The multi-faceted consequences of these historical trajectories have had a major impact on the production and utilisation of the internet. This chapter shows how online mobility became part of the alternatives to overcome that lack of mobility.

The notion of Palestinian mobility is inevitably shaped by the struggle for an independent state. Postmodern redefinitions of national identity have contributed to reducing the importance of state and territory; in the face of everyday (offline) contexts these conclusions have become unconvincing.[1] Ethnographic experiences with immobility have framed the general analysis in this research. During fieldwork in Palestine in 2002, Israeli soldiers drove by in their jeeps when curfew was imposed and repeatedly shouted in broken Arabic: *mamnu' at-tajawwul* – walking outside is forbidden. This was usually followed by: 'It is prohibited to leave your house. If you do not follow these rules, measures will be taken. This curfew is imposed until further notice. Whoever does not abide by the rules will be shot.' Another defining moment happened on my return to Palestine in 2003 for more fieldwork. Hearing the simple words: 'You are denied access', and the subsequent deportation, made a great impact. This double immobility – directly, not allowed to stroll at will, or indirectly, not allowed to cross borders – is familiar to most Palestinians. Yet, while many Palestinians share these setbacks, the diaspora reflects internal differences too. This chapter thus picks up where the narratives and position of refugees in the different diasporic settings were set out in Chapter One. The underlying meaning of 'transnational mobility' in the offline and online narratives is 'forced mobility'. The first section centres on the realities of exile to present a general overview of the Palestinian refugee situation in Jordan and Lebanon.

Palestinians are not a fixed entity in the host countries, but reflect different class and exile trajectories. Transnationalism, with which the notion of mobility and the impact of the internet have become associated, is best deconstructed when, besides dominant global perspectives, it is analysed through the prism of the local (Smith and Guarnizo 1998). Global forces influence or structure local situations (Kellner 2002: 295). The development of ICT amalgamated the evolutions of transnational network societies, but its mobility is highly selective: Palestinian everyday life resonates only a little with free flows of space or place. Indeed, a view from below shows that in fact some have more and others have less mobility (Eagleton 2004).

Having noted the predicament caused by immobility, the discussion moves forward to understand where the internet does offer space for agency and for an outlet. The second section examines how online mobility overcomes offline immobility. Through the internet the diaspora found a tool to talk back and forth, and to see each other via instant messaging, using voice chat and web cam; this involved both interactivity between countries and intra-activity within a country. Internet usage requires a computer and a telephone or cable connection, whereas managing internet content can be learned in community centres, or from friends.

This direct communication, despite its challenges and shortcomings, has led to groundbreaking changes in cyberspace. The diversity of internet usage validates the birth of a Palestinian virtual community. The way local Palestinian initiatives have capitalised on these opportunities is illustrated in the third section. Since individual and local motives also determine how the internet brings about new possibilities, the chapter concludes with a closer analysis: where virtual mobility offers escape, and becomes an idiom of alienation.

Palestinian mobility: forced migration and exile

> The political insistence on the right of return is a demand for righting a moral wrong (Abu-Lughod 2004:35).

> The same American officials and media pundits who thundered then about the inviolability of [Balkan] refugee rights and the immorality of dispossession and forced exile, demanded that Palestinians drop their 'unrealistic demands' about refugee rights (Abunimah 2001:247).

The Palestinian diaspora refers to a displaced community, living in exile, yet sharing the aim of a national home. The right of return (*haqq al-'awda*) of refugees is bound up with the desire to narrate Palestinian experiences, the roots of which unmistakably lie in 1948, as Abu-Lughod (2004) points out. The refugee camps are the painful reminders that the current Palestinian 'transnational community' has in effect been created by forced migration. The minimal services provided by UNRWA in the camps have enabled Palestinians thus far to survive. Ambiguous definitions of the term 'refugee' have further constrained Palestinian rights, causing the propagation of different norms in international law when it comes to Palestinian refugees (Takkenberg 1998: 50). Although the main problem is Israel's responsibility, compliance on particularly the part of the USA and the EU has worsened matters (Talhami 2003). In the quotation at the head of this section Abunimah points to the double standards in that the principles and laws protecting Balkan refugees are denied to Palestinians. The 'inside' and 'outside' have become common classifications; inside or *dakhil* refers to Palestinians residing in the homeland, whether the OPT or Mandate Palestine (i.e. what became Israel after 1948), while outside or *ghurba* signifies the diaspora in exile. Palestine is thus *one* nation in *multiple* states.

The boundaries of belonging and the sense of 'safe spaces' are constantly contested in host states. Notwithstanding the formal praise by Arab leaders, Palestinians at times were used as political pawns or had to flee from these same hosts. This happened for instance during political upheavals with the PLO in Jordan and Lebanon or when whole communities were expelled from Kuwait (1991), Libya (1995) and Iraq (2003).[2] Those who do not have the means to travel elsewhere are forced to live in camps, and when not welcome in neighbouring countries whole family collectives are stranded in deserts between borders.

Thus rather than essentialising 'the refugee', it is important to note the different localities and status of the diaspora. Such differences, and living in multiple states, produce dissimilar experiences, albeit there is a shared desire for Palestine as a homeland, as discussed in Chapter One. Geographical location defines the level and structure of transnational Palestinian networks (Hanafi 2005). Features of geography reveal important differences between Jordan and Lebanon as host states: the former is closely connected via the geographical continuity between the East and West Banks. Apart from location, time (duration) is also significant: many of the Palestinian refugees in Jordan are the result of the 1967 exodus, while in Lebanon the majority of refugees have been settled there since 1948. Whereas the general history of Palestinian exile is sketched in Chapter One, in this chapter I further unfurl the matter with empirical data drawn from fieldwork.

Jordan: between assimilation and segregation

Following the carving-up of the region after WW1 and the weakened British position, Mandate Palestine was promised to both the Zionist movement and the new Hashemite Kingdom of Jordan. After WW2 the UN partition became a fact, and it was agreed that Gaza came under Egyptian rule while the West Bank was to be considered Jordanian. The Palestinians themselves meanwhile had no say in the matter, thus no self-determination; but they soon made up the majority of the population in Jordan, the unification of both banks actually doubling that population at a stroke (Takkenberg 1998: 158). Until the 1970s, Palestinians could move up in the military hierarchy and fill powerful positions in society – such as that of Prime Minister, but tensions grew. Confrontations between the Palestinian national resistance and the Jordanian monarchy led to Black September in 1970 (commonly referred to as *Ailul al-Aswad*), after which many Palestinian political cadres were forced to leave. This partly explains why, up till now – and contrary to the politicised situation in Lebanese camps – there is little or no political activity in the Palestinian camps and communities in Jordan. According to a local organiser in Amman: 'Since the conflict of the 1970s, many people have turned away from political involvement.' After the second massive influx of refugees into Jordan during the 1967 war, the increase in numbers strengthened Palestinian organisations and created more tensions with the Jordanian ruling class, deepening the love-hate aspect of Palestinian-Jordanian relations (Plascov 1981; Wilson 1990).

Jordanian rule over the West Bank and its people lasted until Israel occupied the remaining territories in 1967. As a result, Jordan now hosts different categories of Palestinian refugees: those from 1948; those displaced in 1967; those from 1948 that were again displaced in 1967; and those displaced specifically from Gaza in 1967. The wars of 1967 and the Gulf Wars made Jordan host to one of the largest refugee communities. Despite the fact that the legal status of most Palestinians is similar to Jordanians, i.e. they have Jordanian nationality, there are still important differences between Palestinian and Jordanians, as well as between Palestinian refugees in the refugee camps and those living in the cities.

The first influx of Palestinian refugees, with higher levels of educational and labour skills, was of great benefit to Jordan. Many of the 1948 refugees had access to a pre-existing social capital which helped to set up a nation-wide commercial sector. These Palestinians mainly continued to live their urban/middle-class life in Jordan, and by the time the 1967 refugees arrived the political/power balance had changed, and social stratification had to a large extent already formed. One of the most important differences by the time the 1967 refugees arrived was the change in citizenship policy; this divided the diaspora, and had further implications.

Many of the 1967 refugees came from rural backgrounds, unlike many of the middle classes who 'built' Jordan. With the new policies the new-generation refugees mostly remained in camps, often under difficult conditions.[3] According to one of the Palestinians interviewed in Irbib: 'Children are sometimes forced to study in the street because they don't have electricity at home, or they go to the mosque because it's overcrowded and noisy at home.' Only four of the 13 UNRWA camps

– Irbid, Wehdat, Zarqa and Hussain – date back to 1948. Around 20 per cent of the Palestinian refugees in Jordan live in camps, and the rest in cities. These residential, territorial and temporal elements are tied together, and help to explain the generally closer connection to Palestine. For instance, an estimated 60 per cent of those in Jordanian refugee camps have strong links with Palestinians in WBGZ (FAFO 2002). An interview in 2003 with an IT businessman in his 40s illustrates the different opportunities he enjoyed compared to many of the Palestinians interviewed in refugee camps:

> In 1973 I visited Palestine with my parents. I went back in 1996 after Jordan's peace treaty with Israel. I have two Jordanian passports now: one for the Israeli visa to go to Palestine. I'm not an exception – even rich Saudi Palestinians are granted entry to Israel this way.
>
> Though I very much identify myself as a Jerusalemite Palestinian, in a casual conversation I say I'm from Jordan; the common term is 'Jordanian of Palestinian origin'.

He had never lived in a camp, and was able to visit Palestine. Besides these important differences, how one chooses to identify oneself as a Palestinian also came to the surface during fieldwork in Jordan. In the camps the reference is often 'Palestinian', to which is added the place of origin before expulsion, for instance 'Palestinian from Ramleh'.

One of the consequences of living in the camps is weaker interactivity with Jordanian cities and their society, which for instance affects the possibility of visiting internet cafes outside the camp. During interviews, community workers repeatedly expressed the view that the problems of Palestinian refugees in Jordan are increasing. Despite their legal status – which is undoubtedly better than elsewhere in the Arab world – those in Jordanian refugee camps have no particular privileges but harder living conditions, such as higher concentrations of poverty and lack much basic care (Khawaja and Tiltnes 2002). In particular, some 120,000 refugees who came from Gaza in the 1967 war, and who were not given Jordanian citizenship, face harsher living conditions.

Three main official bodies organise the Palestinian camps, and have authority over those who live there: the Governor of the area where the camp is located, the Camp Committee (CC) and UNRWA. One of the camps researched in this study is al-Bekka, Jordan's biggest; about 20 kilometres north of Amman, it accommodates nearly

100,000 refugees.[4] According to several Palestinian NGOs in al-Bekaa, the Department of Palestinian Affairs (DPA, part of the Jordanian Ministry of Foreign Affairs) intervenes in their work, is sometimes present during the Camp Committee's meetings, and may even select the camp representatives. According to a local activist in the camp, when she was asked to be a representative on the Camp Committee the DPA stepped in. The activist is outspoken and enjoyed broad support among the people, but the DPA usually prefer to select representatives from among the older refugee notables.

Of the larger proportion of refugees who yearn to move out of the camps, only a small number manage to do so, and these people build houses near the camp in order to be nearer their social networks and family. But through the prism of the internet the issues related to control and surveillance, at both physical and virtual levels, become increasingly important, particularly in the context of the camps. Some refugees try to move out, firstly because of the difficulty of living and working in isolated areas, but also because they feel under constant surveillance. As a refugee from al-Bekaa camp pointed out: 'We know that we have the *mukhabarat* (undercover police) everywhere – it is part of our daily lives.'

Interviews with refugees in the camps and with Palestinian students in Amman and Irbid confirmed instances of repression during protests in solidarity with Palestine. Since the al-Aqsa Intifada outbursts of anger and grief have often turned into demonstrations, with increasing criticism of the Jordanian regime for its cooperation with Israel. Riot squads shoot paint bullets at student activists so as to find them easily in the crowd and arrest them. They are later interrogated, and often abused. In one of the camps where protests have broken out the refugees were caged inside the camp perimeter; riot squads threw teargas bombs inside homes and shot at people. Local witnesses reported that at least two women suffered miscarriages from the suffocating teargas. According to one of the camp volunteers riots broke out after the Intifada; when angry people tried to get out of the camp to protest, two refugees, including a child, were killed. Her dismay, she explained, came from the fact that while Israeli forces were responsible in Palestine, in Jordan the suffering was at the hands of an Arab government.

As pointed out above, Palestinians in Jordan are still connected through kinship networks to Palestine itself, and one therefore finds condolences in local Jordanian newspapers for relatives killed in Palestine, or even *biyut al-'aza'* (funeral ceremonies) in the camps. Also, most of the Intifada victims with acute injuries who receive special permission to get medical treatment in Jordan rely on these networks. This type of bonding with Palestine is impossible for refugees in Lebanon. Several interviewees in Jordan wondered what was worse, the well-known deplorable situation in Lebanon or that in Jordan. Murad formulated it like this: 'Do I really want political integrity and freedom of speech, yet be treated like a dog, as in the camps of Lebanon?'

Lebanon: 'two mothers'

In Lebanon the division of Palestinians mirrors that in Jordan: around 80 per cent of the total Palestinian population in Lebanon live as stateless refugees in camps. Their situation can be summarised as bearing a double burden. The colonial divide-and-rule strategy imposed on Lebanon is critical to understanding the current state of affairs regarding Palestinian refugees. Privileges were allocated by colonial powers in a dangerously sectarian way. Social hierarchies were based on religious affiliations – Druze, Christian (Maronite, Orthodox) and Muslim (Sunni, Shia) (Salibi 1988). This meant that the influx of thousands of Palestinian Sunni Muslims (and a smaller number of Palestinian Christians) immediately became a political issue, with grave consequences: most importantly, they were not granted equal citizenship, so as to keep the demographic sectarian balance in control. Hence the exception made later for Palestinian Christians: many of them received Lebanese citizenship in the 1950s.[5]

Lebanon never really had a policy for Palestinian refugees; it did however actively segregate them. Growing fears of demographic changes, because a large majority of Palestinians were Muslim, had initially led Christian leaders and feudal lords to stir up public opinion against the refugees (Nasser 2002). Palestinians were subject to the security service known as the Deuxième Bureau and *al-maktab al-thani* (Sayigh 1979) but in the late 1960s, during *ayyam al-thawra*, 'the revolutionary days', the PLO played a major role in liberating the camps from repression.

Besides suffering socially as a consequence of the sectarian divide, Palestinians in Lebanon also suffered high levels of violence. People in Lebanon confronted Israel in two ways: through their resistance to Israel after its 1967 occupation of south Lebanon, and through the fact that Palestinian resistance movement operated from Lebanon. Israel attacked Palestinian refugee camps in Lebanon as early as 1972, but the consequences for Palestinians were even more dramatic when civil war broke out in Lebanon and reached a climax when Israel invaded the country in 1982 (Takkenberg 1998: 18). With the Tel al-Zaatar massacre in 1976, the 1982 massacres in Sabra and Shatila, and the 'war of the camps' between 1984 and 1987, Lebanon became the site of a painful Palestinian history, to which the camps and their nearly half a million refugees still bear witness. The accounts collected among refugees during fieldwork expressed Palestinian suffering under these conditions.

The policies of the Lebanese government, worried at so-called *tawteen* (permanent settlement), aggravated the already severe conditions arising from a lack of services in the camps. Restrictions were imposed on housing and employment, and the camps made subject to martial law. Palestinian students were not free to choose their higher education specialism: studying medicine or law, for example, was prohibited regardless of academic talent. Due to this, and the high rate of unemployment, many university graduates would end up as manual labourers or taxi drivers.

1982 is a defining year in Palestinian history and is marked as such in poetry, oral accounts and songs. After a two-month Israeli siege of Beirut, the PLO was forced to leave Lebanon. Until then, it had functioned as a shadow state, and a major shield for Palestinians. Most of the services the various PLO institutions had provided eventually stopped. Internal conflicts between the remaining Palestinian factions and various Lebanese groups further aggravated the situation.

Residents of the camps became easy targets, and vulnerable to attack. It was in this context that massacres took place under the then Israeli Minister of Defence, Ariel Sharon, with on-the-ground assistance from the Lebanese Phalange. The Phalange, taking revenge on Palestinians and willing to cooperate with Israel, committed atrocities that shocked the world. Many people still talk of how they were directly affected, either through the loss of family members or by being part of the resistance. These were not clichéd narratives dictated by victimhood, but a living reality still remembered in daily life. 36-year-old Ahmed in Shatila was one of the people who shared his experience of the 1982 attacks during fieldwork in 2004:

> The second time they entered our house and started shooting I hid with my seven-year-old brother Ismael in the bathroom. We came out when the Phalanges left; Suad was shot 16 times, and paralysed; my brother and I couldn't carry her. We saw many

> bodies lying in the alleys, dead people. We weren't the only ones who'd been attacked and shot in their houses. Killing was everywhere – the killers were still in the camp. Everybody in the camp had expected the Israelis would come and do as they did in Saida: arrest the wanted people, put them in the Ansar concentration camp, but leave most of the others alone. This is why we stayed at home in Shatila. We only found out that a massacre was taking place in the evening ... Shadi, Shadia, Fareed, Bassam and Hajar – five children, plus my father – were killed.

During the 1982 Sabra and Shatila massacres, Ahmad's family was literally split in half: five siblings and their father died, and five other siblings and their mother survived.

For many interviewees Lebanon represented heroic resistance as well as great suffering. Samar from Shatila expressed the love-hate relationship people have towards Lebanon, and spoke of the camps as both miserable places and networks of solidarity and protection:

> Lebanon and Palestine are like two mothers. One gave us the soul and the other raised us. Our real mother is Palestine, for we are not of Lebanese blood. Life in the camps is full of contradictions. It's beautiful and at the same time miserable. If you want to see people suffer, come to the camp. But when I've been away for a few days I feel the need to go back to our camp where it's warm and I feel safe.

Israel's main aim was to crush the PLO resistance. After the 1982 massacres, the camps were again under attack: for instance the Syrian-backed and supported Lebanese Shia Amal militia attacked Palestinian refugee camps during the 1985 battles. While the camps were under siege, many Palestinian fighters were in south Lebanon with the Lebanese resistance front, against Israeli occupation and the South Lebanese Army, Israel's ally. The civil war led to further enormous destruction and to thousands of Palestinian deaths (Hagopian 1985). Collective Palestinian and Lebanese resistance against Israel also shaped refugee sentiments with respect to Lebanon. The stories, songs, plays and poems about the revolutionary years in Lebanon are inspirational and still fuel hope.

Palestinian refugees in Lebanon consist of the poorest sector in society. The country hosts an additional 42,000 refugees, unregistered (due to bureaucratic classifications) in approximately 20 non-UNRWA-recognised 'population collectives'. Many of these people are not even entitled to basic UNRWA services, often the last safety net. The houses in refugee camps are cold and damp in winter, and when it rains there is flooding because sewage pipes inside the camps get clogged. During the fieldwork several interviews were cancelled because it was difficult to move around the camp due to flooded alleyways or power cuts. Water pipes are sometimes left above ground, vulnerable to damage: as a result, the water is sometimes contaminated. Abu Basel, local PLO representative in Bourj al-Shamali described the conditions during an interview in 2004:

> In 1974 four schools were built in this camp. Now in 2004 we still have the same four schools – they were never improved. Meanwhile the population has increased from 11,000 to 17,000, and 40 to 45 children are jammed into one classroom. This winter 19 houses are in urgent need of reconstruction. A few days ago pieces of a ceiling fell down on a person who was sleeping.

This background to refugee life in Jordan and Lebanon helps explain the relevance of the internet. The drawings, street posters and songs encountered during fieldwork, and the interviews themselves, all expressed a certain agony, and one of the ways to realise part of the diaspora's dream is by strengthening personal ties with historic Palestine; the *inside* personifies both the loss of and quest for a Palestinian state. Ethnographic examples from Palestine, Jordan and Lebanon will explicate how internet usage becomes a social outlet in light of the everyday conditions laid out here.

Virtual mobility

> I think that if I hadn't had the internet during the Ramallah sieges, I would have gone insane.
>
> *Rima, Ramallah–Palestine, 2002.*

Jordan and Lebanon demonstrate the fragmentation of Palestinian communities across the diaspora. Divisions have also appeared inside Palestine itself, with the wall and the checkpoints paralysing movement between the West Bank and Gaza. The internet, however, facilitates the reconnecting of Palestinian society by offering an accessible space. Having discussed forced mobility in the previous section, the debate now takes a closer look at how virtual mobility becomes an outlet, an escape into cyberspace. The internet is able to transcend space by linking people from geographically separate territories. Online spaces are *vehicles* that assert the dream of a territorial Palestinian space and empower people to visualise their own territorial place. The internet 'glue' has become even stickier as interactive tools have further eased usage at the grassroots.

National sentiments online are a reminder of what is lost offline. Boredom, loneliness or anger, during curfews or because the entrance to a town or camp is closed by checkpoints, profoundly increase the internet's relevance. Thus meeting with comrades, other peer groups or new-found family members is experienced as highly meaningful. Zaina from Bethlehem, for instance, recalled in 2002 her experience of finding family members on the internet for the first time:

> I met family in Austria, Canada and Australia through the internet. I now know people I didn't know existed. I got in touch with an aunt in Australia. It was difficult to decide whether to call her, how to introduce myself and what to say. We mainly email and she urged me to visit her.

Objective conditions, such as the required capital for a PC or the basic infrastructure needed for electricity and cable connection are nevertheless imperative. Grassroots projects form the backbone of online communities and make the advantages of the internet available to other segments of society. Some projects were set up within existing programmes, built on the community support that such programmes already enjoyed.

This section exemplifies, furthermore, how the diaspora is transformed by the introduction of mailing lists, local internet initiatives and chatting. What had evolved from spontaneous and incidental initiatives became professionalised. Internet enterprises such as the Ritaj were crucial for the survival of university education, and have all contributed to a radical leap in the evolution of internet-mediated public spheres. The coming of the internet led to new encounters between Palestinians, at times correcting the idealised imagined community.

Evolution of the Palestinian internet

Direct online interaction between Palestinians had started in the 1990s. Hanafi (2001) discusses one of the first Palestinian internet-based networks – Palestinian Scientists and Technologists Abroad (Palesta) – set up to 'harness the scientific and technological knowledge of expatriate professionals for the benefit of development efforts in Palestine' (ibid: 4). The Palesta network functioned as a discussion group as well as a database of professional Palestinians in the diaspora, many of whom were prevented from returning to Palestine.

Their online discussions covered a variety of issues, from an eventual return to the homeland to corruption in the Palestinian authority. Palesta formed a unique online public sphere. The network was to some extent also a selective space which privileged middle-class and academic Palestinians; and since it mostly consisted of the diaspora in Britain and the USA, the dominant language was English (ibid: 15). Virtual interaction via Palesta offered a new way of 'returning' and connecting dispersed Palestinians; thus rather than suggesting the end of geography, such internet-mediated communication redefined the sense of geography. Palesta can be seen as the predecessor of later popular online forums: an explosion of similar networks appeared a few years later when the internet made its appearance as a mass medium – auspiciously coinciding with the Intifada. What began in the mid-1990s as an elite means of communication for Palestinians became an infrastructure used by the non-elite masses and by grassroots organisations, transcending territorial and government regulations.

The process started off with Usenet groups (Netscape) such as soc.culture.palestine and soc.culture.arab, followed by Yahoo E-Groups such as Free Palestine; and later enhanced with Web2.0 social networking sites such as Facebook. At the time of research mailing lists were a novelty. The Free Palestine mailing list, for instance, started in November 2001 with the aim of connecting Palestinians and their sympathisers; it described itself as 'a secular voice in the electronic wilderness'.[6] These internet tools helped to build new social bonds between individuals and organisations. People were able to get in touch in ways not possible before, transforming the dynamics of interaction – now person-to-person as well as person-to-organisation.

Post-Oslo returnees played a crucial role in the development of the new local information sources, some by starting their own websites and mailing lists. During an interview in 2002 Sam Bahour explained how the need for better communication and alternative information came together:

> When a lot of IT-oriented Palestinians returned from different countries in the world, we were like orphans. A country that was not particularly on the brink of an IT revolution either, we created the ITSIG mailing list as a group of friends. We started with ten guys from abroad. It now has 600 members of IT-focused people in Palestine. It moved from friendly discussions and 'let's meet for coffee tonight' to criticising policy-related matters, bringing up new ideas and providing a sounding-board for IT issues.

At the time of the fieldwork, website data showed that March and April 2002 were the peak months for internet traffic: the period when the Jenin massacre and the attack on Arafat's compound took place. Sam Bahour had returned to Palestine from the USA just two years before the Intifada in 2000. He began sending personal stories to friends and family, but occasional emails became a mailing list with many more subscribers. Other email initiatives started in a similar way.

Palestinian mailing lists

Karima, a 28-year-old Palestinian returnee, was trained as a journalist in Britain and Lebanon. During interviews in 2001 and 2002 she described in detail how she became involved:

> I followed the mainstream media and heard nothing about what was happening on the ground, something that really put me in a panic. Ten people were killed daily with live ammunition to the head. We would hear '10 Palestinians killed in clashes'. But what are these 'clashes'? Children demonstrating – throwing stones that couldn't even reach a tank – are being shot in the head. I call that 'targeted killings'. I'd send emails to anyone who I thought could make a difference, about what was actually going on, with the names of the children killed, how they were killed ... I started by emailing a few friends on a daily basis.

Many Palestinian mailing-lists were started out of frustration over media reporting of the Intifada. Karima and Sam illustrate two different examples of the birth of a new tool to confront biased mainstream news media, their random emails turning into regular mailings. The emails were forwarded, eventually creating a snowball effect. These initiatives soon became more structured, frequent and professional. Karima's new internet enterprise contributed to a grassroots archive of events during the first crucial Intifada years:

> ... I discovered that there's local and alternative news but that it isn't being exported. I spoke the language [English] well, could relate to [American/European] people, and knew how to get through to them. I sometimes have to downplay my stories because the truth is so astonishing that people just won't believe you. Although I also got hate mail, many people encouraged me to continue. It went up from my own five friends to a few thousand subscribers. People started addressing me as 'staff', not knowing just one person was behind it. Now that I look back at the archive, I see that I have a full record of the Intifada because I did it on a daily basis, non-stop, for three years.

Understanding the media as a freelance journalist, Karima diverted her frustration and anger into what she could do best, equipped with computer, radio, newspapers and mobile phone. News from her *Hear Palestine* mailing list made a difference for independent journalists and activists who couldn't get access to such local sources. Filling this gap became more important, as Israel was meanwhile distributing piles of well-written, ready-made texts and full-colour files with background information for journalists. The Israeli (PR) approach works because many international journalists have no sources of their own, in fact: most (Western) journalists are not even based in the OPT (Luyendijk 2006) – and often revert to cut-and-paste techniques.

Karima's *Hear Palestine* briefings were a creative and unique response to the media gap. A number of British and American Middle East correspondents, as well as several Israeli journalists, received her mailings. The briefings developed and improved. From hurriedly written or angry personal accounts, they became widely circulated newsletters. They started with a summary introduction, followed by local news from different cities, often with a particular feature story, and ended with news about international solidarity events. There was clearly a desperate need for this kind of information. One of Karima's subscribers emailed her the following cry of outrage: 'I can't believe people are interested in Britney Spear's virginity while these atrocities are taking place!'

According to mailing lists and website organisers, frequency, tone, language and content were the crucial elements of a successful

Palestinian PR strategy. Like the Free Palestine initiative, the Palestine Monitor mailing list targeted specific audiences with a specific approach. Its database contained the names of European MPs and members of the US Congress, as well as those of various solidarity groups. It dealt with politicians in tactical ways:

> When we first started we had about 50 people on the mailing list. In two years we built it up to 13,000 people. The internet is an unbelievably important tool for us. Only a few [politicians] can come to Palestine but we still want people to see the situation. It's important they get something innocuous, not 'the horrible Israeli army attacked innocent Palestinians' messages, but some 20 readable lines of what exactly happens.

Hear Palestine and *Palestine Monitor* also offered news about demonstrations in Italy and Britain to bring international solidarity groups and Palestinians together.[7]

Obviously not everybody appreciated Karima's work. In July 2001 her site was attacked by pro-Israeli hackers. The *Hear Palestine* subscribers received a short email stating: 'We apologise for recent delays; *Hear Palestine* has been sabotaged.' But despite these setbacks she continued to play her own part in general political activism. At the time of our meetings in 2002, *Hear Palestine* had become a full-time job:

> I start my day very early. First I read the local newspapers, then listen to Palestinian radio Sawt Falastin [Voice of Palestine] for the daily detailed local news and then just write and write, putting it all down in my own style. I switch off my mobile, take a pen and paper, and make notes. I try to listen to Israeli Arab radio stations and the BBC Arabic service every hour. I check Wafa [the Palestinian press agency] to complete my stories. I know the staff by now, so I phone them, and I sometimes get the news before it's published.

The military violence accelerated in 2002, and the dramatic events shaped her work, almost to the point of obsession:

> What I see and hear is insane. We Palestinians seem to stop realising how drastic it actually is. *Hear Palestine* became an

> obsession. I stopped seeing people because it made me feel guilty just to be out with friends. I almost fell into despair and eventually had to take a break from everything.

Anger about media bias was turned into something useful with *Hear Palestine*. Here we see how the Second Intifada differed from the First: more than ever, information from Palestinian sources went out across time and space. Those involved were at the same time conscious that this did imply the end of occupation. Patricia at *Palestine Monitor* offered an important insight: 'We don't know how much better it is, but we also don't know how much worse the situation would have been had we not done this.'

The *Palestine Monitor* mailing list continued its work during the sieges of Palestinian cities, even when the office was attacked in March 2002. The webmaster escaped to Jerusalem and with her team managed to put out urgent appeals and local news stories that were clearly barred from the mainstream media. To get the message across they would send an urgent action appeal. For instance their alert entitled Attacks on Medical Services, which described in detail the killing of people like doctors, ambulance drivers and nurses. The mailing list showed that the Israeli attacks deliberately prevented medical personnel from reaching civilians; and reminded readers that this was a serious violation of the Fourth Geneva Convention, which was completely ignored when Israeli soldiers attacked marked cars, or after the Red Cross coordinated its arrival in advance with the Israeli army staff.

Soon this virtual alternative progressed beyond the initial level of mailing lists. Virtual mobility also created a method of survival for one of the crucial standards in Palestinian society: education.

The Great Portal

> Universities managed to hold classes and students graduated throughout the crisis – crucially, because education is a major priority in Palestinian life. Closures, military roadblocks and checkpoints between students and their school or university, accompanied by curfews, added to the existing complexities ... Sharon is sentencing younger generations to illiteracy.
>
> *Sam Bahour, Ramallah–Palestine, 2002.*

Education is important for Palestinian social mobility in the context of occupation and exile, and in the OPT the intellectual milieu is fairly open and independent. Apart from an all-pervasive determination to overcome the occupation, the connection between IT and education has given the internet an extra legitimacy in Palestine. The example often given to emphasise this is of a Palestinian father who is willing to buy a computer for his children, or allows his daughter to visit internet cafes because it helps her education. The importance of the internet can only be fully understood when contextualising Palestinian education. The mainstream context usually associated with Palestine is that of (Palestinian) violence and (Islamist) terrorism, but it is first and foremost a context of war against Palestinians and of their forced displacement that is the perspective taken here. The ability to offer some form of distance learning must be seen in the light of war-like conditions (Halileh and Giacaman 2002).

Baramki's biography *Peaceful Resistance* (2010) gives a startling account of what this special context actually entails. Baramki not only notes the persistence with which Palestinians hold onto education, and how Birzeit University in the West Bank evolved from a small school to become, against all odds, one of the most prestigious and progressive universities in the Arab world. The thousands of students and staff who have been arrested, injured or killed unveil the dark side of Palestinian education. For years it was common for Israeli soldiers to march into a campus, surround its buildings and raid the student dormitories. Although the long closures Birzeit suffered during the First Intifada eventually ended, and it gained (partial) autonomy after Oslo, the university was still confronted with great impediments during the Second Intifada. The occupation was less visible, but in other ways more intense. F-16 jets and colossal walls replaced the M-16 guns and flying checkpoints. The school system was not spared the traumatic impact, on an already poverty-crippled nation, of environmental and infrastructural destruction, the demolition of homes and institutions, death, injury, disability and the arrest of loved ones (Giacaman et al 2002).

In terms of the relevance of technology, Baramki's chapter on 'Networking Around the World', for example, illustrates not only a context where fax machines were forbidden and direct communication with the Arab world made illegal, by military order (2010: 124). But we also read about their creative survival strategies during the First Intifada: how one fax machine was hidden on campus; how academics held secret telephone meetings via a three-way call; how documents were slipped in and out of Palestine; how back-up plans for holding clandestine lectures in private houses were implemented when the university was forcibly closed; how students and teachers rebelled by sitting on the bare ground to hold their lectures at the military Surda checkpoint during the Second Intifada. The tactical use of the internet builds on these earlier forms of everyday agency and allows some of the oppressive conditions to be overcome. Bearing in mind Israel's potential to control access to internet communication (and to monitor its content) and the fact that it has asserted its power by disconnecting Palestinians (see Chapter Two), e-education offers Palestinians an escape via scholarly search engines, and online libraries and tutorials.

E-learning – combined with early ICT development, yet in time to avoid some of the infantile disorders – was born out of this great necessity. This combined and uneven development symbolises that the revolutionary effects of the internet relate directly to the occupation. Ritaj shows that sometimes the extremely negative can lead to the exceptionally progressive. Ritaj, an internet portal for students and faculty members at Birzeit University, was originally initiated to ease procedures for admission, registration and course selection, as well as to improve communication between staff and students.[8] But the project was stalled by the constant disruptions from curfews, and especially by the Surda checkpoint between Ramallah and Birzeit.

During fieldwork in 2002, when military occupation forces had entered Ramallah and imposed a strict curfew, access to the University was extremely limited. Something had to be done or there would be disastrous implications for both students and the University in general. People in the University's Computer Centre realised that the internet-based portal that they had envisioned before the Intifada could be adapted as an effective tool in combating the extreme implications of the new situation. The initial system was restructured to become the first online learning system in Palestine. The IT team worked day and night for two months to develop a seminal system. The house of one of the engineers was turned into the primary workstation to enable the programmers to work round the clock and to avoid further delays caused by curfews. The system was finally named Ritaj: 'portal' in Arabic.

Almost 30 per cent of the students were computer-illiterate at the time Ritaj was launched, and in response the IT Department developed computer-literacy courses. The various faculties soon realised that, in effect, Ritaj would not only resolve the curfew and closure crises, but could instigate a revolution in general learning processes in Palestine. The willingness and enthusiasm of the University community motivated the staff at the Computer Centre. Despite occupation, closures, curfews and other disruptions, the University managed to complete two out of three semesters of the 2001–02 academic year. It also enabled over 3,300 students to register online for the first semester of the following year, saving them dangerous trips to the University, and avoiding humiliating treatment by Israeli soldiers when crossing the checkpoints.

A context-dependent analysis is also relevant in terms of momentum. At the time of fieldwork in Palestine (mid-2001 to end-2002) the West Bank was suffering extreme restrictions on mobility, and danger when trying to defy curfews and closures and reach work or school. Hence Ritaj was about circumventing the strangulation of education by offering some of the essential conditions, such as registration, mediating between staff and student, and listing class and examination requirements. A later study by Landon (2009) shows that when the checkpoint between Ramallah and Birzeit had disappeared and curfews were not as dominant, Ritaj was no longer a portal operating as an academic access point but more an administrative tool, showing the greater relevance of the internet as a community tool in war-like conditions.

The results of using Ritaj were astonishing, but it also provided Birzeit University with the ability to participate in the IT era – both because of and despite Palestine's many political and economic disadvantages. Professional initiatives like Ritaj and *Palestine Monitor* were not the only markers of the internet's evolution in Palestine. There were also grassroots and informal internet engagements that inspired local Palestinian encounters.

Local online encounters

> The Intifada gave additional momentum to the impact of the internet on people's personal and social lives. People felt they deserved to live and dream. They weren't able to do so in actual life, so they found a substitute for this on the net.
>
> *Abu Mujahed, Shatila–Lebanon, 2003.*

A significant virtue of internet technology is its dual ability, at once to transnationalise and localise. While the flow of emails and mailing lists have shed light on Palestinian politics, culture and news, chat rooms, voice chat and web cams have become the ears, voices and eyes of everyday life. A 21-year-old from Shatila camp, Nuhad, had a great interest in local Palestinian culture, and the internet enabled her to familiarise herself with Palestinian songs and folklore. Websites giving information and pictures of traditional Palestinian costumes, such as the Palestine Costume Archive, fascinated her in particular:

> When I'm at the internet cafe I surf the websites about Palestine. It helps me understand more about Palestinian culture, music, etc. We knew songs and stories about Palestine before, of course, but only the basics. I also want to know which traditional costumes and dresses belonged to which city – from Ramallah or Nablus? I didn't even know where that city was located in Palestine. It's remarkable; there are photos and explanations about what the costumes represent and where they originate.

Fig. 6 Palestinian Costume Archive website.

Nuhad's experiences clarify how the internet provides the infrastructure for a Palestine represented in cyberspace. As Abu Mujahed in this section's opening quotation suggests, Palestinians deserve to dream even when these dreams sometimes go beyond the possible. While a Palestine online mirrors people's actual dreams and national desires, a wide variety of Palestinian websites and internet forums epitomise the different Palestinian cities and communities, and online forums and digital newspapers reflect a critical public sphere. And while Palestinian national identity is represented, promoted and shared on the internet, Palestinians inside and outside the homeland come together – though for the deprived communities in the diaspora the challenges have a different character.

For instance, 16-year-old Sanaa only recently came to Lebanon. She knew very little about the country, let alone about life in the refugee camps. In Italy, when her friends asked about 'their country', she and her sisters would describe the beauty of Lebanon and the excitement of Beirut; but then the family was unable to stay in Europe due to a toughening of immigration laws, and returned to Bourj al-Barajne camp. But camp life had little to do with the (favourable) image Sanaa had formed of Lebanon:

> The first day we returned to Bourj al-Barajne there was no electricity. It was dark and they kept saying that it would come back. We asked our parents from where will 'it' come? Now we're used to it. Sometimes when there's no electricity and TV, I go to the internet cafe because they have the extra [UPS] electricity.

Her language disability was sometimes a problem too, as some of the popular websites she wanted to view were in Arabic.

The internet also assists the inclusion of deprived members of society and those who are computer-illiterate. Local initiatives were developed with innovative ways of including Palestinian refugees; one such initiative was a poll amongst refugees. PNA decision-making and negotiations about the future of Palestinians and their land had been essentially undemocratic, because the largest group (the refugees) had no voice. But, to the initiators' surprise, such a proposal was like opening a can of worms, as became clear during interviews in 2001 and 2003 with coordinator Mona Abu Rayan and local Palestinian NGO allocating-surveys in Bourj al-Shamali camp. The idea behind the new initiative was to hold an 'election poll' amongst Palestinian refugees in Lebanon, offering a more democratic and just procedure. Election ballots were distributed by local organisations and offered via the internet. Although they were aware that the polls had no direct political effect, I was told that at least the refugees' opinions on the right of return, compensation as part of a possible agreement, and other political arguments were being documented. This was one of the first examples of what will in later sections be formulated as the 'scratches' that direct internet engagement also entails.

Capturing the history of the Nakba and making sure factual accounts and witness statements are documented and remembered has been a great motivation for many more initiatives. The Beirut-based Palestinian NGO Arcpa (Arab Resource Centre for Popular Arts, which became known as Al-Jana), for example, organised a project to collect personal stories from refugees in the camps. Children interviewed the elderly about exile in 1948, using the computer at the small Arcpa office for additional work via the internet. These oral histories were digitised to be preserved as archives and made accessible via the internet. According to Mu'taz Dajani, the coordinator: 'This way history will stay alive and the Palestinian diaspora can communicate their experiences.'

Ten minutes from Arcpa is the Beirut-based youth and research centre Ajial, which took the initiative to debate with Palestinians abroad. Abu Rabi', founder of the centre, held online meetings with young people in other Arab countries. During an interview in 2004 he emphasised the importance of providing alternative analyses of the Palestine-Israeli conflict, and explained how such online debates were prepared:

> We use voice chat and the two PCs here. We first prepare the debates with our own youth members here and then invite others for the online discussion. There will be young people participating online from different places in the Arab world.

Samir, a young Palestinian in the United Arab Emirates, was one of the participants; he had his own website, with a chat room, and invited Abu Rabi' in return to give an online lecture for his contacts in the UAE about the situation of Palestinian refugees.

International NGOs fund some of the new internet projects, or choose Palestinian camps to participate in their existing projects. Although it remains a question how much of the funded projects are about Western idealisation of ICT as a bridge to (free-market) 'development', numerous experiences did lead to Palestinians in exile tapping into the everyday lives of their compatriots in Palestine. One such project for Palestinian children was Save the Children's *Eye-to-Eye*. These children live in Ein al-Hilwe (Sidon), and they acquired their own website through which they could talk to other children in the world. The journalist Robert Fisk (2003) reminisced about their activities:

> There are 32 children in the class, all Palestinian, all new experts on the internet ... where do they all come from, I ask? And the answer is, of course, not Lebanon – even though they were born there. 'Safad,' says one. 'Hitin.' 'Tabaria.' 'Nimerin.' 'Sminya,' says a little girl wearing a scarf. All are towns that are – or were –in what is present-day Israel.

Before the Ein al-Hilwe project the Palestinian youth organisation Nabe', in Nahr al-Bared refugee camp, organised the first *Eye-to-Eye* project. The children introduced themselves with the following message on their *Eye-to-Eye* website: 'We want to tell you what our lives are like as Palestinian refugees, using our photos and stories. We were cut off from young people in other countries, but through *Eye-To-Eye* we can make links worldwide.' For the first time the children in Nahr al-Bared got in touch with children elsewhere. The project was simultaneously mounted in Balata refugee camp (Nablus, Palestine), and so – beyond disseminating their stories to an abstract 'world out there' – the refugees in Nahr al-Bared were connected to Palestine as well. The project raised awareness and the participants received hundreds of responses from all over the world.

The success motivated Nabe' to set up a computer centre and to continue with similar internet activities. The children actively portrayed their stories with pictures and drawings which were then put on the website. By making new discoveries, talking about their lives and taking photographs of the camp, they expressed themselves more intensely than they otherwise could have. Yahia was one of the key figures; he explained how one of the indirect goals was to alleviate the sense of frustration among the refugees, and added half jokingly: 'A colleague discovered that the children become more aggressive when we have no internet connection; so when the connection is up the fighting goes down.' For many projects the use of the internet is driven by political realities and the need to offer an alternative space for exiled Palestinians. The double attraction lies in internet space offering both information (content) and contact (medium) with other Palestinians.

Technological developments can thus reshuffle the relations between Palestinians in the diaspora, yet direct interactive communication is not always considered the right instrument. Adding a forum page was met by some with reservations. *Palestine Monitor* decided not to add one because 'most of our audience is related to NGOs, academia and the press. Flashy attributes make our websites seem less serious and informative'. Ramallah Online initiator Maroufski explained that 'the problem of having facilities for fully open discussions relates to issues of online flaming and aggression ... Over the years I have had to ban many members for inappropriate and generally malicious behaviour'.[9] Thus while mailing lists were important in countering media bias and offering a 'counterpublic' voice in the public sphere, local grassroots initiatives provided an interactive framework for refugees to participate in Palestinian cyberspace. One of the supreme upshots of the internet's evolution that benefits local encounters is live, anonymous, chatting.

Chatting

The first thing one sees on entering most internet cafes and centres in Palestine, Jordan and Lebanon are the tiny letters and strange-looking symbols on the computer screens. Initially, visitors chatted in English or in colloquial Arabic transliterated into the Latin alphabet; when the chat programmes were 'Arabised', many could finally chat in Arabic. Palestinians in chat-room discussions cover romance, lifestyle and sports. One-to-one chatting and one-to-many forums via the internet have become one of the main communication channels for Palestinians. While the online conversations show commonalities between Palestinian and non-Palestinian internet users, socio-economic, local and real-time constraints also have specific consequences on internet usage.

On a personal level interactive (and anonymous) chatting was the main way of overcoming a personal sense of immobility. Chat and discussion forums boomed, penetrating everyday life, as the internet became more accessible and the interface more user-friendly. Forum sites such as *Palvoice, mIRC, Zorono, Al Buraq, Arabia, Maktoob,* and *3oyoon* began to offer chatting in Arabic interface-script.[10] *Maktoob* was one of the first companies to recognise the potential of Arabic chat, and made this its primary aim. Sameeh Toqan, the general manager, explained during an interview in 2003 that the target was: 'The spread of Arabic language on the internet, and to be the force behind facilitating communication among Arabs ... We cannot go into competition with Messenger [Hotmail] but we offer a new email edition that can simultaneously include Yahoo and Hotmail chat.' *Maktoob* became the fastest growing Arabic-language website in the region, with the largest number of members.

Most of the Arab chat forums at the time had separate rooms for Palestinians, and numerous online forums had a particular Palestine focus. This was partly due to the fact that the founders were themselves Palestinian, and thus inclined to offer Palestinians a meeting point in their own cyberspace. *Yahoo Messenger* and *Hotmail MSN* services were the most popular instruments for direct chatting, while popular forums and chat sites were often used to find new contacts; chatting on *MSN* or *Yahoo messenger* tended to be reserved for closer contacts and family. Palestinians who have never used the internet themselves are also part of these virtual communities, not only the technically-savvy internet users. A 15-year-old from Bourj al-Barajne camp, Samah, brings her family to an internet cafe, where she shows them pictures of friends and family, and connects them via the web-cam to family members living elsewhere. One day she located one of her uncles online:

> The first time I entered a Palestinian chat room I said 'Hi, is there anyone from Palestine?' And I got many reactions. Once I chatted with a person from Nablus, I kept asking if he knew an uncle who also lived there. It appeared that eventually he did. I was so excited and went home to tell my grandmother. The next time I took my whole family with me to the internet cafe.

Aside from bringing family members along to the internet cafe who would otherwise not visit it, online communication sometimes takes place in the home setting, although in the refugee camps this was still the exception. One December evening in 2003, we were all enjoying the stories and jokes of Sanaa's family (with whom I usually stayed overnight when on fieldwork in Nahr al-Bared). The brothers, sisters, parents and cousins had a supportive and open relationship, but it was clear they missed those of their family members who were studying or working elsewhere. They had a computer that Sanaa' used for her work as a teacher, and with only a few technical adjustments, I suggested they could be having internet meetings with their loved ones. This made Sanaa' laugh: they had had such internet meetings all along. She said:

> One evening we were all sitting together like this: with *argilah* [a water pipe], coffee, etc. We invited my brother's friends, our sisters and cousins. We put the speakers on and connected the computer to the internet via the cable. We stayed up all night chatting, cracking jokes and talking about the latest news in the camp.

Many of the cases encountered reveal that immobility is a pertinent factor in Palestinian's internet usage. However, claiming that these virtual encounters are the online equivalent of offline reality is not the point of departure. Abu Mujahed, in Shatila camp, explained that the importance of the internet for diasporic communities lies in its potential to include those who are otherwise cut off. A 17-year-old from Shatila, Samar, expressed a longing for Palestine that goes beyond the virtual:

> People want to go back but don't believe any more that they can. If you cut the hope of returning to Palestine you're nobody: a person without a homeland is like a tree without roots.

For a great many Palestinians, an alternative online Palestine, however fascinating, is unsatisfactory. Maher, repeatedly mentions that it is important for Palestinians always to identify themselves as such when chatting online; he sees this as an aspect of their steadfast and stubborn refusal to give up the struggle, but adds that this should also be a part of their message online: 'We didn't sell or abandon our homeland. We didn't pretend to be different, twist our tongues to look and sound Lebanese, we are still living as Palestinians.' What are the implications when those who are cut off and dispersed are reconnected to the land and the people? Virtual mobility has led to fascinating experiences, but also unexpected and unintended effects. Being on the internet is in many cases a social outlet from the practical and everyday difficulties illustrated in the previous sections. Moreover, rather than idealising the online, cyberspace encourages a virtual community built on collective strength, but also one that excludes or restricts participation.

Floating in cyberspace

> I feel I want to jump into my computer and run into those fields or play in that snow; I want to enjoy the beauty of my land. Maybe you've seen many beautiful countries. But this is the first time I've seen how beautiful my land is. All I want to say is, despite what Israel is doing, we'll keep these pages in our mind.
>
> *Dali, Shatila–Lebanon, 2004.*

This quotation describes the moment when Dali received a collage of pictures by email. Her reconnection with Palestine was a virtual experience: through a series of picturesque images on a computer screen; she had never seen such pictures of places in Palestine before. She forwarded the email to her friends with the title *Here is our past, present, and future*. The symbols, and personal expressions, are shaped and given significance in locally specific ways before finding their way into global cyberspace.

Until now, the transformations in Palestinian cyberspace were viewed through the upsurge in online mobility. Dali clarifies that online mobility is used to escape everyday reality – she dwells in an imagined Palestinian world made up of images and stories. Escapism here is not used in its narrow dystopian sense, as suggested by notions such as 'simulation'. Online escapism is caused by the need to escape everyday miseries, and the wish to experience online pleasures. How can the unintended or dark side of the internet be understood, but simplistic conclusions about the evaporation of real life avoided? How is the worry to be addressed that online participation will create problems of simulated experiences that depoliticise and alienate? In the preceding chapters the notion of escapism offered a framework within which to understand the complex relationship between the internet and its users. This final section will examine people's experiences by questioning what the internet means to exiled Palestinian diasporas, i.e. to those for whom the offline nation is unavailable, and whose feelings of nostalgia are ignored.

Online traversals

In 2000, Maisoon gathered a group of youngsters in Shatila camp in Lebanon with the novel plan of connecting them with refugees in Dheisheh camp in Palestine. Initially they communicated through Maisoon's own email account; she would print out the emails and pass them around. During interviews in 2001, 14-year-old Samer and 13-year-old Shiraz from Shatila camp described how they started this unique adventure:

> We got to know each other by writing emails and then became friends. Now it is more than friendship, we are like brothers and sisters. Everybody in our group has a friend in Dheisheh. We talk about personal things and problems, about school and what we do. And we email each other on birthdays, Ramadan and the Eid.
>
> A week ago we emailed our friends in Dheisheh and told them that we had memorialised the Sabra and Shatila massacres,

> which happened exactly 20 years ago, and that we had a big demonstration.

The enthusiasm for the internet among many children in Shatila and Dheisheh began with this initiative in 2000. Making their own website about the camp became their next project. Shiraz helped write stories about their life in the camp, and proposed ideas for the design of the homepage. When asked about their motivation in using the website during an interview in 2002, Samer and Shiraz explained:

> To let our voice be heard, to let people know how we are living, what our feelings are. This is important – we know how they live [in the West], but they must also know how we live.

> It's to let people know that we still hope to return to Palestine and that living in the camps is different to living in Palestine. We want to work together in order to return.

Samar and Shiraz wanted to use the internet to reach out and express their grievances. This explains also why chatting was extremely popular among young people in the camp. Although pop culture and romance were favourite topics, the political situation at the time dominated discussions. Eventually, the young people wanted to be heard, to break through the walls that excluded them from public debate. When asked who in particular they were curious to chat with, many answered that next to Palestinians, it was Israelis. Shiraz was the most explicit:

> Once I battled with an Israeli on mIRC. She said there is no country called Palestine. I said: 'Do you agree there are "Palestinians" from a country called Palestine?' She said that Palestinians are terrorists because they are suicide bombers. I said it was the only way to make Israel return our freedom. She said: 'They kill civilians.' I said: 'Many Israeli civilians have weapons and kill Palestinians, or take other peoples' houses and steal the best land in Palestine.' Maybe I was too rude, but it made me feel stronger.

Contact between the refugee camps in Lebanon and Palestine strengthened as many more discovered these new opportunities, through either friends or grassroots projects, as mentioned in the previous section. After having only been in touch by email, young people in Shatila were rewarded in a way they had long dreamed of. After the Israeli withdrawal from South Lebanon in May 2000 the borders could again be reached. Dheishe and Shatila now planned for those who had emailed each other for a year to meet face-to-face at the border. Palestinians from both sides shouted their family names and some held up pictures of missing relatives. The refugees from Lebanon tasted olives that the refugees from the West Bank had brought for them.[11]

These spontaneous meetings were soon replaced by coordinated visits between Palestinian communities on both sides of the dividing fence. The hope of returning was rejuvenated by the internet and eventually revived by the (almost) physical contact for which most had been waiting so long. But according to Dajani in 2004, such new opportunities will lead to closer connections, potentially creating expectations that cannot be fulfilled:

> The presents that were given at the [Lebanese-Israeli] borders represented the soil: olives, oil and bread. But this combination, their unfulfilled hopes to return and a confrontation with the land, is precarious. First, there was one fence, so people could stand very close, touch, hug and kiss one another. Then they erected another fence, which made it difficult to meet physically, or give each other presents. When the refugees tried to break through anyway, Israeli soldiers reacted violently. Eventually they even divided the borders by a no-man's-land between them, making it impossible to meet. People from both sides could only shout to each other from a distance. As the Intifada continued, visiting the borders was prohibited; soldiers shot at anyone who tried.

Indeed, it did not take long before the Israeli army intervened. After the border meetings, the children's longing for historical Palestine, its land, its houses and its trees grew stronger. The chance to escape via the internet is of great importance with respect to immobility. Yet the cautiousness of some local organisers like Dajani is that with intensified online communication, the desire to return to Palestine becomes stronger, whereas a solution for the refugees is as far away as ever. These are the circumstances that generate escapism.

Virtual escapism

As argued above, everyday conditions of Palestinian life, for exiled refugees in particular, strengthen the double-edged characteristics of virtual escapism. As reconnection with family in other parts of the world has shown, the internet has become a direct, practical solution for a divided community. Reconnections have also taken place with a land, by those who can only imagine it. As Dali shows, maps, pictures and audio references to Palestine represent the juxtaposition of the virtual and the territorial. A parallel life in cyberspace allows an escape from everyday living conditions, yet this online escapism can also have undesirable effects. It can cause a sense of alienation because virtual participation is often an individual experience, which may increase the sense of loneliness or even exclusion.

For some Palestinians the internet mobilises engagement with the Intifada, for others it leads to greater fatalism. Rannia, in Jordan in 2003, explained her attempts to help Palestine by way of the internet:

> There's a danger that after spending two hours' emailing you think you've done the fight for the Palestinian cause for that day. You might not go out and participate in a demonstration, which might have a more direct effect. It's a tool, and you need to look at it in that perspective. The internet isn't going to save Palestine, but it is going to contribute to its liberation.

From Rannia we learn that escapism can be anathema to dissent and protest, since it negates the need for social change.

Nevertheless, the intensity and frequency of internet communication during the Intifada gradually decreased because the (worsening) Intifada had alienating effects on internet use as well. For instance, Nuhad in Shatila camp was fed up with emails full of rhetoric and pictures of massacres in Palestine: rather than enthusing or empowering her, they mainly left her angered and frustrated. She preferred softer pictures, such as stone throwers, or even Palestinian folklore and songs. This change in attitude was apparent among other interviewees too, a dynamic mainly caused by two factors: an important one lies in the fact that online engagement is shaped by political developments, and reflects particular triumphant or despairing stages of the uprising. Nuhad's shift partly reflected the hopelessness felt on the ground: a victory was not in sight, and many people became as it were politically exhausted. A second factor is that these virtual escapisms show Palestinians a world that could have been theirs, but is not. Dali told me that the internet was like a glass wall, referring to her online boyfriend from Gaza: 'I wish to see him for real but I can't. It's like you can see someone but are unable to touch him. It makes it sometimes even worse.'

Isolation, entrapment, boredom, humiliation and homesickness fuel escapism. Hence, for Abu Mujahed in Shatila, turning to the internet has further meaning, since the Lebanese government provides no significant services for refugees:

> [It] treats the camp like a leaf in autumn – just leave it, it'll fall off by itself. They know how miserable and inhumane the situation in the camp is, and that there are criminals and drug addicts hiding in the camps. They know, but they'll just leave it until it collapses by itself. That's why we find girls and boys on the internet so much: they're escaping to another world. One writes love letters, others discuss politics, or even look for pornography. They're spending time there [online], to run away from reality here.

The flip side of internet participation is the unfulfilling outcome, which can cause further disillusionment. This can become alienation, conveyed by the overuse of online activities and excessive correspondence with Palestine. Dajani too fears that increased communication and the desire to return to Palestine has led to disappointment, and thus has deepened the disillusionment: 'Sometimes it's better not to know.'

As illustrated throughout this chapter, the virtual *conveys* rather than *escapes* reality in the context of the Palestinian diaspora. For some, online engagement meant activism, but for others it was political escapism which also led to a sense of isolation. All this captures the first reactions and experiences with the internet and with the novelty of online communication. Virtual mobility, with all its pros, cons and uncertainties, is another way of coping with the offline reality characterised by immobility.

Conclusion

Israel imposes a double restriction: it prevents the flow of people and censors the flow of information. These restrictions have been partly overcome by the birth of grassroots internet projects and online discussion forums. Palestinian publishers, commercial entrepreneurs and government bodies have capitalised on the possibilities of the internet. Virtual journeys have had a tremendous impact in breaking the isolation, and the subsequent alienation, from mainstream Palestinian politics.

Focusing on Palestinian online and offline mobility, the internet has helped overcome immobility in two ways: as a medium of communication and as a message. People's responses, stories and encounters in Palestine, Lebanon and Jordan mentioned in this chapter have shown what the internet has meant in a context marked by the Palestinian struggle for self-determination in the first phase of the Intifada. For communities barred from national autonomy, forcibly divided and sent into exile, the internet offers a platform for the exercise of collective identity. Moreover, it has improved the confidence of refugee communities by helping them to reassert themselves and to proclaim an independent state as a central axis of Palestinian politics. With the internet becoming a normalised medium, the impact of the online encounters discussed in this chapter also changed.

As the debates in cyberspace between Ajial in Beirut and Arab and Palestinian young people across the region shown, Palestinians can communicate with each other simultaneously from different places, altering the offline conditions of time and space; and the content of such communication is often based on the fact that the participants are part of a united Palestinian diaspora. The narratives and analyses presented here reconstruct a time when the internet was a novelty for Palestinians – the initial euphoria at the impact of the internet was meaningful, in that it was related to the political impact of crossing (virtual) boundaries. This new phenomenon was made possible for the first time since 1948.

Many Palestinians regard themselves as belonging to one nation, and continue to express their wish to return to their homeland; indeed, this is one of the main topics of their discussions on the internet. For those on the outside, their notion of a collective national Palestine is mostly based on how Palestinian life, culture and society were when their grandparents left the country; so what is being recalled is an idealised Palestinian homeland. Does the practice of traverses in cyberspace and forming online relations have offline repercussions in the construction of national identities? Does this lead to a re-examining of 'Palestinianness'? Palestinian culture, particularly for those on the inside, has gone through many phases and challenges since 1948. The following chapter is concerned with how the internet strengthens as well as questions Palestinians' national identity and their call for an independent state.

4

VIRTUAL SPACE, TERRITORIAL PLACE

> *Li kull al-nas watanun ya'ishuna fihi, wa lakin nahnu lana watanun ya'ishu fina.* (All people have a country to live in, but we have a country living inside us.)
>
> *Dali, Shatila–Lebanon, 2003.*

While representing the imagined nation, new technological innovations have also reshaped Palestinian self-identification. New styles of connectivity have combined with grassroots interactivity to redefine the relationship between territorial place and virtual space. Being denied civil rights and citizenship, yet claiming and disseminating national identity via an 'electronic passport' on the internet, signifies a fusion of politics and mass-mediated practices in concrete ways. Mobility, space, place and time are often interrelated concepts in internet studies. Having discussed in the previous chapter the tension between mobility and immobility with regard to the reality of forced migration, occupation and exile, this chapter argues that in the Palestinian context virtual space is a reminder of the absence of a shared territorial place.

The 19-year-old Dali shared what having a nation and country meant to her when we met in Shatila refugee camp in 2003. Talking with her and others prompted issues varying from life in the camp to personal experiences on the internet. Contact between Dali and myself intensified – we became friends and added each other to our Hotmail messenger. We enthusiastically greeted one another on MSN the first time we met online when I had left Lebanon. While we chatted, her long and poetic 'nickname', like a signature or ID (and quoted at the head of this chapter), intrigued me. She explained that a 'country living inside us' refers to coping with exile. She chose this as her online ID because: 'Many people don't realise what it means because they are used to having a country; we don't have this luxury. The message is that despite not having a country, it lives very strongly inside us.' Such cases concretise the juxtaposition of virtual and spatial spaces, highlighting the dialectics of state, nation and (imagined) community: contrasting the celebrated and assumed 'free-flowing' post-state societies.

Zionism was (and continues to be) the primary 'other' that strengthened Palestinian national consciousness: Palestinians considered themselves part of a sovereign entity *'Shaam'* (the Levant: Syria, Lebanon, Jordan and Palestine), and within that as a Palestinian people. Thus although the affirmation of a Palestinian national identity enhanced in response to Zionism, it already existed in addition to regional identifications. The development of a collectively imagined Palestinian community stems from the end of the 18th century and was further consolidated in the colonial Mandate period. In dialogue with Anderson's (1991) analyses Khalidi's (1997) study on the local Palestinian press shows that a national identity was well-grounded by the 1920s and 1930s. As argued in previous chapters, delving into notions about nation, state and national community is necessary because they have become an integral part of the discussion about mediated identities. Moreover, the nation-state is a potent frame of reference in analysing the creation and regulation of media networks (Abu-Lughod et al 2002: 11).

Research about the social impact of media can be extended to analysing the internet and questioning how national narratives or communities flow in Palestinian cyberspace. The internet fills an important gap; whereas the classic media are formed in hierarchically organised (state) schemes, the internet has a decentralising (global) character. This is the main reason that the internet becomes more relevant for dispersed and exiled communities. Discussing diaspora communities online, Eriksen distinguishes four forms of internet nationalism: state-supported, surrogate, pre-independence and multiculturalist, each exhibiting different styles and methods of online interaction (2006: 12).[1]

However, as discussed in Chapter One, a nation-state framework for dispersed or occupied communities brings up new dilemmas. What state is there for Palestinian media production and in which public sphere can Palestinian media production play a role? Not only did

Palestinians lose the territorial battle through colonial occupation and settlement policies, moreover: the basic notion of 'Palestinianness' was long denied via the propagated myth that Palestine was 'a land without a people for a people without a land'.[2] Therefore, electronic media, in the context of colonialism and apartheid – as well as of resistance and solidarity – are equally important references. The question is now what exactly is framed as the national point of reference for a community so dispersed, after 60 years of exile? The strong politicised reality explains why regional and class differences are considered, overall, secondary. Expressing a Palestinian national identity online is not about an existential nationalist feeling or about ignoring the role of the individual, but about the practice of coming together collectively, about sharing a platform.

Answering part of these questions, the first section of this chapter discusses the notion that *anti-colonial* nationalism – not nationalism as such – forms the premise of a Palestine Online. Several case studies will demonstrate that a mediated national consciousness does not depend on possessing sovereign territory. Other ethnographic examples will further illustrate how the online dissemination of Palestinian identity and belonging has been greatly affected by the political upsurge since 2000: the Intifada, in short, boosted the online interactions and reconstructed the diasporic identity. These counter-narratives are shaped both by denial of the ethnic cleansing and exodus (the 'Nakba', also referred to as *al-nakba*) and by remembering them. Again, these motivations were given fresh impetus by the outbreak of the Intifada.

This kind of an imagined national community, one promulgated by the internet, will be examined in the second section. Online communication and representation introduced an *online public sphere* and in turn also created the conditions for a commodification of identity, which resulted in the ultimate configuration of a *Made in Palestine* label. The Palestinian nation is globally imagined through a myriad of novel online encounters such as the formative Across Borders Project as the final section illustrates. By challenging the online-offline divide these virtual crossings not only confirm but also have the ability to alter Palestinians' ideals *vis-à-vis* the nation.

Counter-narratives

> Do we exist? What proof do we have? The further we get from the Palestine of our past, the more precarious our status, the more disrupted our being, the more intermittent our presence. When

> did we become a people? When did we stop being one? Or are we in the process of becoming one? (Edward Said 1986)

Live communication and online mobility are the key elements of virtual communities. Before studying the collective (imagined) identity on the internet it is important to review the underlying conceptualisations with regard to Palestinian national identity. As evocatively suggested by Said (above), Palestinianness is in a continual process of 'becoming', while simultaneously 'preserving' itself as a national community. The making of collective identity is a dynamic process, shaped for instance by people's dreams about the land. How are these dreams imagined, constructed and contested through the internet, - a technology that has become one of the pillars of the diasporic nation-building process? Answering this will help trace how 'Palestinianness' is expressed online.

At the start of the research it became immediately clear that intense political developments were shaping online-mediated communications. On 29 September the second (al-Aqsa) Intifada broke out, affecting all Palestinians one way or another and wherever they were. For them, the internet is not a *tabula rasa*, but has been fuelled by these experiences and shared histories. This alternative online space is not a strict replica of an imagined Palestinian nation, but assumes a re-structuring and re-imagining of a nation in flux between contemporary and historical memories and symbols.

This section continues the debate about national identity whose premises were set out in Chapter One, in order to unravel several contextual difficulties. It will be shown that Palestinian identity is formed by being a nation without a state, and hence inspired by anti-colonial nationalism. Furthermore, Palestinian identity in this context relates to an imagined community coming together via the internet; this section exemplifies the paradoxes of online Palestinian identity.

Imagining the nation

A striking example of state manipulations of the political national identity is the way academics and others have used historical archives to justify the creation of the Israeli state. There is for instance a fluid relation between the security apparatus and faculty members at Israeli universities (Forte 2003), and the notion of state security became strongly linked to the notion of national identity (Zureik 2001). However, the release of previously unavailable documents tarnished the authoritative nationalist narratives of Israel's foundation. Many patriotic academic practices were challenged, from the 1980s onwards, by the so-called 'new historians', who were among the first Israelis to shed light on the Nakba, effectively making the Palestinian narrative become more acceptable in mainstream analyses.

Palestine was fragmented, and rendered a nation of displaced refugees. It is the uniqueness of the settler/colonial project in Palestine that meant that Palestinians became systematically excluded from all facets of what became the colonisers' society (Shohat 1989). Zionism is a form of colonial oppression that combines capitalist exploitation and racist claims of superiority. Zionism implies exclusion and ethnic cleansing of the native followed by a settler-colonial occupation of those who remained. These particularities have shaped a Palestinian persistence in forming and celebrating their identity, language and resistance movements. Colonial and revolutionary histories are therefore important components of the collective self-identity. According to Khalidi (1997), Palestinians therefore identify themselves differently:

> [g]iven the lack of such a state or unified educational system, the Palestinian would be more likely to refer identity to a number of 'historical' narratives, each carrying a different valence and a somewhat different message (1997: 146).

Khalidi argues that because Palestinians were not allowed to form an independent entity, self-definition often took place in relation to 'the other': the remark made by the then Israeli Prime Minister Golda Meir – that there are no Palestinians – is the best example. This logic displays a colonial attitude towards Palestinians that has nevertheless become commonplace in Western discourse (ibid: 147). Palestine is a nation that exists in multiple states, as argued in Chapter One; since a territorial or judiciary framework is absent, Palestinians are 'non-state' people (Eriksen 1993: 14).

The importance of this 'otherness' does not mean that Palestinians are defensive, passive subjects: national identity has become connected with Palestinian resistance. Colonial subjugation transforms the expression of national identity into a political act. Palestinians have to struggle for recognition because they are contested as a people. Palestinian collective identity, nationalism and struggle are therefore interrelated (Shulz 1999; Y Sayigh 1997). As argued before, this does not imply that Palestinian identity can be reduced to a mono-national representation; in fact a collective identity also harbours contradictions. Furthermore, online topics not only relate to politics or identity but include romance, art, music and business. A good example is the website initiated with the acronym PEBBLES: *politics, economy, business, bizarre, lifestyle, entertainment, sports*. During an interview in 2002 in Ramallah Sam Bahour explains that it is important to know 'Palestine is not just about politics ... however, while we are all of this (pebbles), the last suicide attack is the only thing people in the West seem to associate with Palestine.'

Since several decades Palestinian identity and public perceptions have become 'Islamised'. Islamic movements indeed grew in popularity and political presence. But its uncompromising discourse and on-the-ground resistance matters more than religious content. Historically, political identity was prompted by *al-qawmiyya al-'arabiyya* (Pan-Arab ideological framework) of which *al-qawmiyya al-wataniyya* (a Palestinian national ideological framework) was an important subcategory (Kimmerling 2000: 71).[3] The defeat of Pan-Arabism, the PLO's move away from analysing the occupation conflict in terms of a regional conflict, and the general collapse of the secular left after the Cold War, channelled Palestinian resistance and identity from a secular Pan Arab nationalist to a more Islamist and local framework. Hamas rejected the peace process and revolted against the demands of non-violence, while Fatah became increasingly associated with political impotence, and while Hamas provided basic healthcare and education in the poor refugee camps, Fatah got trapped in corruption scandals; this was to give Hamas political credibility and led to its electoral victory (Hroub 2006).

The history of forced exile and social uprisings illustrate that anti-colonial nationalist discourses matter greatly in Palestinian identity formations. Non-state communities maintain a strong degree of longing for national independence despite as well as because of injustice and forced displacement (Eriksen 1993: 125). Notwithstanding an important critique of essentialist representations of (ethnic) communities (Baumann 1999; Hall 1990), nationally-motivated identities prevail in contexts where the very people and their histories are contested, and deprived.

Nakba denied, Nakba remembered

Palestinian nationalism, memory and identity are very much intertwined, as meticulously unfolded by Swedenburg (1995) and

Khalidi (1997). The history of Palestinian life and culture provides important reference points for the collectively imagined nation. These cultural lifelines and geographical reference points are epitomised in a number of important studies, such as Abu Sitta (2004) and Sa'di (2002). *Al-nakba* is the strongest Palestinian symbol of the 'tragic fate of men and women whose lives had been shattered, and about their descendents who continue to suffer its consequences' (Sa'di 2002: 176).

One reference point is particularly important: *al-nakba*, 1948. Even after the defeat in the 1967 war (*al-naksa*), Black September (1970), Land Day (1976), the Sabra and Shatila massacres (1982), the First Intifada (1987) and other events, *al-nakba* has remained the main site and point of reference of Palestinian collective memory. The tales and consequences of the Nakba are masterfully brought to life from different disciplinary angles in important collections such as Masalha's (2005) *Catastrophe Remembered* and Abu-Lughod and Sa'di's (2007) *Nakba: Palestine, 1948, and the Claims of Memory*.

People who have been colonised, exiled and occupied, and denied national institutions and archives, resort to different constructions of identity. Homelessness is a powerful element of the Palestinian collective consciousness; here Palestine differs from other nations that have suffered during struggles for independence. Whereas many colonised nations have experienced a decolonisation process, Sa'di sees the Nakba as an *anticlimax*, a promise of independence that turned into a nightmare (2002: 186).

The Nakba has become a constitutive element of Palestinian identity, and Palestinians have begun to use it as a temporal reference – marking both an end and a beginning. It is 'a Palestinian event and a site of Palestinian collective memory; it connects all Palestinians to a specific point in time that has become for them an "eternal present"' (ibid: 177). Palestinian community and identity, formed through the prism of the Nakba and present in a large part of Palestinian literature, conjure up feelings of how Palestine was *before* the Nakba. Saloul's work (2008) deals with the cultural memory of *al-nakba* in present-day Palestinian exiles' consciousness through an analysis of literary, cinematic and oral narratives.[4] These stories and recollections of individual and collective everyday life form an important layer in the construction of the national narrative.

Literature is an important contributor in the construction of long-distance imagined communities. Literary projects mirror the shifting impact of political discourse at particular moments. For the Palestinian context Hassan shows that the repositioning of Palestinian literature is illustrated by a move towards aesthetics, as opposed to politics and resistance. The under-representation of writers from 'inside' was for instance not explained in terms of political conditions but by its aesthetic quality (2003: 21). Palestinian politics during the transformation of the PLO between 1982 and 1993 shifted from *resistance* to *appeasement*. While Palestinians in the OPT organised a massive uprising during the First Intifada, PLO officials in exile who also determined the political course of action ultimately weakened the collective grassroots political unity. In his critique Hassan links the trend of literary studies in the 1990s to the 'politics of appeasement', arguing that it neatly coincides with the compromises of the peace agreements (2003: 22).

The sense of belonging is reproduced through traditions, commemorations, national canons and museums. But the construction of Palestinian identity is not only mediated through top-down processes; *localised* experiences, practices and sentiments also lead to the Palestinian community being imagined as a nation. As Moors (2001) shows, representations of the past and of Palestinian identity tend to be selective, Khalidi's (1991) beautiful photographic history *Before Their Diaspora: a Photographic History of the Palestinians 1876–1948,* for example, uses sources and images that are predominantly of upper-class Palestinians. Sa'di (2002), who also studied Khalidi's photographic history, as well as Hisham Sharabi's *Jaffa, the Perfume of a City* (1991), with the personal testimonies of Shafiq Al Hout and Yousef Haikel, calls for a bottom-up analysis; because the local social context gives deeper meaning to concepts of national identity and nationhood.

Shifting political realities as well as local identity formations in the diaspora communities or those lacking a territorial centre of gravity are especially reflected through online media outlets. While sovereignty, and having a voice in the official public sphere, are lacking offline, they are perceived and voiced in cyberspace, where new spaces for solidarity are formed and counter-narratives voiced. Interesting similarities can be found between the Iranian and Palestinian diaspora. The reconnection of the diaspora and the homeland offered Iranians a transnational public sphere, an alternative to the traditional public sphere which was marked by social segregation, political tensions and state control. Through an online ethnography of Iranian websites such as www.iranian.com, Khosravi (2000) discusses how the internet reshaped the landscape of the Iranian diaspora. There is a fascinating resemblance between the virtualised memory of the Nakba and the way Iranians remember *pre*-revolutionary Iran and express strong nostalgia for the past in the cyberspaces studied by Kosravi. Nevertheless, a major difference is that Palestinians have not only been exiled because of their political engagement or ideological stance, but mainly because they were expelled under a settler-colonialist project and a continuous context of forced land appropriation.

This difference strengthens the importance of 'return' as an alternative; also of a virtual return to the homeland.The expression of national identity through online encounters is more poignant in the context of the actual loss of land, and in that of being confronted by a colonial other. Continuing from the quotation at the head of this chapter, Said (1986) asked: 'Are there really such things as Palestinian embraces, or are they simply intimacy and embraces – experiences common to everyone, neither politically significant nor particular to a nation or a people?' Most probably there are particular Palestinian embraces, to answer Said. For Palestinians in the occupied homeland the internet offered new ways of sharing the experience of living under colonialism, and to those in the diaspora this new medium of communication offered reconnections for a nation in exile, while to both parts of the Palestinian national community it offered a platform from which to call for a just solution, to uncover political deadlocks and to organise resistance. The massive uprisings became central online issues and a massive turn to the internet in turn coincided with the al-Aqsa Intifada.

Intifada boost

> That day [29 September 2000] I didn't feel like seeing anyone. I went home. I was so angry I beat up my brother; my father hit me for that. He has been through this – war, revolution, invasions – before. But for me, this was all new, so shocking. Seeing those scenes, of killings and bombings in Palestine ... So I ran away. I went to my grandfather's house, where I slept on the roof, I was so angry.
>
> *Rami, Nahr al-Bared–Lebanon, 2004.*

The al-Aqsa Intifada not only mobilised worldwide support but was also the impetus for Palestinian internet use. A similar push towards the internet had taken place in Lebanon after the liberation of southern Lebanon in May 2000, only five months before the outbreak of the

Intifada (Gonzales 2001).[5] Disseminating information and images about the Israeli retreat from Lebanon was a demarcation point.

In Palestine this push was a requisite, as Karima in Ramallah explained: 'The curfews without the internet would have been a real nightmare; if I didn't have my *Hear Palestine* to work on I would have gone mad, like those who became suicide bombers.' The 16-year-old Shaker in Beirut said: 'Watching news was like breakfast, lunch and dinner: checking the internet and Palestinian websites was as necessary as having your three meals.'

The Intifada reactivated the urge among (especially young) Palestinians to resist the status quo. It meant a reorientation of attention towards the Palestinian territories, and the internet provided the means to guide people through cyberspace. Interviews with refugees showed the importance of distinguishing between Palestinians present in the territorial centre of the conflict and those who were left to deal with their fate without any means in the (diasporic) periphery. As Dali in Shatila recalls:

> When the Intifada started I wanted to be in touch with my people, so I entered the Palestinian room in mIRC.[6] I did not know anyone from Palestine. I was happy each time I entered the internet and discussed with Palestinians. When I go home I tell my mother I talked with Palestinians from inside.

Palestinian internet usage was motivated by the political context, revealing that Palestinians voiced their counter-narratives in different ways.

Images of the Intifada from Palestine affected Palestinians in Jordanian and Lebanese refugee camps. The death of ten-year-old Mohamed al-Durra in Gaza, captured by a French cameraman and transmitted worldwide by television, became a prominent symbol of the Intifada. Associated Press photographed another child from Gaza, 12-year-old Faris Odeh as he stood in front of an Israeli tank attempting to halt it by throwing stones. These children became icons of the Intifada: the image of al-Durra stood for a victim of oppression, while Odeh symbolised the Palestinian rebel. Both images were reproduced as murals, posters in narrow alleys and stickers in the Lebanese refugee camps. Kindergartens, scout groups and streets were named after them. A third category of this symbolic depiction is also present. Despite being very cruel the picture of nine-month-old Iman Hijou from Gaza with a bullet hole in her stomach was not only circulated on the internet but also reprinted as a postcard. Also the images of young men blindfolded and stripped to their underwear, or of the man who was buried until his chin under the ground and blind folded is part of this type. Rather than as Palestinian *victim* or *rebel* in the first two examples, these pictures symbolise the indiscriminate *cruelty* of Israel.

Fig. 7 Visual rhetorics.

All these images were widely distributed on the internet, evoking anger and mobilising support. The images discussed here were for instance displayed on the website www.intifada.com, sometimes meant to reinforce the textual/content of a commentary about the Intifada but often just to confirm the saying that 'a picture is worth a thousand words'. The combination is a powerful one, especially when combined with famous slogans – such as *Give me Liberty or give me Death* and *I Die Therefore I Exist:* when visual and textual representations online come together a virtual rhetoric emerges.[7] The impact has reached beyond the internet cafe: human-rights appeals and political communiqués are reproduced and spreading from one website or forum to the other. Popular images in particular are printed from the internet circulated in universities and mosques, or put up on the wall, sometimes in a frame, as part of the house decoration as I noticed in several refugee camps. New Web 2.0 internet developments influenced this virtual rhetorical representation by allowing the merging video, photographic and textual applications, for instance on YouTube. It is not about merging technical function in the first place, but a merging of Palestinian cultural icons such as in the case of the late famous Palestinian poet Mahmoud Darwish and Mohamed al-Durrah. Darwish dedicated a poem to the young boy and then the recording of the recitation was used and reworked with pictures of al-Durrah in the background and distributed on the internet.[8] In the same fashion, Palestinian singer Rim Banna dedicated a song in memory to Faris Odeh. This was made into a video clip showing the epic Intifada image of the little Odeh in front of the huge tank throwing stones (Figure 7). [9]

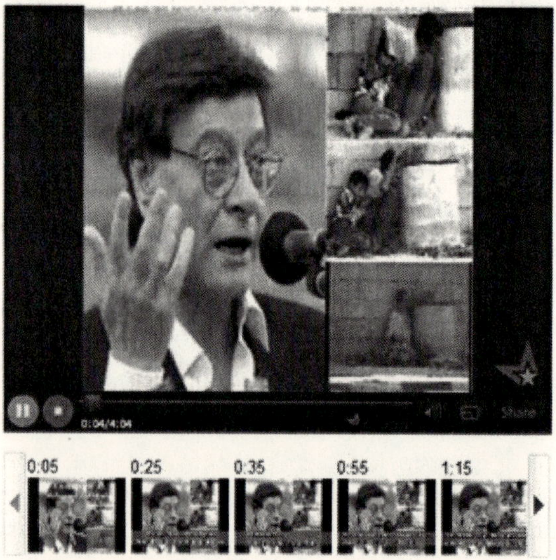

Fig. 8 Mohammed al-Durra in poem by Mahmoud Darwish on GoogleVideo.

Despite such illuminating examples of the power of virtual rhetorics, the style and content of the internet *vis-à-vis* the intifada showed ups and downs between 2001 and 2005. Some interviewees expressed that they simply had to cope; to feed their families in conditions of social devastation, occupation and war. At times, a sense of frustration seemed to lead to a kind of numbness, and can also be interpreted as a coping strategy. The shifting states of mind also caused a decline in political online activities or a rise in virtual escapism as discussed in the previous chapter. Samar from Shatila during an interview in 2003 said that over time the Intifada changed her:

> In the beginning I had to know everything, I kept track of how many fighters died and people were killed. I'd shout when I saw a Palestinian child killed on TV. Now it's become normal. Something inside of us snapped; is destroyed. I want to fight, to do something, but since I'm outside what can I do?

Not only did they want to know everything as Samar says, young people were also anxious for direct physical contact with Palestinians. As Samar continued:

> I started to use the internet and speak to guys and girls in Palestine. When I meet Palestinians from Palestine I want to hug and kiss them, something inside me grows: 'He's from inside', 'She has the smell of Palestine.'

Maryam, from Shatila, took pride in being identified as a Palestinian. Although this was for her a recent phenomenon, she added:

> Some Palestinians, especially girls, used to introduce themselves as Lebanese on the internet, mostly because they think Arab men like it. But after the Intifada, everybody said: 'I'm a Palestinian' or 'I'm from Shatila camp.'

When Karima visited Lebanon after having lived and worked in Ramallah, she suddenly realised how important it was for Palestinians 'outside', in exile, to be in touch with those inside:

> I understand how sacred it is to have direct contact and information from inside. It's almost something holy... when I

> returned to Lebanon and people knew I'd been in Palestine, they got all excited and emotional, and wanted to hug me (Ramallah, 2002).

For people explicitly to present themselves as belonging to a political community of course draws attention to them. But with regard to Palestinian identity being contested by pro-Israeli propaganda, the first online introduction and identification to the outside world is a political act in itself. This happens mostly through a personal nickname or email address. Dali's nickname on MSN referred to at the opening of this chapter is a telling example. Other nicknames were: *al-thawra hatta al-nasr* ('revolution until victory') and *Happy Birthday Intifada*, or long poetic ones such as *Wail lil 'alam itha imtalaka al-Falastini qararahu bi yadihi* ('beware the time when Palestinians take decisions into their own hands'); and *Ma btuchmud nari wala btib jrahi ila biruj'ek ya falastin* ('my fire won't be extinguished and my wounds won't heal until you return my Palestine'). Email addresses were also explicit: *Palestine4ever@hotmail.com* (from Lebanon) and *hatem115@hotmail.com* (from Gaza), here 115 symbolises Palestinian unity: (19)48 + (19)67 equals 115.

In this politicised context it was no surprise that Palestinian political websites were popular. Motivation in Lebanon differed little from that in Jordanian refugee camps. Hiba, a 16-year-old from Bourj al-Barajne camp in Beirut, wanted to go beyond mere virtual participation, *to do* something for Palestine:

> I visited all the sites: PFLP, Fatah, Hamas, Intifada.com, all of them. Once I entered the website of Azzedine al Qassam (the military wing of Hamas) in Palestine. I felt I wanted to do more, and become a member of a party through the internet.

But the Intifada boosted not only Palestinians. The whole region and beyond saw a new online and offline commitment. Academic and activist Ibrahim Aloush, in Jordan, explained how the Intifada, beside sparking the sympathy of Palestinians inside and outside the OPT, also awakened a general sense of rebellion on the Arab street: 'Whether in terms of peace with Israel or in succumbing to the dictates of the World Bank and IMF in our countries, the Intifada got back the vitality it had missed for 25 years.' Aloush sketches a situation in which online engagement with Palestine began to take on a regional character.

Maktoob, a pan-Arab website, offered a concrete means for pro-Palestinians to become politicised through the internet.[10] It was naturally prevalent in the Palestinian room of the website, but the Intifada soon became the main topic in other countries' rooms on *Maktoob*. The website's statistics showed that the Intifada caused an upsurge in its membership. Social and political imperatives prevailed despite the commercial interests of many such internet projects. *Maktoob* initiated Palestinian solidarity, responding to growing anti-Israeli sentiments amongst its members. *Maktoob* explicitly called on its members, who spanned the entire Arab world, to express solidarity with Palestine. It set up an online fund for Palestinians and urged members to donate money to the Palestinian Red Crescent. Sameeh Toqan, a Palestinian Jordanian and one of the initiators of *Maktoob*, said: 'We will use *Maktoob* to its maximum capacity to express our support and dedication to our brothers and sisters in Palestine.' The website's opening page was temporarily redesigned to express support for the Palestinian people during the climax of the Intifada in 2002.

Internet participation by Palestinians themselves was shaped by real-life conditions. Violence and suffering were daily phenomena affecting the vast majority of Palestinians. Discussions with web designers, internet-project coordinators and internet-cafe employees in the West Bank and Gaza about the siege and reoccupation of the cities were some of the most intense moments during fieldwork. The invasion and occupation caused immense destruction – everybody paid a price, as public places were indiscriminately destroyed during the sieges.

Visiting the organisations affected by this violence during fieldwork in 2001-02 gave direct insight into the impact on the ground, and eyewitness reports were indispensable during heavy attacks. The press could hardly report what was taking place because the IDF declared the OPT a closed military zone. Some fieldwork contacts were specifically targeted: Ma'an Bseiso of Palnet explained:

> At 2.30 a.m. the IDF invaded Palnet. Soldiers searched the whole building, blew up doors and abused our employees. They eventually found the room where the main power source was, and completely shut down the connection – all Palnet internet lines in Ramallah were cut. Why was only our company in the building attacked, if it was not deliberate? I think they came for us: they wanted to turn us off. They don't like what we're doing on the net.

The widely read *Palestine Monitor* (PM) website was a thriving source of information, and one of the most popular websites in and about Palestine between 2001 and 2004.[11] This non-violent Western-funded NGO also suffered a great deal. Patricia, coordinator of PM at the time, talked about the distressing experiences that had taken place. Her breathless reminiscences during interviews in 2002 betrayed how shocking the siege had been:

> The soldiers used our offices as their outlook post and stayed here for three weeks. They destroyed absolutely everything, including the hardware. It was particularly bad to discover they stole our computer equipment. The day before the invasion we heard rumours and expected something would happen. British and American foreigners were warned to leave the city. We sent our website coordinator to Jerusalem and hurriedly made backups before the borders were closed.
>
> It wasn't a coincidence. They knew PM, as part of HDIP [the Health, Development, Information and Policy Institute], is very effective and we don't threaten Israeli security. They monitor everything we send out on the internet. The goal of Sharon and his government is to destroy every aspect of Palestinian democratic society. They have destroyed the PA technically by bombing the entire infrastructure, and politically by undermining Arafat's position. There is no official authority left, so civil society, which is also critical to the PA, became an important threat for Israel.

The experiences Patricia described were documented on the website, including pictures and personal testimonies. According to Joki, the webmaster at PM in 2002: 'We suffered a lot from the sieges; the soldiers really went out of their way. Some colleagues broke down and cried when we returned to our offices. I felt raped'. Those events taught them important lessons and also prepared them for next time, said Joki:

> We started taking away our things. Whenever we hear rumours of a possible invasion or attack, we take as many documents and files as possible to our homes. As an NGO we're not rich, we can't afford laptops. Yet we managed to do a lot of work during the sieges and curfews.

Besides ISPs and NGOs, the websites of internet cafes were also targeted. *Al-Carma* in Ramallah, which also had a website, was attacked and severely damaged.[12] According to Hisham, the owner of the cafe and the initiator of the website:

> Around the same time that the IDF invaded Ramallah in March 2002 and occupied *al-Carma*, the site was hacked and replaced with Israeli propaganda. Unfortunately we had kept the website's back-ups in the cafe, which was destroyed completely. So the website and our portal project are irreparable.

Upon walking through the buildings and what was left of the IC, the traces of the attacks just described in the interviews came to life. The following message was given to the visitors of *al-Carma* website and IC:

> **We're Closed...**
> During the last incursion of the Israeli occupation forces into Ramallah (29 March - 21 April 2002), trash soldiers broke into al-Carma Offices. Criminal troops were not able to gain entry through the main door, which was closed from the outside. Therefore, they blew up a hole in the wall to break into our offices.
> Two servers were stolen, while one was deliberately damaged. Furthermore, evil troops stole and damaged almost all computers and accessories that they reached. Occupation army thieves also stole cash money, personal belongings and other items including cigarettes and refreshments. In brief, other than the photocopy machine and few PCs, savage troops either stole or damaged all what was inside our offices.

The demolitions by the Israeli army aimed to undermine intellectual and civic life in Palestine. These cruel realities also clarified how an active online counter-response and a (re)construction of the imagined Palestinian nation online is motivated by real-life events offline and for these offline realities to be channelled through. The internet became *the* medium through which the Palestinian national community was imagined.

Transforming the nation

> I am from Akka. The Palestinians I meet online tell me it is beautiful. I keep a diary about Palestine, and I found many things

> about Akka on the internet. Sometimes my online friends help and email me pictures of my country.
>
> *Samah, Bourj al-Barajne–Lebanon, 2003.*

If online mediation of national collective identities is strongest amongst politicised diaspora communities such as Iranians, Kurds or Tamils (Eriksen 2006: 7), then it is self-evident to add Palestinians to the listing. The internet shapes national identities, and the aims of many websites and discussion forums can be described as nation-building. Palestinians hook up with other Palestinians to express, share, debate, listen, view or negotiate. And precisely because of this, the internet has the potential to challenge national identities concurrently. The synergy between technological developments, diaspora participation and political identity has led to an online public sphere where these identities are negotiated on the internet.

Like all public spheres, this online public sphere is not just defined by unified opinion but by debate, and by dominant vs marginal struggles over the content of such debate. The scope of participation has widened, gone beyond territorial boundaries, and deepened, crossing different sections of society. Forums and chat rooms have become important meeting points. Through a myriad of interactions – using the internet as a tool to collect and transform national identity – Palestinian communities online have been (re)constructing their collective identity. The experience and expectation of what it means to be a Palestinian or refugee is a constant part of the narratives. Diasporic local and *sha'bi* (popular) relics also entered online public spheres. The internet offered new spaces to make and share music, stories, recipes, fashion and images. They formed the ingredients that structure transnational identities and made real what is meant by 'Palestine Online'. Transnational online communication here did not erode the meaning of a Palestinian state, but reconfirmed it.

One example of a stimulus for these virtual networks was a television programme in 2004 called *Online*. Keen to motivate Palestinian internet use, it demonstrated all sorts of possibilities offered by the internet, in an uncomplicated way. The presenter used concrete examples while he explained how to surf websites or to use search engines such as Google. Fascinatingly, most of the examples were framed within a Palestinian national context; it was a sign of the times that the presenter chose to show a children's website depicting drawings of Mohamed al-Durra and websites about Palestinian history. Participants in the studio and viewers at home were shown historic and contemporary photos of Jerusalem and Jaffa on the *Palestine Remembered* website,[13] and it was explained how many more could be found via a Google image search. Moreover, the programme was made and aired in Palestine, but viewed by the author during fieldwork in Lebanon. This trans-local access was unattainable before satellite and internet media were available. Many Palestinians in the refugee camps have a satellite dish, and the internet is no match for television when it comes to reaching/targeting a mass audience.[14] But the power of internet technology is that it has expanded the public sphere by allowing participation *and* by connecting diverse publics. Beside the Arabisation of the internet, mentioned before, the easy, graphic, mouse-controlled interface on the World Wide Web popularised the internet even more (Terranova 2004: 41). The upshot for those who have directly or indirectly managed to join in Palestinian cyberspace is that locally-based identity has become part of a transnational Palestine. It will be argued that the online public sphere led to the discovery of different lifestyles and attitudes, and that this created cracks in the idealised visions nurtured for so long by exiled Palestinians. In due course, the online public sphere also inspired the commodification of Palestinian identity, as will be illustrated.

The online public sphere

Ethnographic fieldwork in the refugee camps allowed for accompanying people to their homes and internet cafes and to witness their responses at first hand. When pictures of Palestine or nostalgic pre-1948 images were viewed, the reaction was often full of excitement. Akram, one of the first owners of an internet cafe in Bourj al-Barajne, told of the first moments when people started surfing Palestinian websites:

> One of the guys whistled and said in amazement: 'Wooooow, this is very nice.' I looked and saw it was some hills, mountains, a few houses – you know, probably just like any picture from a village in for instance Tunisia.

Akram continued recalling those first encounters:

> When they started to chat with Palestine you could hear them shouting in the internet cafe: 'He's from Palestine! Look, I'm talking with Palestine!' They proudly told people they met that they'd 'talked with Palestine'.

These responses unveil how some internet users in the refugee camps responded. But surprise for the refugees was also apparent when discovering that the Palestinian person on the other side of the virtual line lived a comfortable life, was free to travel and to live the kind of life only dreamed of in exile. This at times led to disappointment, if not disillusionment, especially when a chatter learned that the other person was uninterested in the plight of refugees. One of the young women in Shatila camp had been chatting with a Palestinian from Gaza – one of the most deprived, isolated and destroyed places – but this particular person did not care much about the Intifada, in fact told her she was fed up, they should just reach an agreement with Israel, anything was better than the present situation. There was shock, but she had no idea how to respond – she was talking to a Palestinian on the inside, after all not the enemy. It was as if little cracks had started to emerge in the idealised imagined nation. Another interviewee in Bourj al-Barajna camp had for instance chatted with a Palestinian who supported the US-led agreement, with no concern for the right of return she herself is longing for. These cracks are painful but not necessarily negative. According to Palestinian sociologist Muhammad Ali Khalidi interviewed at the American University of Beirut in 2004, at times it is necessary to challenge romanticised visions:

> New confrontations create new paradoxes. Sometimes we need to correct the one-sided representation, for instance of the historic struggles for self-determination. The liberation movement was far too nationalistic and submerged in internal or local differences. You will find many nationalist myths in the PLO narratives. We must sometimes admit mistakes, take responsibility and continue. Only lifting up morale isn't necessarily the best strategy. Sometimes it's good to bring some of the fantasies down to reality.

Also heated debates between Palestinians and pro-Palestinians in online discussion forums took place, for instance on whether state terrorism could be compared with individual terrorism, and what are or not accepted as forms of resistance. Such confrontations in the online public sphere signify that the construction of an idealised, imagined nation online is not without its problems. It inevitably also means different kinds of internal confrontations, i.e. a re-construction at the same time, for instance where it concerns internal political and class differences that cannot be simply compressed into a unified identity. Aforementioned Ibrahim Aloush in Amman talked about these internal differences during an interview in 2003. Although there is broadly shared sympathy for the struggle for Palestine, he stressed that there is not one kind of Palestinian agenda, and the social stratification in Jordan confirms this for him:

> Certain sections of the Palestinian population have assimilated into the system and developed interests not dissimilar to those of the Jordanian regime. They promote economic or cultural normalisation by facilitating connections between Arabs and Zionists. You find a spectrum of views. Intellectual liberals try to foist on people's minds the idea that Arabs and Zionists should be friends.

Aloush's observations were not strange – the arguments about Palestine, how the situation affected Palestinian national consciousness and what the solution should be, were shaped by whether in Amman I was sitting with someone in Wehdat refugee camp or in Abdoun.[15]

One of the local activists remarked that the Amman candle-vigils for Palestine were mostly attended by upper and middle-class Palestinians or by foreigners: the refugees and working class did not bother to come or were simply not informed nor mobilised to join. In refugee camps in Jordan Palestinians dealt with the Intifada as if it literally affected them: it was not about solidarity 'with them', it was about 'us'. This does not mean that there was no activism in the country: many Palestinians in Jordan are in close contact with their surviving relatives in the OPT, some of whom were imprisoned, tortured or injured. Internet possibilities in a sense compensate for the absence of the territorial, but they do not replace it.

Social and economic conditions and the specific realities of refugees influence the level and form of internet participation. And these differences also have practical implications for the way the internet functions as a tool for escape, as illustrated in Chapter Three. For Kholoud, a mother of two teenagers from Bourj al-Barajne camp in Beirut, the internet was an important outlet she had to use 'at least once a week'. Kholoud also illustrates how she hooked up with people via the internet. She makes clear how the internet has a different meaning for someone in Lebanon like her, and for most Palestinians in Jordan:

> The first time was amazing. When I received my first email I even shouted in the internet cafe ... We need this more than others. Palestinians in Jordan are closer to the land and some can even go to Palestine, but for us this is impossible.

The new internet initiatives have induced wider sections of society to use the internet. Here the Arabisation of websites has helped to motivate Arab audiences in particular. Multi-media websites with access to radio channels, television stations, and (banned) newspapers have particularly strengthened online interactivity. The online Palestinian public sphere eventually merged with, and commodified, political representation and thereby Palestinian identity.

'Made in Palestine': Palestinian identity commodified

So far this chapter shows that Palestinians have increasingly been sharing national loyalties because the internet facilitates this transnational encouragement between members of the imagined community. As argued, national identification does not assume fixed identities or that people will always act in unison. Nevertheless, the internet was eagerly used as a way to recollect and transfer a Palestinian heritage that was broadly shared. With references to Palestine's geographic territory, oral narratives, traditional local cultures and Nakba experiences, and of course the Intifada, a politicised Palestinian national identity was revived. Pre-1948 pictures, those of the 1948 and 1967 exoduses, and then pictures of the new Intifada, were the most popular images downloaded and forwarded on the internet. The first two sources articulate a certain nostalgia and loss, while the latter expresses resistance and hope.

The anti-globalisation movements that galvanised after the Seattle protests in 1999, and the post-9/11 anti-war protests, made Palestinian symbols like the *kufiya* (the national black and white shawl), along with other political gimmicks, part of a new activist trend. The *kufiya* has long been a political symbol (Swedenburg 1992) but Palestinian solidarity movements lifted it to the point of becoming a standard activist garment.[16] This emphasis on 'Palestinianism' as an activist symbol became global through the internet.

Most Palestinians felt connected to the cause, if only at least in a spiritual way. The (better-off) Palestinian diasporas (and their sympathisers) could purchase Palestinian goods that were usually unavailable in their host country. The commodification of Palestinian identity flourished as Palestinian ICT entrepreneurs engaged in e-commerce projects involving local Palestinian products such as olive oil, Dead Sea products, Nablus soap, flags, posters and t-shirts. Palnet started an online store with *PalTime*, offering Palestinian products – i.e. locally produced by or about Palestinians, although the website was hacked several times and the business did not take off. *Palestine Online Store* by Haithem al-Jabiri (who also co-founded *Solidarity Design*), however, further developed the branch and sustained the business more successfully.[17] There was great interest in Palestinian history and culture amongst Palestinian internet users and supporters – according to Ma'an Bseiso (manager of Palnet at the time), during an interview in 2002, 'especially those who have difficulty in accessing the homeland'. It was not always easy to purchase goods via the internet because it meant a credit card was needed, and sometimes only certain credit cards were acceptable. *Maktoob* facilitated such e-commerce projects, stimulating online shopping by offering 'Cash U' cards – prepaid cards that worked like credit cards.

Fig. 9 Palestinian identity on the internet: 'Online Commodification'.

The aforementioned Palestine Costume Archive (Figure 6) is an example of how local identity, tradition and culture were intertwined online, reconfiguring the *transnational* diaspora through the *local*.[18] This websites exemplifies what Benedict Anderson meant when he wrote that:

> This emerging public sphere is not only one of talking back to power but also one of a wider range of public actors who talk to each other sometimes about power and often about the power of the new media in their communication (2001: 3).

As Jenni Allenby of the Palestine Costume Archive said during a telephone interview in 2005: 'Palestinian women can email us prior to their wedding to ask how to acquire a traditional dress, or what type of costume was worn prior to 1948[19].' As a medium which allows a combination of direct participation and visual representation, the internet is superior to any other form of mediation and a key communication tool for such projects as Jenni Allenby's.

It is this combination that has created space for new interpretations and new interpreters, and for the construction of an internet-mediated Palestinian nation, a *Palestine Online*, as part of the 'imagined' Palestinian community. Interwoven in the texts and images that are produced and disseminated in cyberspace are re-articulated narratives of Palestinian culture, history and national identity. The internet is not only a network that puts Palestinians in contact with other Palestinians or communities: it also reconnects them to their history. During numerous interviews, Palestinians in Lebanon and Jordan pointed to the fragility of the collective national heritage. There were projects with children in Lebanon coordinated by Moa'taz Dajana (discussed in Chapter Three), and a cutting-edge initiative, the Nakba Archives. In this project, coordinated by Diana Allan and Mahmoud Zeidan, survivors of the Nakba were filmed, and their testimonies were digitalised and put online.[20] The exiled diaspora has entered its fourth generation, and those who actually remember Palestine before or during the Nakba, are slowly disappearing. The next section will discuss how an important grassroots Palestinian project on the internet came to life, and recalls how this initiative was experienced during its first stages in Palestine and subsequently in Lebanon.

Palestine online and offline

> People in Palestine used to think that the Palestinians outside are cowards, that we abandoned them and the land. The Palestinian body was divided. The idea seemed that we, outside, are cut off from the main body. As if we had assimilated or melted into the societies where we took refuge – the Lebanese, the Jordanian, the Syrian, etc. And that they inside [Palestine] continue fighting while we here outside do nothing. Not everybody inside knows about the massacres that took place against us here. The internet is slowly correcting such notions, and showed that we – by our thoughts, struggle, money, everything we have, are devoted to the

> Palestinian cause. The internet is the tool to gather the scattered Palestinian 'body'... this way we create a new society.
>
> *Mohammed, Nahr al-Bared–Lebanon, 2004.*

Palestinians have taken an active approach to the internet, and some refugees can be regarded as the first grassroots Palestinian internet producers. One of them is 24-year-old Mohammed from Nahr al-Bared refugee camp who actively contributed to the virtual interactions. He spends days and nights working on his website. Not only does the internet help people in Palestine to be heard and noticed, it is used to reconnect the 'divided body', as Mohammed's powerful allegory points out. But how exactly do the birth of Palestinian cyberspace and the success of local initiatives help to effect this reconnection? Mohammed played a role in this when, with a few friends, he set up Albareek.com. Friends from Nahr al-Bared helped him, just as he helps others when they need his expertise. One of the local websites Mohammed helped set up was Nahrelbared.org; this unique website is part of the Across Borders Project (ABP), or *Raghm al-hudoud* as it was known in Arabic. This project epitomises the revolutionary potential of the internet at the time. ABP made it possible to cross borders that divide the refugee diaspora in all aspects. The IT department at Birzeit University launched ABP in 1999 to provide the Palestinian community with access to a global audience, but foremost to facilitate Palestinian reunification by linking refugee camps scattered across the region.

The first ABP centre was launched in July 1999, at the Ibdaa Cultural Centre in the Dheisheh refugee camp, Bethlehem. It was also the first internet cafe in a Palestinian refugee camp. It can be considered a follow-up to Muna Hamzeh's community-based website project.[21] In September 2000 the management of the ABP was taken over by Birzeit University's Centre of Continuing Education (CCE), where it was to be further professionalised. The closing section of this chapter looks at the background and process of setting up the ground-breaking ABP project, first describing the main development of the project itself and then analysing it from the perspective of its inception in the camps of Lebanon and Palestine.

Crossing borders

The diaspora in the West was able to access Palestine via the internet, but soon also those in refugee camps tried. It makes sense: many families were torn apart. Most have never met their

> families again. We felt the new project had to come down to these people, the most affected, the refugees.
>
> *Alaa', Ramallah–Palestine, 2001.*

The first initiators of ABP were young and active IT professionals and students at Birzeit University. As Alaa', in Ramallah, one of the first initiators, recalls above, some of them were in touch with Palestinian refugees and with exiled Palestinians for the first time. After the success in Dheishe, the opening of additional ABP centres in refugee camps was scheduled for 2000: four in Palestine (two in the West Bank and two in the Gaza Strip), two in Lebanon, and one in Jordan. In 2001 ABP announced the opening of a centre in Bourj al-Shamali refugee camp in southern Lebanon. The opening of the Lebanese centre was a significant achievement since it marked the first regional online network of Palestinian refugee camps. The coordinators' enthusiasm while recalling the first online meeting during interviews reflected its importance.

Via a big screen and internet link-up, ABP set up a live connection between Bourj al-Shamali and a refugee camp in the West Bank. Among many activities a poem by Kamal Nasir, about the importance of keeping the memory of Palestinian history alive, was recited. These stories from Lebanon during fieldwork in 2003–04 resembled those I had heard before – in Palestine in 2001. During an interview with ABP coordinator Labiba at that time, she described the launching of ABP in Jalazone camp. Via the live link-up with Lebanon some families were reconnected with each other for the first time in many decades. It was an emotional event: people repeatedly enquired about possible family members and requested the camera to move around in order to show them the camp. After hearing the stories in Bourj al-Shamali for a while, it became clear they were talking about the same virtual meeting that Labiba had described to me about the camp in the West Bank; I now met those on the other side of the wire and discovered the (unintended) historical continuance in the ethnographic narratives.

The first stage of the project was the 'initiation phase'. For this, the central management offered training in web design and financial management, provided internet lines and servers, and of course computer laboratories, where the refugees connected to the internet, participated in the training and worked on computers. The camp elected a board to represent the local ABP, which would for instance nominate which organisation would host it. The second phase concerned the sustainability of the project, so that it could continue without the help of Birzeit's CCE. Users would pay a small fee for internet access and for the training courses, to create a self-supporting system. During an interview in Palestine in 2001, Labiba explained the idea:

> An important motivation for this website is to let refugees themselves talk, to allow them to deal with their issues in their own way. The second reason is to be able to communicate, despite the many checkpoints and physical obstacles between Palestine inside and outside, and between the different refugee camps.

ABP was all about promoting refugees' rights, while simultaneously offering an online platform through which to assemble people, as a way of disseminating a Palestinian voice in the outside world. Nur, ABP coordinator in 2005, stated:

> The goal is ultimately to give an alternative image, to show the other side, of Palestine and Palestinians. This is for instance why the section on poetry was included. The aim is to show that Palestinians are not just poor refugees that have nothing to offer, but are in many ways like the rest of us – and they also write poetry.

A website was set up for each refugee camp, connected to the general ABP website, which also offered a discussion forum. The ABP website is well-designed, with a user-friendly front page linked to various refugee camps. The website consists of three main parts: life stories, photo essays and interviews. The logo of ABP is a figure walking through barbwire (Figure 10). One part of the page offers Arabic and English links to files with UN documents (for instance resolutions related to Palestine), interactive maps of Palestinian camps in the region, and video material, such as interviews with refugees.[22] The language of the discussion-board option on the website is an indicator that the ABP website is mostly geared towards Palestinian refugees in the camps, and that its foremost objective is grassroots participation there. Nur explains: 'The language of communication is mainly Arabic. The forums are in Arabic, while the homepage is bilingual. The Arabic-speaking people are the priority.' By participating in the creation of the camp website the refugees opened a window onto the history, society, culture and everyday life of the camp.

Fig. 10 Across Borders Project Logo.

Between 2000 and 2002, when the second phase of ABP was scheduled to begin in the camps the project faced many difficulties, its staff was confronted with serious technical and financial problems. With the reoccupation of the OPT, the APB was forced to shift its focus: rather than developing the project through further innovative ideas, it was necessary first to survive. The military and financial problems were unavoidable. In some cases the infrastructure – computers, internet cables and software equipment – was wrecked by Israeli soldiers. Moreover, the staff and volunteers were not able to travel inside the OPT to organise training and assist local staff. Bassem, one of the field coordinators during our meeting in Ramallah in 2002, explains why they were forced to downgrade the project:

> It's not even possible to go from Ramallah to Birzeit, let alone give training and special courses in remote camps. Our donors initially understood the deteriorating situation and were flexible. But in general, the priority of funders changed from sustainable projects like ours, to 'bread and milk' projects.

Yet the need for the project increased with the Intifada, and the organisers received more requests from other camps to join the ABP project. Some offered to cover their own costs if the CCE would carry out the general coordination, prepare the training and organise the technological and administrative infrastructure. But according to Ivan (CCE's general coordinator of ABP) during an interview in 2002, rather than broadening the project it would be wiser to upgrade existing camps and save the remainder of the project, although by then the ABP was in greater financial crisis: 'We don't have field officers, camp or district coordinators any more. Only two employees are available: me and the webmaster. ABP funding is gone: we can't even pay the salaries of current coordinators.'[23]

Noor Shams camp, north of the West Bank, and Nussairat camp in central Gaza were provided with just five computers, instead of the usual ten plus additional hardware. The sieges and imposed curfews made it difficult to carry out even the simplest requirements. Ivan continued:

> Due to closures and curfews we couldn't pay the website provider on time. At the time, a lot of the post going in and out of Palestine was lost; our cheque probably never even arrived there. The website provider stopped our subscription and then sold our name. As a consequence we had to change acrossborders.org to acrossborder.org, including all the existing hyperlinks.

In the light of these financial problems two newly planned ABP centres in Palestine were aborted, and the scheduled launches of centres in Syria and Jordan could not take place. Important meetings planned in Jordan to discuss the future of ABP-International were cancelled because many coordinators were not allowed to cross physical borders to discuss crossing virtual borders. Meanwhile, the general frustration of the coordinators in Lebanon and Palestine led to friction between the groups. Ivan explained:

> In April we had an international conference planned in Amman with all ABP coordinators to finally discuss our international work, internal relations, how the process in Lebanon was going, and our plans to extend our project to Jordan and Syria. But the situation deteriorated in March and April 2002, and no travel permission was given any more.

ABP Lebanon was eventually decentralised, to be run by the host organisation while assisted by NGOs in Lebanon. Looking at these and other experiences of ABP is particularly important in understanding how internet development in the refugee camps of Lebanon and Palestine has evolved since its inception and what the specific challenges the camps in host countries encounter.

Across borders in Lebanon

Amid many difficulties, the Lebanese section managed to launch ABP centres in two camps: Nahr al-Bared and Bourj al-Shamali. The hosts were al-Najde, a women's centre in Nahr al-Bared, and Beit Atfal Sumoud, a youth centre in Bourj al-Shamali. Educated young people, rooted in the respective camps, were recruited to manage the project. They understood the relevance of the internet as well as anyone because they were themselves experimenting with its possibilities. The enthusiasm, personal effort and creativity of these local coordinators saved parts of the project at times of crisis. Cooperation between APB in Lebanon and Palestine decreased, and coordination between the two countries reached its lowest point. Sami, the ABP coordinator in Bourj al-Shamali camp, was searching online for people in Nour al-Shams in the West Bank, one of the camps that was suppose to launch APB and be hooked to this centre before the Intifada broke out and much of the planned activities were aborted. But their virtual meetings were revived when Sami managed to find a contact via MSN. From the outset ABP in Lebanon was born into a politicised setting. Bourj al-Shamali camp started ABP on 30 September 2000 – the very day the Intifada broke out

Although the ABP was not the first to set up an internet line and allow the camp to join cyberspace: Al Karameh offered the internet, and two other small internet cafes leased from Al Karama had also opened; visiting these other places showed immediately that the age and gender composition of their customers was different to that of the ABP centre's.

Some level of reluctance to join the project was also anticipated by ABP and therefore it sought to prepare the community for the new and ground-breaking project. Introducing ABP in the camp requires broad support, but neither Nahr al-Bared nor Bourj al-Shamali was the easiest place to start pioneering internet projects. Some locals were suspicious of the internet, and did not welcome it. On top of the local disadvantages, the troubles in Palestine further complicated the work. One of the ABP coordinators in Nahr al-Bared, Ibrahim, explained:

> We ourselves also passed through difficult times setting up the required infrastructure, due to problems with electricity and phone lines in the camps. When the situation got better here, it worsened in Palestine. We used to set up internet meetings but they [in Palestine] couldn't show up due to bombings. ... This all weakened communication and we lost contact with many people.

An ABP project operating under the umbrella of an established organisation was important in structuring the activities and maintaining a policy of sustainability, but it also offered 'protection'. The selection of the hosting NGO was therefore an important issue in the camp, an internet centre inside an NGO having a better reputation than the commercial internet cafes. Young women were often employed by the host organisation to participate in the management of the project; they were in the internet centre to offer assistance to female clients, and this made an important difference.

The computer courses offered by ABP in Bourj al-Shamali provided an insight into the gender and social dimensions. The group during fieldwork in the winter of 2003–04 consisted of men and women from both inside and outside the camp. Some female participants were veiled, others not; several men looked as if they had just come from construction work, with cement still sticking to their shoes; others came dressed as *muwazzaf* (office employees). The atmosphere was relaxed: when for instance someone – and especially the teacher himself – made a mistake, laughter and joking broke out. The course was unique and affordable, and therefore also attracted several Lebanese participants. According to Sami: '[T]his is the first time they have intensively participated *with* us and in our camp. During the course training in the camp some of the previous, negative ideas about Palestinians and refugee camps were challenged.' After the final examination participants could apply for internships at an ICT company, in a computer shop in Sour or with ABP in the camp itself. Besides educational courses there were also gatherings to organise online meetings with other camps.

Not all refugees readily participated in the ABP, and the coordinators had to think of special ways to approach people. They used encouraging leaflets with such lines as: 'Would you like to talk with your relatives and friends abroad, or even to Palestine?' This approach was powerful because the potential participants clearly preferred to have contact with Palestinians inside Palestine. Online reconnection with Palestine through the ABP strengthened the dream of *al-awda* (return). It can be argued that online meetings between Lebanon and Palestine were a fundamental part of the formation of Palestinian virtual communities. ABP hoped for continued contact with their new online friends or a search for others after they had finished a meeting. Sami described the method of the 'virtual group meetings' as 'Palestinians in one camp in Lebanon meeting another group in a camp in Palestine'. Sometimes three groups even met simultaneously, such as the meeting between Nahr al-

Bared in northern Lebanon, Bourj al-Shamali in southern Lebanon and Jalazone in the West Bank. Participants were first introduced by the coordinators, after which a discussion on a specific topic usually followed. One of the topics discussed during fieldwork visits was the role of the Geneva Agreement and what refugees themselves thought of it. The participants shared their ideas with each other.[24]

After the official part of these virtual meetings, young people were allowed to chat informally and to exchange emails with their counterparts. The coordinator would sometimes go out to smoke a cigarette or prepare the next activity with a colleague, but more often it was actually the case that he or she had to run from one participant to the other and explain how to add someone to a chat-room, how to send attachments, how to open music files, and so on. Sometimes the meetings were organised between girls, often at their request, when they wanted to raise topics they would hesitate to discuss in a mixed group.

Unlike Bourj al-Shamali, where the project was broadly welcomed, Nahr al-Bared was faced with local issues which had not really been anticipated. Many negative rumours about internet cafes had already been circulating, and people also started to complain about al-Najde women's centre, where the ABP was hosted: the centre had become a target of widespread gossip, with some wanting to prohibit children and young people from going there. Ahmed Hadj, a local sheikh and respected imam of a mosque nearby, decided to see and judge for himself before giving his advice in public sermons: his cooperation or opposition could be crucial. After his own assessments he publicly referred to al-Najde as a 'clean' place. This incident will be further discussed in Chapter Six; in the discussion about the ABP it is important to note that his intervention contributed to an acceptance of the internet centre in the camp.

Those attending the ABP centres experienced their new internet opportunities in different ways. Hanging around the centre in Nahr al-Bared for a while, 19-year-old Rami drew my attention. He was not just chatting like most of the young people around him. Swiftly surfing websites through different search engines, he was copying and saving files to a disc, as if he was creating his own archive. Asked how he usually started his internet voyage, and to explain simply to me what he was doing, he answered:

> I start about 4 pm, so there is always someone online in some part of the world to talk with. Then I open Google. I usually have a specific

> subject I want to research. Today it's about smoking hazards. I found some websites and papers I want to read, so I'll download them ... The other time I wanted to know about the meaning of 'logic' – what's the philosophical meaning of it? I asked my friends, but they all had different ideas. I write some of the answers in my notebook, and continue to search for more online.

Reading everything online takes a long time and thus would be too expensive for Rami. So instead of paying another LL 1.500 (US$1) per hour in the internet cafe, he saves the documents on a floppy disc and goes through the material on his uncle's computer, selecting what he wants to keep.

The website was one of the ways ABP mobilised the participation of the local community in the Nahr al-Bared camp. The website had its own coordinating team to update the website with local news, feature stories, personal contributions, etc. According to the ABP website coordinator in Nahr al-Bared, Mohammed: 'We have a section on the site called "an elder and his village", where we interview an old person who tells about how he/she remembers Palestine before the Nakba. This is important because they were the eyewitnesses in 1948.'

Besides connecting Lebanon to Palestine, ABP opened a gateway between the Nahr al-Bared and Bourj al-Shamali camps and the transnational community. During fieldwork in Bourj al-Shamali a brother and sister were on 'voice chat' in the ABP centre, talking with their family and friends abroad (Figure 11). The brother talked with Tulkarem in the West Bank, and the sister with her cousin living in Libya, from whom she had just received pictures, through MSN, of the latter's engagement. It took some time to download these, but eventually she saved them on a floppy disc with the help of one of the ABP volunteers; in this way she could show the pictures at home.

While it crossed borders miles away, ABP did not necessarily form a bridge between the camps and Lebanese society, i.e. people in their everyday environment. Some of the Lebanese volunteers and activists such as Bachir addressed the issue during an interview. For him it was imperative that ABP was set up in such as way as also to overcome the gap between Palestinians and Lebanese. During an interview in 2004, Bachir argued:

> Refugees in Lebanon are meant to stick to a dream, instead of fighting for change and basic rights; they are not supposed to

intervene in the society surrounding them. This is a contradiction: on the one hand helping them [Palestinian refugees] and on the other not changing their structural situation.

Camps are embedded in the local settings of the particular host countries, which means that the ABP project is affected by the specific realities of the camp, and by a general discrimination against Palestinians – in Lebanon Palestinians were for instance not allowed to have independent internet or telephone lines. In Bachir's approach, overcoming the lack of infrastructure and other problems must therefore be an integral part of the project's goals.[25] The later Digital Solidarity Project (DSP) was set-up by some of the same activists involved with ABP.[26] The project matured, after ABP experiments and the technological possibilities improved, especially in overcoming the infrastructure problems. Besides online content, DSP also organised offline projects, such as film-making in the camps. The struggles with insufficient funding and the challenges of coordinating ABP in Lebanon bring us back to Palestine, where the project originated.

Fig. 11 Brother and sister in ABP internet centre Nahr al-Bared.

Across borders in Palestine

Hands and bodies were penetrating the fence, the thorns of the wires were piercing its teeth [sic] inside their hands, chest, even faces, tearing their clothes, but they did not mind as long as they could have one touch from an outstretched hand. Letters,

> addresses, and dates were flying everywhere. Bottles of water were exchanged across the fence, but tears were the masters of the occasion. They couldn't cut the iron fence for sure, but they made it more flexible.[27]

Following the Israeli withdrawal from southern Lebanon, Palestinians on both sides of the border seized the historic opportunity to reunite with other Palestinians, from whom they had been separated for nearly six decades by a border fence. This was not going to be a complete unification in the sense of being able to visit each other and spend time together, but physically meeting each other at last was nonetheless a small revolution. The initially random meetings at the border became coordinated visits, arranged by Palestinian organisations in both countries. The Israeli army started to obstruct the reunions, eventually forbidding the two refugee groups to approach one another, backing this new rule with a shoot-to-kill policy. Between 2001 and the longer fieldwork visits in 2003, three Palestinian teenagers attempting to reach the border to see Palestine, and throwing stones at Israeli soldiers, were killed by Israeli snipers. Their deaths, funerals, memorials and tributes, were all dealt with in the same way as those of the *shuhada* (martyrs) of the Intifada in Palestine. Yet, before this all started, and as soon as the opportunity was there, children of the Ibdaa' centre in Dheisheh camp took the opportunity to meet face-to-face with the children from Shatila camp in Beirut whom they had got to know via the ABP. Prior to such border meetings, the reunifications were prepared for online.

After starting in Dheishe, ABP stretched across the rest of the OPT, to become available in the north (Nablus/Jenin), the central area (Ramallah/Bethlehem), and the southern parts of Palestine (Gaza). Stories were circulating in the Palestinian camps about the Raghm al-Hudoud wonders, for instance, the family that found some relatives in Bourj al-Shamali in Lebanon, or the woman who met a man on the internet and married him. At the time of fieldwork in 2001-02, the ABP in Khan Younes (Gaza), Jalazone (Ramallah/Birzeit) and al-Ama'ri (Ramallah) were up and running. Refa, the ABP coordinator of al-Ama'ri, considered the awareness and use of the internet as particularly important in her refugee camp: 'It's important for political reasons. Refugees feel they must strengthen the relationships between the camps. We face the fact that nobody else is concerned about our rights.'

The ABP in al-Ama'ri was hosted by the Ama'ri Women's Centre, and opened its doors in July 2001, in the middle of the Intifada. Although the internet centre was open to all, it paid extra attention to women and girls. The team offered special courses for women, many of whom worked as hairdressers, designers or wedding make-up stylists in the camp. During the courses they learned how to find new information or new, inspiring styles on the internet to improve their skills. Labiba, coordinator of the ABP in 2001, describes how it helped to empower women:

> After the women finished the internet and computer courses offered through ABP some of them took a loan to purchase a computer and started doing administrative work at home. This way they managed to generate extra income without having to leave the children or the elderly.

The centre was reserved for females from 9 am till 3 pm, and from 3 pm till 10 pm for males. Offering separate courses and internet hours proved to be an increasing success. The initial courses and later attendance helped to normalise mixed participation. Labiba mentioned one particular participant in Ama'ri camp: '70-year-old Yasser al-Azaa types his stories and ideas about the camp and the Palestinian issue and has involved young people to post it for him on the website.'

The story of Yasser al-Azaa exemplifies the local participation of young and old, men and women. Nevertheless, it was the young people in Ama'ri camp who most enjoyed the availability of the internet: they used it for school assignments, to make new friends online, and to email those they already knew. According to the grapevine, however, there was also indulgence in other, less seemly activities, and not all these rumours were without substance. The organisers at first did not believe the stories, but eventually took them seriously. A colleague of Refa said:

> At the start there was a large group of internet users – it was really crowded in the internet centre. It was a bit too enthusiastic, though: we didn't realise that many teenagers were surfing sex sites. We notified ABP, and the [IT] people of Birzeit University tailored a security system that blocked these websites.

This does not imply a default situation of problems emerging as soon as the internet was introduced in the camps. ABP in Jalazone was very active: training, courses and services were offered, and the host organisation managed to generate capital with which to sustain the project. This local success relied to a large extent on excellent grassroots participation and creative leadership. In Ama'ri the problem was not merely lack of efficient coordination or good leadership: the camp was located on the poor outskirts of Ramallah, near a checkpoint; this made it an attractive place for demonstrations, and thus vulnerable to Israeli army attacks.

The women's centre that hosted the ABP provided internet access to a large part of the camp. When military operations were to take place, the army usually entered Ramallah through the checkpoint near the camp, which latter was also known for high levels of resistance, with many of the *tanzim* activists living there. When soldiers rolled into the camps with their tanks and jeeps, much of the infrastructure was destroyed. But the attacks went beyond material destruction of the projects: in one incident in June 2002 two children were killed and seven others injured by explosive devices the Israeli soldiers left behind. Some of the children in the internet centre showed me shocking pictures on Ama'ri's website. The ABP, as well as the host organisation, whose building was also destroyed, suffered enormously. Refa', one of the coordinators of the women's centre, explained that after a while:

> ... the centre just could not continue. The Israelis attacked our camp many times. Tanks came all the way to the entrance of our centre and damaged the camp's telephone networks; we were disconnected for 23 days, and had to stop internet services for three months. The contract with CCE ended, but we weren't able to take over the whole responsibility and coordination of the project as had been planned.

According to the original plan, the camps had to finalise the start-up phase in July 2002. But Israel's 'disproportionate' military response to the Palestinian Intifada greatly disrupted life. The practical consequences of the re-occupation of the OPT increased immensely: instead of self-sustenance the continuation of the project depended more and more on its headquarters and external funding. The ABP coordinator needed special permission from the Israeli army to visit the centres across the territories – permission that was rarely granted. This immobility increased the problem that places like Gaza were already enduring, and reduced its ABP centre and website to a deplorable state. However, the first phase of the project had been a promising experience and it sowed the first seeds of internet usage in the deprived and isolated camps.

For Khan Younes camp the ABP was its first internet project. In a similar fashion to Ama'ri and Jalazone, the launch of the ABP project in Khan Younes camp, in the very south of Gaza, also occurred by live connection with Lebanon. Iyad, the ABP coordinator in the camp, recalled the launch as they hooked up with other camps in Lebanon and used a web-cam to see each other. Iyad supplied his participants with a list of email addresses of Palestinians in Lebanon that they could contact. According to Iyad:

> We need to have connections with Palestinians outside, and especially Lebanon. Through the online meetings we know that Palestinians in Lebanon are distressed and angry because they don't live inside Palestine and can't even play a role in resisting Israeli oppression.

Flyers and posters in the camps announced courses and activities in the camp centre. The extreme entrapment and isolation of Gaza also meant there was a stronger conservative and socio-religious tendency than in the West Bank. After some initial suspicion, in fact very similar to the rumours in Lebanon, people eventually became enthusiastic. This explains the different attitudes towards male and female participation in public life and in internet use. The centre offered separate activities and provided two internet rooms, one for men and boys and one for women and girls. As Iyad explained: 'We cannot just neglect the culture and traditions.'

This camp faced extraordinary problems due to divisions created by the Israeli military even inside Gaza itself. The Khan Younes website offered news about the camp to overcome these divisions. The internet helped to overcome the isolation between Gaza and the West Bank, and allowed them to communicate directly with Palestinians in the diaspora as well. Iyad again:

> We discovered that we're living in similar circumstances as refugees in Lebanon: first as Palestinian refugees in a camp and second with very bad economic and social conditions ... Gaza is like an Israeli prison. We're isolated and surrounded by army ships on the sea, Israeli soldiers on the land, and the air force in

> the air. On top of this separation we are separated even internally because they have divided the Gaza strip into three parts, with checkpoints.

Only two years after the first ABP centre had introduced the internet in Gaza there were well over 20 internet cafes. People continued to chat about their circumstances and engage in online activities. Many could not escape the offline reality with which they were daily confronted, but projects like ABP and its legacy at least provided a gateway for the dissemination of stories and images about these everyday realities.

Conclusion

The internet profoundly changed internal and external communication dynamics. Chat, email and websites provided accessible instruments, and to some extent overcame the fragmented nature of the Palestinian diaspora. Internet users in refugee camps felt compelled to seek contact with their long-lost brothers and sisters. The internet provided a longed-for meeting point – but it could not replace a (still strongly present) focus on the desire for a non-virtual state and face-to-face contact. This chapter questioned how everyday political life stirred Palestinian cyberspace, how it hampered, advanced and explored events that illustrate the creation of transnational Palestinian linkages and imaginations.

Tactical and strategic internet usage was motivated by the aim of sharing messages and directing them towards an international audience, as well as communicating inside their own Palestinian communities. The imagined national identity configured online was framed in the desire to return to a homeland. Internet projects were clearly shaped by Palestinian national politics, largely because the outbreak of the Intifada gave a significant political boost to mass internet use. The experiences of the 2002 invasions motivated organisations and individuals towards instrumentalising the internet even more. They set up websites, reported on the incidents and used video-conferencing to continue their businesses. Palestinian national politics were expressed in idealistic unison, while online meetings and virtual encounters were contested. People's motivation to use the internet related to their condition: for Palestinians in the homeland, inside, the internet provided a new outlet to communicate and express events; for Palestinians outside, in exile, it provided a new medium for gaining knowledge about the homeland and for strengthening internal communication.

The ABP participants in Bourj al-Shamali and Nahr al-Bared, as well as the stories from Dheishe, al-Ama'ri and Jalazone, portrayed how Palestinian communities were introduced to and are influenced by the internet. The Nahr al-Bared website became an archive of the camp, and through people writing their own stories, the project also had a community-based aspect. The ABP offered Palestinian refugees a voice and opened a window onto the world,

Some of the activists in Lebanon who were involved with these projects had no pro-active and organic link with local political dynamics. ABP provided an important platform for communication, but not a pro-active body for political change. However, in Bourj al-Shamali ABP was becoming more directed at voicing protest and writing statements about conditions in the camp; it was mostly focused on the outside world, questioning Lebanese policy *vis-à-vis* the refugee camps.

Internet access and usage provided the structure and motivation for the creation of a transnational virtual community. *Palestine Remembered*, *Maktoob*, *PalChat*, *Mirc*, MSN, email and local projects are repositories of virtual Palestinian interactivity and illustrate how this 'virtualisation' was made operational. In due course, it promoted the development of more Palestinian websites, blogs and online outlets. Some of the most popular websites, collected while doing interviews and spending time in ABP centres and internet cafes, also included those about Palestinian martyrs, of movements such as Kataeb al-Aqsa', or of Hamas' military wing Izzidine Qassam. These virtual representations, in their online and offline settings, and especially the contrast and overlap between the offline and online will be analysed in the next chapter.

5

THE MAKING OF PALESTINE ONLINE

> Our philosophy is that greater awareness of the Palestinian issue leads to greater support for the Palestinian cause. The advent of the Internet has presented an unsurpassed vehicle for achieving this.
>
> *Haitham El Zabri, Solidarity Design, 2003.*

The internet consists of electronic infrastructures that make it possible to avoid territorial borders and to overcome the limits of state-media broadcasting. The global space maintained and hosted by the internet offers a unique platform for dispersed communities. As illustrated in the previous two chapters, Palestinians separated by national borders and roadblocks or by geographical and political barriers were able to exhibit new modes of connectivity via innovative grassroots projects. Here, interactive websites and forums were the mediating spaces through which the Palestinian nation was imagined. Most refugees had never seen their homeland, but now it was possible to exhibit virtual traversals to Palestinian cities and villages. In due course, alternative virtual spaces started to blend with an idealised vision of a free Palestine.

Concurrently, the internet motivated the emergence of hundreds of websites about – and in support of – Palestine. The story of this development, and the infrastructure that has accompanied it, is the theme of this chapter. The outbreak of the al-Aqsa Intifada in 2000 is the background against which the rapid increase of internet developments in Palestine is to be understood. The first section illustrates how the Arabisation of websites and public-relations strategies towards Western audiences became ground-breaking markers of the expansion of Palestine in cyberspace. Further key markers in this evolution were obtaining the *.ps* country code and the initiation of a Palestinian blogosphere.

How websites are classified, according to which categories or codes, largely determines how they are valued. The second section of this chapter discusses which methods can be applied to classify Palestinian websites. The websites are categorised on the basis of their *globalising* or *localising* nature in order to locate which audiences are being targeted. The globalising websites have an international focus; born during the Intifada, with the goal to counter dominant media biases, *re-humanising* Palestinians was an important factor in this. Besides these quantitative collections, respondents were asked about their favourite websites during interviews in internet cafes; these websites were then added to my list.

A crucial part of the analysis during this categorisation exercise was the discovery that Palestinian websites do not only focus on the international (Western) community, as a first glance would suggest. The third section therefore shows websites that have a local perspective related to or formed by grassroots communities: they are the *localising* websites. The earliest of these emerged around 1996, and were mainly created by professional Palestinians from the media or IT sectors. More people participated in the production of Palestinian websites as internet technology became more user-friendly. The grassroots websites articulate locality in two ways: in outlining a personal objective, in the case of a family website or personal blog, and in being shaped by a particular geographical location, as exemplified by *Beit Rima* and *Remembering Jenin* from the West Bank.[1]

Mapping and studying Palestinian websites according to the methodologic guidelines laid out above raised additional questions. Why, for instance, was there a discrepancy between the popularity of certain websites mentioned in the internet cafes (ICs) or during interviews, and the way or the extent to which these websites were linked or referred to online?

This chapter's two-fold ethnography of Palestinian cyberspace – online and offline – shows what takes place behind the scenes. After researching the mode of operation as a starting point, the chapter ends by illustrating how websites were grounded, who were the people behind them, what motivated those people, and the extent to which they considered online projects to be part of the struggle in everyday Palestinian life. Special attention is given to the personal experiences of the people who engage with the internet. An insight behind the scenes facilitates the understanding of the potential offline implications, and in turn hints at the reality of making a Palestine Online.

Tracing Palestinian websites

Online Palestinian representations can be traced back to the mid-1990s. Despite the 1993 Oslo negotiations, the discrepancy between the rhetoric of peace and the reality of land confiscation only increased. Tensions mounted as the gap widened between lived realities on the one hand and available images and news sources about these realities on the other. Yet, with the agreements, ICT infrastructures (telephone and internet) became to an extent available for Palestinians. The juxtaposition of these two sets of factors proved to be crucial.

The first institutional manifestation of the internet came when Birzeit University (BZU) launched its website in 1994.[2] An early marker of local Palestinian internet use was Muna Hamzeh's website for Dheishe refugee camp in the West Bank. Set up in 1998, the latter website gave a voice to those living in the camp – the first opportunity for Palestinian refugees to share their stories, in cyberspace, with the outside world.[3] Now efforts to create awareness of the Palestinians' cause and to help them network with each other were being exploited via the introduction of the internet.

I Am a Palestinian for instance exemplified a website that targeted the international community with the apparant goal of raising political awareness. In its introduction it proclaimed: 'Palestinians have names and faces. And now they [also] have a voice.'[4] The increasing number of websites can be traced according to different targeted audiences, which shaped the strategies of style, language and technological applications. Such strategies will be evaluated through an analysis of ground-breaking techno-political developments: the Arabisation of the internet, personal homepages, the rise of blogs and the struggle for Palestinian recognition in cyberspace with the *.ps* code.

Ground-breaking developments

El Zabri's comment quoted at the head of this chapter reflects the specific strategy of utilising the internet for improving and strengthening the Palestinian presence online. *Solidarity Design* (Figure 12) kept its word by developing websites such as www.alaqsaintifada.org (with daily news about the Intifada), and www.rachellcorrie.org (homage to the American ISM activist who was crushed to death by an Israeli bulldozer in Gaza). The potential of websites should be viewed in the broader context of technological developments, such as investing in multi-lingual and user-friendly interface options. Such investments increased quality and accessibility, which in turn helped to broaden the scope of the audience. A good example is the *Adalah* website launched in May 2004, known at the time for appealing to the Israeli Supreme Court over the use by the IDF of Palestinian civilians as human shields, and especially for its legal battles against the structural discrimination suffered by Palestinian Israelis.[5] To reach as many people as possible, the website is in English, Hebrew and Arabic. A press release on the website stated: 'Disseminating this news and opinion, and bringing it to the public's knowledge is especially important in a state where gross human rights violations against Arab minorities occur.' This multilingual method was preceded by an important trend-setting breakthrough for Arab websites: the Arabisation of the internet.

Fig. 12 Solidarity Design.

Many respondents had mentioned *Maktoob* as an important initiator of an online Arab community. It was among the first to take the major step of Arabising its internet services and played a vital role in assembling large numbers of Arabs world-wide, and hence became instantly successful as the first multilingual web-based email service.[6] According to the Palestinian-Jordanian manager: '*Maktoob* provided a virtual community for Arabs around the world.' The website served the Arab public in various ways, and became an example for many initiatives that followed. People could send musical or poetic dedications, or engage in heavy political debates, but the chat section was probably the most popular, reaching up to 1,000 participants simultaneously. The most dynamic discussions concerned Palestine, and at times events would spark intense debates: for instance, *Maktoob* set up a live chat session with Souad Srour from Shatila refugee camp while she was at the Brussels Tribunal (as a witness of the 1982 massacres) during a campaign to indict Ariel Sharon. It also initiated *mabrook.com*, the first initiative to offer Arabs the opportunity of finding a partner via the internet.

Besides the multilingual aspects of the service, as the example of *Maktoob* already suggests, the political context was the other main determining factor for the ground-breaking development of Palestinian websites. In addition to the professional websites, Palestinian homepages gave cyberspace a personal focus. Palestinian academics and journalists in the Palestinian diaspora were among the first to create these homepages; while the BZU *Guide To Websites* offered a list of Palestine-based homepages at the time, it offered only a selection of personal homepages from Palestinians in the diaspora – there were already too many to be listed.[7] The timing of the research covered the first-generation internet, but towards the end of the period Palestinian internet developments had reached a new stage: Web 2.0. Informal and personal homepages progressed and professionalised and turned into blogs.

From homepage to blog: stages in a virtual (r)evolution

The homepages themselves formed a virtual network by providing hyperlinks to other local and personal websites, emphasising the links within the online community of Palestinian homepages, as the later bloggers would do. Mazen Abu Hajleh, who was raised in Lebanon and lived in Australia, said on his homepage: 'Sometimes you have to read about Israel to know Palestine, but you always have to read about Palestine to know about Israel.'[8] He had a special section devoted to Palestinian homepages; this collection later became an important source of information about Palestinian cyberspace pioneers.

Daoud Kuttab's *www.amin.org* was also a pioneering website, popular for its accessible information with articles about Palestine in both English and Arabic.[9] The local homepage produced by Hanna Safieh from the West Bank, on the other hand, offered a beautiful collection of pictures of historic Palestine between 1920 and 1967. And as an ode to his home town, Beit Sahour, George Rishmawi presented a biblical history of the town on his homepage. These are but a few examples that helped shape the evolution of Palestinian websites and in themselves they confirm the fusion of personal and professional motivations: the personal was political.

Websites became easier to maintain and therefore increasingly created by people who were not necessarily ICT professionals. These homepages evolved into what became known as 'blogs', which started to become more popular in the Middle East around 2005.[10] Many Arab blogs are political because of the highly politicised context in which they have evolved, and because they represent par excellence a counter-hegemonic tool. As a new virtual subculture, bloggers were engaging in innovative forms of democratic self-expression. They networked with other activists, were involved in global political and media critique and provided local, alternative journalism.

Rafah Today was one example of a new type of political counter-culture, and *Tabula Gaza* also became a well-known Palestinian blog. These personal media sources have become an important part of the Palestinian 'counterpublics' (Warner 2002), and the technologies have increased the internet's relevance to political activism. The growth of such blogs in the Arab world, exceeding many expectations of the Western media, gained legitimacy. By 2006 *Open Arab Internet* estimated there were 40,000 Arab blogs.

Many reports appeared about Egyptian bloggers, some of whom became well-known internationally. Others were part of social movements and mobilised for the protests in Cairo's Tahrir Square in support of the Palestinian Intifada or against President Mubarak, while some were active in the new opposition and protest groups such as *Kifaya* ('enough'). Several of these bloggers suffered harassment or were prohibited from travelling (Hala al-Masry), imprisoned (Kareem Amer) and even tortured (Mohamed al-Sharkawy).[11] The dialectical relationship between online activism via blogs, the offline political developments of the protest movements, and general political mobilisation in the Middle East is crucial. It encouraged many others to create blogs, to reveal stories and news that would otherwise have been concealed or bypassed by the mainstream media.[12] What is it that these blogs in Palestinian cyberspace were representing?

The Palestine Information Society Project (P@ISP) traced 192 Palestinian blogs, coded them according to eight basic categories, and subsequently applied a content analysis of the retrieved websites.[13] Several phenomena were revealed by a comparative study of the blogs. Online network analyses based on category, issue and alignment relations illustrate how blogs correlated according to category, issue and alignment. The line shapes show which links transmit or receive links, while the size of the nodes indicates the quantity of links.[14] The findings show that, in general, blogs were framed by socio-cultural issues, and that those from Palestine tended to highlight political topics in particular. Within Palestine there were also differences. It appears that blogs from the West Bank focused more on education and health issues, while those from Gaza leaned more towards advocacy and Islam. Linguistic differences also appeared to be relevant indicators in our analysis. Palestinian blogs in Arabic more often focused on socio-cultural topics, while those in English were dominated by politics.

Interestingly, websites based in the OPT had a much stronger presence than those by Palestinians living in Israel. While the internet connectivity of the latter group of people is potentially much higher, and certainly cheaper, their web content was much lower than that of Palestinians in the OPT. This difference exists because Palestinian web development in Israel finds itself, like Palestinians themselves, caught between a rock and a hard place– an expression of their status within Israeli society and of their continued alienation, as Dahan (2003) shows. This important observation also indicates that everyday politics, including personal experiences such as bombings, curfews and invasions, defines the style, the content and the quality of internet development.

A crucial stage in ICT development in Palestine was the *.ps* domain name, which added another level to the revolutionary development of Palestinian websites. Palestinian experts and investors worked together to put *.ps* on the world-wide cyber map, and its approval provided important legitimacy – the internet was regarded as a new gateway for Palestine when the *Internet Corporation for Assigned Names and Numbers* (ICANN) finally approved the new country code. The pressing question, of course, is whether that approval symbolised any territorial/political legitimacy.

Re-territorialising Palestine: *.ps*

> It is the gateway for Palestinians, something we have all been waiting for. It will back Palestinian IT, and introduce Palestine to a wider scope of the world; it is the address of Palestine.
>
> *Sabri Saidam, Gaza–Palestine, 2002.*

During fieldwork in 2002, resistance against invasions, curfews and occupation peaked, dominating daily life. But a similar struggle was taking place in cyberspace too: the fight for 'dot PS'. When the *.ps* country code was finally approved as the top-level domain for the OPT, in March 2000, the struggle to reach this point had taken five years (Cisneros 2001). ICANN's approval was based on a United Nations verdict in which Palestine (defined by the 1967 borders) was recognised as a country. Since the 'dot' and the characters following it identify and confirm the territorial or state origin of web pages, it was a symbolic change. It put Palestine on the map in cyberspace, an internet signifier that marks national boundaries, a code indicating the 'nation of origin' of the connected computers and websites. ISOC played a major role in the formation of *.ps* and of the regulations governing its use. Palestine evolved in cyberspace from the a-political *.com* community to the *.ps,* national, community. According to ISOC-Palestine the new country code meant the reconnection of all Palestinians, whether in Israel, the OPT or the diaspora. They could all identify and register with it and it was certainly an alternative to the Israeli *.il*.

It was also assumed that people would express interest in websites with their national initials, and help direct others towards specific Palestinian sources. Several interviews illustrated that this marker did indeed promote a sense of pride and a feeling of independence. Like the international telephone dialling code, *.ps* offered an aspect of anti-colonialism in cyberspace that altogether eradicated the Israeli country code as a domain name for Palestinian websites, and asserted their independent existence.[15] Interviews and debates concerning the online domain suggested that it is the virtual equivalent of offline independence. Yet *.ps* still faced many obstacles on its path.

For Palnet and other IT companies gaining the *.ps* code was a frustrating project, the never-ending discussions over it leading to quarrels; the implementation of the code was further complicated by continual delays. Palestinian society at large had reached an impasse as a result of Israeli policies; for example, the import of equipment was sabotaged by Israeli border control, or made difficult by curfews, closures and travel restrictions, and the re-occupation was beginning to take its toll. Although the *.ps* code was approved in 2000, it did not take off until 2002 due to internal disagreements, and this delay in setting up the official Palestinian internet had consequences: many websites had already been established as *.com*, *.org* or *.net* in the meantime. However, it was still expected that many would switch to the *.ps* code. Qadah, senior technology advisor to the PNA, expected at the time that most Palestinians using *.com* or *.org* would move to *.ps* (Cisneros 2001). The predicted switch would demonstrate the national values ascribed to the new code.

One way to show whether the *.ps* mirrors the values ascribed to territory and national identity is the trajectory of websites changing to *.ps* from an earlier *.com*, *.org* or *.net*. Checking Palestinian websites collected at the beginning of the fieldwork, with the addition of further quantitative collection in 2006, it appeared that, contrary to Qadah's expectation, many websites did not move to the *.ps* code. Only a small number of the Palestinian websites collected between 2002 and 2004 migrated to *.ps*. Furthermore, *.ps* is now predominantly used by political parties and commercial concerns. In other words; *.ps* was not the main domain of Palestinian cyberspace.

Over 1,200 *.ps* URLs within the Palestinian IP range were collected and coded in the P@ISP study. The websites were analysed according to the following classification markers: content, alignment, location, orientation, audience and language.[16] To grasp their 'centre of gravity', the *.ps* websites were coded within the Palestinian IP range as well as outside it by noting the locality of the owner, via a 'who is' domain-name search of all the *.ps* websites to identify them. The analyses of websites hosted inside and outside of the Palestinian IP range did not show significant non-Palestinian registrants in the *.ps* domain.[17] After thorough consideration of the bulk of the data, P@ISP found several other particular factors. The majority of those *.ps* websites are registered within the Palestinian territories yet are hosted outside it, mainly in the USA.

The extensive analyses confirmed the hypothesis based on 2006 preliminary *.ps* data of 733 URLs and revealed that the link between location, ownership and national identity does not necessarily make *.ps* a significant online political marker. This conclusion was also confirmed by tracing Birzeit University's comprehensive old list of links via the 'Way Back Machine'; P@ISP found that of the 172 BZU links from 2002, only five had migrated to *.ps* (one of which had kept its domain name but with differing content). Seven websites had bifurcated, migrating to *.ps* but also keeping the original; and five more websites had planned to migrate, i.e. they had reserved the *.ps* domain name without activating it. Figure 13 offers a visual conversion of the migration of Palestinian websites to *.ps*.

One of the most surprising results concerned the 'Government and Services' sites listed by BZU at the time. It was expected that, more than other types of websites, these would adopt a *.ps* identity. But of the 35 websites listed, just one migrated, with two bifurcating (sustaining the original). However, it is important to bear in mind that many of the early websites were inactive. Earlier ethnographic analyses of the 2000–04 manual collection showed that by 2007 one third of the websites were either 'dead' (i.e. completely inactive) or 'stale' (inactive for more than a year. The argument here is that many did not plan to survive, and so felt there was little point in moving to *.ps*.

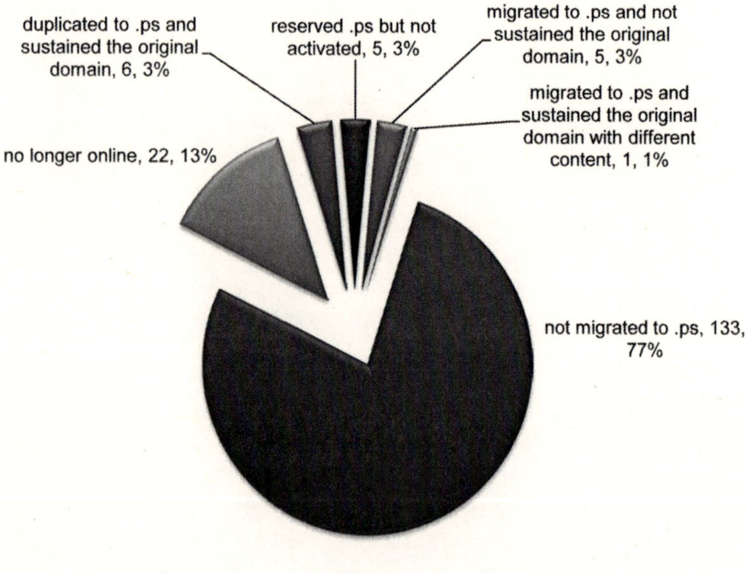

Fig. 13 Migration of websites to .ps.

The discussion about *.ps* is significant since one of the crucial implications of website relocation is the expectation that websites will eventually be followed by their networks. P@ISP retrieved data for the three main Palestinian universities: Birzeit University (Ramallah/Birzeit), Najah University (Nablus) and the Islamic University (Gaza), which had the option of using either *.edu* or *edu.ps*. The network analyses of the links to *.ps* websites by the three institutions (see snapshot in Figure. 14) illustrate which websites have a *.ps* policy.[18] Of the different networks of the three universities, the Islamic University gave a higher value to *.ps*, as website traffic was automatically redirected to its *.ps* site. The map showed only a few links pointing to the *.ps* websites for Birzeit and Najah Universities, which seemed to undervalue the *.ps*.

The results of the study concluded that the physical or offline location of a website is not based on territory, but rather on the degree to which the mechanism makes sense for technical or financial reasons. Besides it being troublesome to move a website, the risk of doing so is that the more casual visitors can lose it, so the site will be ranked lower by search engines and possibly attract even fewer visitors. Despite a push by the Palestinian community to adopt the *.ps* domain name for Palestinian websites as an expression of 'patriotism', its adoption by existing websites was largely unsuccessful at the time. It is not awkward as in many countries the national domain name only started to be used after the more generic *.com* or *.org* were already widespread. But in the case of Palestine – with *.ps* amongst the few internationally recognised markers of its 'sovereignty' – the *.ps* is a point of interest. Therefore a qualitative and political layer needs to be part of any quantitative analysis here.

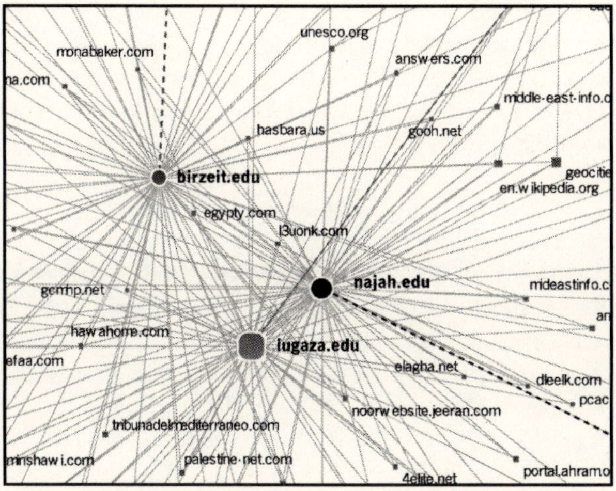

Fig. 14 Migration of .edu to .edu.ps: 3 Universities compared.

During the collection of data on locality and *.ps* migration two important facts came to light: first, offline territorial struggles are not necessarily mirrored in online struggles; and secondly, the revolutionary leap from Palestinian absence to presence in cyberspace happened *before* the *.ps* code could operate. Thus the low migration statistics *also* relate to the historical conditions that shaped the evolution of websites. Had Qadah made this statement four years earlier – around the time *.ps* was requested by the PNA, i.e. when many websites were in the process of being created, and before the Intifada-created boom – we would probably have seen a different outcome.

The virtual trajectories discussed here are thus characterised by the political conditions faced during the period in question, mirroring real-life migration. Assuming that *.ps* website ownership is indeed a reference to Palestinian national identity, the location of the owners is one indication of the 'grounded' characteristic of Palestinian cyberspace. However, considering the highly transnational Palestinian community – the large number of Palestinians living in the diaspora – the location of a Palestinian website owner cannot be considered a marker of possible national-political references in sites or domain names. Most exiled Palestinians do not feel less Palestinian because they are not present on Palestinian soil; rather, they share an imagined community with other Palestinians inside and outside the territorial centre, while simultaneously considering historical Palestine a very important point of reference. The following section discusses how the different types of websites, located inside Palestine or in the diaspora, can be classified according to codes and categories that reflect their overall identity.

Classifying and categorising exercises

> A truly public sphere for Palestinian opinion is lacking. There needs to be a repository of all Palestinian-oriented websites. Many Palestinian websites try to dump everything into one thing. It doesn't work, it's as if you walk into a library and find all the books on the floor. If it's not departmentalised and categorized, it won't help anybody.
>
> *Sam Bahour, Ramallah–Palestine, 2002.*

The longer the list of websites became during the fieldwork, the more necessary it was to categorise them. It was soon clear that the way audiences were being targeted related to particular goals. In fact, part of the initial critique expressed by Palestinian internet producers and critical internet consumers concerned the failure to target specific audiences, mostly the Western public. It was stated in many interviews that clarity and focus were key elements in catching the web surfer's attention. This methodology, as the above quotation by Bahour also implies, was applied to the research itself: classifying all sorts and sizes of websites collected in internet cafes and during face-to-face interviews in Palestine, Jordan and Lebanon.[19] Classifying Palestinian websites made it possible to analyse them in detail and over different periods of time. The first part of this section assesses the impact of *location* as the reference point of a website's content or target. The following part analyses the main mission of the internet – to 'rehumanise' Palestinians.

Many of the websites encountered at the time related to chatting, news or the Intifada. But the all-encompassing politicised atmosphere led to overlapping categories. 'Politics' was present on many non-political and commercial websites, for instance through posting explicit solidarity with Palestinian victims or salutations to international protesters. And whether activist, governmental or news-related, the dissemination of critical information turned out to be a shared objective. Religion-inspired manifestations are also part of the collective national political agenda. Hamas, for instance, is simultaneously an activist, religious and parliamentary movement. But as offline activism began to decrease, online activities were also toned down. Some websites even disappeared from cyberspace, and several were hacked.

With these underlying developments the (one-sided) quantitative exercise shifted from viewing and collecting websites to a dialectical study. This exercise was reflected in studying *how* the content and images of websites were evaluated and reshaped by internet users. In order to analyse the numerous websites I first identified them by content and goal. Table 5 delineates six markers: Activism, Religion, Entertainment, Government, Personal/Family and Information.[20] Besides political tendencies, websites also have global or local tendencies – they can be operating from local/Palestinian (e.g. *Palestine Monitor* in the OPT, mentioned above) or diasporic settings (e.g. *Jerusalemites*, based in Jordan).

While categorising and sub-dividing websites is important for hermeneutic reasons, it is not a static methodology. Table 6 maps how the markers can be further sub-divided. This allows for a more dynamic, processual, analysis. The way websites are interpreted, and thus classified, for instance depends on particular points in history. A definite time-marker being the al-Aqsa Intifada – with extreme periods between 2001 and 2004 – showed a peak in pro-Palestinian activism around the world in 2002. While many websites were produced in that heat of the moment and when the experiments were still fresh, the boom gradually decreased, reflecting that the novelty of the internet and the political momentum were the defining drivers.

TYPE					
Activism	Religion	Entertainment	Government	Personal/ Family	Information

Table 5 Palestinian website classification

Originate From	TYPE			
	Intifada Activism	Civil Society Activism	Media Activism	Refugees' Activism
PALESTINE	Hamas ISM	Palestine Monitor Miftah	Rafah Today Ramallah Online	Palestine - Remembered
DIASPORA	Arab Nationalist Taht-i Ramad Electronic Intifada PSC	Jerusalemites Solidarity Design Dying 2 Live	Palestine Chronicle	Al Awda

Table 6 Sub-divisions among websites marked for Activism

Globalising Palestine

As the preceding chapters have suggested, the Palestinian community is very much politicised and so it is not surprising that there are many newspapers and political magazines. With respect to websites, however – as several respondents argued – the Palestinian performance was initially considered to be weak: while the quantity of websites was growing, internet producers were rarely impressed by them. ISP employees, for instance, explained that some websites were only viewed by their creators or direct networks. 'Websites are being created for the sake of being created' was a comment that was often made.[21] Active/critical internet users also criticised the Palestinian government for its weak use of technology and content flow. A different nexus can be followed analysing the shape and evolution of Palestinian websites. Here the main differentiation is that between localising and globalising pro-Palestinian websites.

It is important to study locally-based representations to understand the contributions of internet users themselves. From this perspective, two types of contributions were discerned: personal homepages by Palestinian individuals, and websites based on a particular local view. These local sites do not necessarily have a local target: some specifically address international audiences with the aim of building solidarity, as will be shown; and such websites, characterised by their global self-representation, seek in particular to reach out to broader audiences. It is this global dimension of virtual Palestine that will first be examined. According to several interviewees, to become successful – or even to survive – Palestinian websites need to provide good content, a clear focus and user-friendly applications. Several internationally-oriented and professional websites have understood this very well; those mentioned as prime examples of what is possible include *Electronic Intifada* and *Palestine Chronicle*.[22] Both have clear-cut profiles and provide a commentary on Palestinian life and politics in a way that is accessible to international audiences. A successful approach is recognisable by the way journalistic (often Western) frameworks have been applied. These transnational websites have also shown that access to material resources is essential to maintaining high-level quality, as is routinely working with experienced employees and volunteers. These strategies were less visible in the governmental sector. Following up his general assessment of websites in the quotation introducing this section, Bahour continues:

> The worst are government websites. For instance when the Ministry of Education posted a letter on their website, the appeal was emailed as a scanned fax. They used the internet as a medium without understanding that the audience is looking for flat text, and it took half an hour to download the thing because of the size of the Ministry logo.

At some point, however, the PNA realised its weaknesses, and the Ministry of Information for instance set up the online *Palestine Media Centre* (PMC) service.[23] The PMC's overall strategy was to supply professional and up-to-date news and to shape international public opinion on the political realities of Palestine.

The target audience often shapes the style and, accordingly, the principal rules of a website. It was considered extremely important to offer a simple framework for an English-speaking audience. The web-design company InterTech, which set up the initial plan for PMC, pointed out how important user-friendly browsing technologies were, especially in Palestine. Marwan, web designer at InterTech in 2002, illustrates why interface is crucial, though often ignored:

> A particular graphic design relies on the preferences of our clients, but simplicity is our priority. We want accessible websites with the easiest navigation. Since we have to connect through Israeli-controlled telephone lines, heavy images and downloads are not practical for those accessing our websites inside Palestine.

Another feature of successful websites was mentioned as being able to organise effective international mobilisation. *Palestine Monitor* (PM) – created right after the outbreak of the al-Aqsa Intifada in 2000 by Palestinian NGO collective PNGO, and maintained by volunteers closely linked to international solidarity groups – conformed to these requirements, and PM reached massive audiences all over the world. During an interview in 2002, one of the volunteers described the website's unique impact, which was especially encouraging amid all the difficulties:

> I console myself by knowing that all regions are included in our audience now. The monthly registration of the top geographical regions on our site shows Western Europe, Australia, Northern Europe, South America, sub-Saharan Africa ... Of course we've been getting hate mail from Israel and America as well, but we don't respond to that. We basically have the whole world visiting us. This is very important (Hani, Ramallah, 2002).

Analyses of the statistics relating to the PM site showed that the countries accessing the site were mainly the USA, the UK, Australia, the Netherlands and Canada. The type of audience accessing PM varied from media, commercial, academic and, unsurprisingly, the military. The fact that internet visitors from the Western hemisphere accessed these news sources does not mean that people from the Middle East are not interested, but rather substantiates the expectation that the mainstream Arab media already provide sufficient references to Palestine. The September 2002 statistics on PM demonstrated that the site had been visited more than a million times that month, the highest ever reached by any website from Palestine at the time (20 September being PM's most active day that year). When comparing these statistics with news reports and fieldwork notes, the highest number of visitors was traceable as coinciding with the IDF attack on Arafat in the PA headquarters, Muqata'a, in Ramallah, where he was under house arrest.

The most frequently requested PM pages were those with on-the-ground chronicles, latest updates and pictures. The timeline mentioned here points to a direct correlation between extreme political moments and internet hits. This confirms that existing and dominant gaps in Western media are partly overcome online. Particularly when deconstructing the often-assumed dilemma between technologic determinism and social construction, Palestinian websites exemplify that the importance of a policy on 'style' is not only a matter of aesthetics or technical sophistication but conveys strategic political choices and motivations.

Re-humanising Palestinians

> It's basically their [American] money and their votes that determine what happens to me as a Palestinian ... The internet is the first mass tool that provides us with direct access to the end user, without falling victim to pro-Israeli editors ... So we must use it properly to convince the American people.
>
> *Murad, Books@IC, Amman–Jordan, 2003.*

While explaining the story behind *Jerusalemites.org* during an interview in Amman, Murad unfolds his own inspiration to get started with the website:

> When I went to Jerusalem I walked around with a strange feeling: for the first time in my life I realised that if anyone asked me, 'Where are you from?', I could say, 'From here.' I thought, 'Fuck it: these are MY people.' I never had this feeling before. When I later found the house my family owned before 1948 in Jerusalem, I had the same feeling.

Two years after the idea came to him and after his last visit to Jerusalem in 1999, the website went online. It is not a surprise that *Jerusalemites.org* was based in Jordan: Amman has a high concentration of Jerusalemites because most of the Palestinians that escaped from the city during the 1948 or 1967 wars ended up in Jordan. The Amman-based Jerusalem Forum then adopted *Jerusalemites.org*, logically as this organisation was geared towards Palestinians' attachment to their land and this holy city. The outbreak of the Intifada, a year after Murad's visit, triggered the foundation of the website as well. For Murad: 'The fact that I am still alive as a Palestinian means I have to contribute, even in the smallest manner: first of all for my self-respect, but also for my country.' His website appealed to the West, the aim being to portray a more 'civilised' image of Palestinians:

> I deliberately put the image of a synagogue next to one of a church and the al-Aqsa mosque. The site promotes the idea that Jerusalem is not only for the people who inhabit it at present but for all religions, just like Vatican City is for all Roman Catholics.

The website clearly did not aim to target the Middle East. The explanation was simple: 'I don't want to convince those who are already pro-Palestinian.' Murad's goal is to highlight the positive aspects of Palestinian culture, and in this first impressions are important: 'The opening line on the homepage is a quote by the famous Khalil Gibran, because we know people in the West will react to that.'

Formulated with the slogan *Let Palestine hug its people*, the website also reminded its viewers of the dispossessed and stateless Palestinians. By disseminating this message online it sought to strengthen Palestinian unity: to 'hug its people' then means to let the website or the internet reconnect Palestine in a virtual embrace. The website is intended to tell the story of the Palestinian people, and 'to make a connection between people inside and outside because we all belong to Palestine and Jerusalem'. This need to represent Palestinian realities, or as Murad said 'to civilise', can be explained as the double goal of appealing to the West and of correcting the Palestinian image.

Many websites seek to *humanise* Palestinians in this way. An example is a website created in 2002, in a period when Palestinians were suffering heavily under military sieges and curfews. The website was called *Dying2Live* , and was set up as a collective effort of Palestinian advertisers, graphic designers, writers and art directors. *Dying2Live* portrayed Palestinian children in the image of their hero or idol, such as Albert Einstein, Ghandi or Che Guevara. Each of the pictures is associated with a child's personal story, with the sections introduced by the following text: 'We are not a statistic. We have faces. We have names. We have hopes. We have dreams. JUST LIKE YOU'. This message was directed at a non-Palestinian audience whose image of Palestinians needed to be reframed, and the stories also attempted to generate support. The wider impact of the website is shown by the feedback pages: hundreds of people and organisations from all over the world responded with comments expressing solidarity, and that the website has shown them the human side of what seems like a complex or far-away issue.[24] Another website that appeared shortly after *Dying2Live* was *I am a Palestinian* which described itself as 'A place for Palestinians to share their stories with the world, to learn more about what life is like for Palestinians.' The contributors were Palestinians from different places in the USA and the Middle East.

Fig. 15 Dying to live: rehumanising Palestinians.

As already mentioned, Palestinian websites can have the characteristics of a global website while appearing local. *Ramallah Online* and *Rafah Today* are good examples of such websites where the local and global features overlap. *Rafah Today* was successful both in 'rehumanising' Palestinians and at the same time, with persistence and personal effort, informing the outside world and overcoming the Western media bias.[25] This website was set up by a young man living in Rafah, the part of Gaza bordering Egypt. Pictorially rich, exhibiting high-quality photographs which he himself took of everyday tragedies such as home demolitions and homeless families, he succeeded in penetrating the deafening silence about the tragedies unfolding in Gaza. Within a few years his website gained international acclaim, and he was asked to do features and photographic work for international press agencies. During a telephone interview in 2005 Mohammed in Gaza had the following to say about the pictures on his website:

> The photographs document what I'm saying. I'm sad when I can't document or corroborate a story with a photograph because I feel the picture is proof of the reality ... most important is that I report what is happening on the ground in Rafah ... The site does not serve any real function for people who live in Palestine because they're already there: they know what goes on here ... So I don't target Palestinians at all. Perhaps there are some Palestinian NGOs who refer to it, but the site is directed towards people outside, who don't usually get such information.

Mohammed backed his on-the-ground portraits and stories with official data; it is the combination of these factual reports, his unique insider's view and the use of internet technology that hit a particular nerve. Based on his website's traffic statistics he worked out that roughly 80 per cent of his audience was tapping in from Europe and North America.

The assumption that 'a picture is worth a thousand words' is the general motivation for including photographs of local places, faces and events. Real-life documents and online portraits allow viewers to perceive Palestinians as real people rather than being put on for aesthetic purposes or as pawns in a political game as argued before. The images and stories floating in global cyberspace testify to the everyday realities experienced in local places. Like Mohammed with his *Rafah Today*, Palestinians use their websites while living the everyday colonial reality. The relation between text and image is explained on his homepage: 'On this website I present photos and reports about my hometown. About our life, our community, the home demolitions, homeless families, the children in our camps. About the tragedies that happen here every day.' Personally experiencing the impact of a house demolition in Gaza, he stoically photographed house after house being demolished by the Israeli army. Mohammed's talent, combined with the fact that he lived in and was a victim of the war against Gaza, shows that grassroots participation from inside Palestine is of great importance.

Websites such as *Palestine-Net* linked to local places to promote the special significance of Palestinian cities.[26] The struggle over the history and memory of Palestine has already been partly won by those Palestinians who managed to by-pass the traditionally limited official broadcasting media and created websites and mailing lists. Much of their effort was devoted to offering alternative sources of information to counter the silence about (and neglect of) the Palestinian exodus in 1948. This coincided with an important moment in history: in 1998 the Israeli government set up websites to celebrate the country's 50th anniversary. Unsurprisingly, yet no less unjustly, there was no reference to the Palestinian sacrifice which had accompanied the birth of Israel. For the purpose of commemorating 50 years since the 1948 catastrophe, *alnakba.org* was launched, and the website *deiryassin.org* also went online.

Subsequently, websites became easier to maintain; this development benefited non-corporate and individual actors, and thus those towards the local end of the local/global spectrum outlined above.

Localising Palestine

The localising websites are different in terms of ownership and status; this becomes clear, for instance, when combining institutional and personal websites. Then there are also localising websites with more of an official look, such as *Al Bireh Municipality* or *Nablus Municipality,* giving information about the town's art, culture and geography, for instance through articles and online galleries.[27] Compared to these municipal websites, *Ramallah Online* is more informal and not initiated by web designers linked to local government, yet still offers information about the city's history and society. A clear difference is that it also offers interactive communication through its forum.

Remembering Jenin was set up dedicated to recounting the destruction following the invasions ordered by Israeli Prime Minister Sharon in 2002. The audio files of eyewitness stories are like online testimonies, together with a timeline of events, photographs, reports and analyses. These websites seem to say *this history will not be erased or denied again.*

Websites like these nurture the memories of Palestinians inside, and while doing so share them with those outside. This dynamic is a concrete example of how by functioning as virtual platforms the internet empowers dispersed Palestinians and allows them to meet in cyberspace. Territorial references are always important components of Palestinian identity: the map of Mandate Palestine (1948) is a popular shape on websites, as it is on necklaces and embroidery, and in art. Cultivating the *imagined* nation is a unique component of the localising Palestinian online traversals; the discovery of Palestinian cities through online pictures by Dali in Chapter Three beautifully demonstrates this. *Hanaa.org* was mentioned during interviews in 2001–02 by many young Palestinians in Jordan and Lebanon. It combines Palestinian culture and politics, as in the *100 lives/100 Shaheed* (martyrs) section, and was particularly popular for its downloadable virtual cards, with images of Palestine to send to online friends. These online traversals further shaping existing national imagination are an echo of Benedict Anderson's (1991) references to the role of traversals in the 'pilgrimages' that colonial civil servants undertook in the New Americas of the 18th century. Through their travel experiences, these (educated, male) explorers co-defined the territorial contours of the nation and in due course contributed to the construction of what the imagined community entails. Surfing to Palestinian places and meeting other Palestinians online is like a virtual pilgrimage, as Khalili (2004) noted with regard to teenagers who use the internet cafes in Bourj al-Barajna refugee camp in Lebanon.

Nevertheless, while Anderson's traversals are related to real, offline travel experiences, Palestinians do not enjoy this kind of mobility, and it is of course important to differentiate between physical and virtual mobility. The point of reference, however, is clearly historic Palestine. As argued, the internet's defining characteristic inhabits the possibility to, simultaneously, by-pass time and space, i.e. there is an online-offline divide but no direct inside-or-outside divide. The problem regarding Palestinian virtual traversals is the lack of a concrete meeting point, of a centre for the exiled. The fact that exiled Palestinians do not have the option of entering such a centre gives more value to the territorial inside.

Although the notion of an imagined community and Palestinian nation-building are not identical, scrutinising new forms of interactivity in the absence of walking through the territorial landscapes provides creative ways to 're-discover' Palestine. The localising websites constitute key junctions during the diasporic traversals. In the illuminating words of Shaker who finally 'found' his roots:

> I visited Tarsheeha after I found a website with pictures and documents about it. I had never seen pictures of my village before. It was different – I had imagined it like my grandfather described it, with small houses and large fields. Now it looks more like part of a city. It shocked me because of the difference with how I imagined it would be. I had mixed feelings in the beginning. I forwarded it to friends and family and wrote: 'This is the village my mum comes from.'

Shaker described the event as 'visiting Tarsheeha' and the place as 'my village'. Websites were employed to locate and visit these places, and to meet with Palestinians inside. Moreover, it mattered little to Shaker that it was more than 60 years since his village had been lost – the relation felt stronger because of the confrontation. Interactive communication is one of the major blessings for communities separated by walls and barbed wire. Marwan, from Ramallah, helped set up *alnakba.org*; he elaborates on the necessity for Palestinians to have this online interaction. He expands on the context during an interview in 2002:

> We worked hard on alnakba.org. It's important because many deny the Nakba. My mother was born in Lod [Tel Aviv] but she had to flee. We can find a lot of information about her village and history on the alnakba.org website now. It also became popular because of the guest-book: many Palestinians in the diaspora have no opportunities to talk to each other, so we offer this interactive technique to bridge the gap.

Hence, as depicted in Chapter Four, the Nakba is a continuous issue that keeps recurring online and is addressed on several global and local websites. The *nakba.org* website, for example, was a direct response to Israeli propaganda. *Virtual-Palestine* also published a detailed list of towns, villages and cities in Palestine.[28] Clicking on a name would provide a direct link to information on demographics, photographs of scenery, stories and memories associated with the town. But *Palestine Remembered* in particular became a virtual testimony of the history of the Nakba, offering personal narratives, recorded and downloadable, from 1948 survivors and current camp dwellers. Mahmoud from Shatila told me about his experiences with *Palestine Remembered*: 'Through that website I could see where my family fled from. I found pictures of Balad al-Sheikh, our village near Haifa.' Shaker and Mahmoud compared what their grandparents told them with what they found online. Through these examples, Palestinian websites can be interpreted as *localising* tools for Palestinians cut off from each other. In other words, behind the scenes, the local utilisation of Palestinian websites is experienced in specific ways and contexts.

Behind the scenes

As mentioned in the introduction, Palestinians in Lebanon and Jordan often directed me to websites they regarded as important and which they personally valued. They referred to websites about Palestinian towns, such as *Beit Reema*, mentioned above, and as the previous section illustrated, about Palestinian towns their families were expelled from, some of which no longer exist. Because of these new discoveries and interactions, locally-made websites by refugees in Lebanon, such as *Gaza Net* and *Children of Shatila*, also came to the fore.[29] The motivations in setting up these diasporic websites were very diverse. Young people in Shatila simply wanted a website to portray their realities definitively. Besides disseminating a political message, it felt comforting to write 'our own story', as it was usually phrased. The local websites made and evaluated by people in the camps showed that it was not only the 'fancy' or official websites that represented or defined the Palestinian presence on the web.

Many of the locally produced websites offered a mix in terms of content: music, politics, culture, religion and history often fused. These overlaps are not unique – for globalising websites with a 'rehumanizing' PR target a clear-cut focus is imperative, whereas for their localising equivalents such overlapping is more common. The local production of websites reflects in particular an intimate relationship between producers and their websites. For instance, when 22-year-old Nazih from a refugee camp in southern Lebanon was searching for information about his village in Palestine, al-Bassah, he was inspired to construct a website himself, with much of the content – writings and pictures – coming from the internet. While it could be said that he was simply reproducing content from similar sources, it still meant a great deal to him and to others from al-Bassah to have a specific, territorialised entry point in cyberspace.

Mohammed from Nahr al-Bared expressed a sense of pride in his website, and invested a great deal of work in *al-Bareeq* ('shining'). He mounted an online forum for people to hold discussions with each other, and it was his specific aim to attract other Arabs as well as Palestinians. He estimated that 60 per cent of visitors logged in from outside Lebanon. The website engaged with matters that concerned Mohammed, a Palestinian refugee in Lebanon. As the name of the site suggests, his aim was to shine light on such matters. Besides informative links about all the refugee camps in Lebanon and an interactive link to the Quran, a cartoon of the week, and a poll, the Arab forum was the core of his website.[30]

His aim was to convince visitors to the site about the Palestinians' plight in order to mobilise as broad an audience as possible. For him,

Arab unity is crucial for a solution for Palestine: 'So instead of changing the way the West sees us, let us first strengthen ourselves as Arabs.' In 2004 Mohammed added voice chat to enable visitors to talk with each other. During the course of constructing *al-Bareeq* he made friends in several countries, and moderated the forum page in direct coordination with two other young men, from Syria and the UAE. Showing his latest subscribers on the forum to me, he said:

> I think I achieve something for our cause, you know. If convincing one person is a good thing, how about when I reached 126? And how about when they come from different countries? That's what I call change.

It enthused him when new people joined his website, and this in turn made him put extra effort into the project. The website also cost him money – not a minor issue for a refugee in a camp. Apart from costs that were needed to update the website with technological developments, he paid US$50 in subscription costs alone. With the help of his online friends, he managed to rebuild the website when it was hacked, remaking the forum and continuing to host debates, mostly about Palestine and the conflict.

22-year-old Ali from Bourj al-Shamali camp also yearned to reinstate the 'other side' of Palestine, arguing that:

> The camp was a forgotten place for a long time. But with the internet this does not necessarily have to be the case any more. So I made a website about the camp, its conditions, our life etc. Now we can reach the media, tell our story. We can exchange information with our people in Palestine and disseminate their photos and letters about the suffering here.

Akram from Bourj al-Barajne camp in Beirut also could not resist the urge to make his own website. Unlike others mentioned here, Akram's website was not dominated by national politics, but mostly dealt with promoting his internet cafe: 'When I sent the site to my friends in Canada and Europe they were even surprised that there was an internet cafe in the camp.' The site was built gradually by adding textual references and pictures of his activities or those of the customers in the internet cafe. When his clients were chatting they sometimes passed on the URL of the website so that those they chatted with could see pictures of the cafe, and in this way Akram's clients became an organic part of the website.[31]

These and other diasporic cases from Lebanon show the grassroots dimension in the early development of the internet. Plenty of local informal initiatives in Palestine itself started with the same incentive. One of the examples is *al-carma.com.* Just as the al-Aqsa Intifada broke out, this website, run from Ramallah, was featured on Abu Dhabi TV, a regional satellite channel, and this resulted in many new visitors. Hicham set up the website with friends who contributed with news stories, and people from elsewhere in Palestine also emailed him with their additional local news, for instance about arrests, clashes and other incidents. In Hicham's words:

> If someone from Jenin studying in the USA wanted to know what was happening in his neighbourhood, he could go to our site and see. We also had an announcement board where people could celebrate birthdays or send their regards.

Live radio programmes, for instance the popular radio stations *Angham* and *Ajyal,* were broadcast via the *al-carma.com* website. What matters in the ethnographic assessment of Palestinian websites is how they were evaluated behind the scenes, by their users. The latter expressed a variety of opinions about the value and impact of online sources, shaped offline as they are in multiple ways.

Offline implications

The ability to move from one place to another and to visit Palestinian places during virtual traversals caused a wave of excitement. These practices raised my curiousity about the experiences of internet users themselves and the challenges they face. Wandering through online and offline spaces looking at Palestinian internet participation in different contexts showed the internal differences. It seemed that there was less engagement online by Palestinians in Jordan. One of the reasons given by Palestinians living there was that telephone, post and border exchange between Jordan and Palestine were relatively normal – the kind of direct communication unimaginable for refugees in Lebanon.[32] This provides some explanation as to why Palestinians in Lebanon engaged so strongly with the internet in contacting Palestine. In Lebanon the internet was an outlet and fulfilled the need for (virtual) escapism among refugees.

Palestine Remembered was very much the most important global reference point. It was often referred to as the place to 'see Palestine'; people would surf there to collect specific information about particular family/village/city histories – to satisfy a visual need that text or narratives could not. By providing pictures, maps of localities and profiles of prominent Palestinian figures and places, it preserved many Palestinians' memories. And by allowing them to attach stories, memories or pictures to the site, it generated a medium for sharing in the production of these sources. The online sources of *Palestine Remembered* are indeed impressive: there is for instance detailed information on all the 420 villages that were ethnically cleansed in 1948.

Internet cafes have dealt with increasing demands by eager customers wanting to be hooked up with Palestine or requesting they be shown a website about their original village. The relevance of adopting a local perspective goes beyond listing names of websites: not only those referred to by major websites, or by interviewees mentioned above, but also others such as *Hamas, Ezzedeen, Amr Khaled, Arab48* and *Gaza Press*.[33] The announcement of an electronic gallery by a young artist in Palestine made an impact on some of the interviewees in a Beirut internet cafe. This young artist, Sami al-Haw, from Gaza, presented his online exhibition in February 2004 with a collection of surrealist paintings reflecting Palestinian endurance.

Cyberspace has presented many opportunities, but also new challenges. The difference between the offline and online web analyses exist because free virtual cyberspace also represents systems of *exclusion* (Rogers 2002). Webomatrix, in particular, can be applied for these online methodologies as Thelwall shows in his important contributions about affects of links and source mechanisms (2008a, 2008b).

Some of the websites that were popular among those interviewed – for instance those linked to Hamas or Hezbollah – were not referred to by the leading (often globalising) websites. Some avoided association with what were assumed to be radical sources. Such underlying sentiments further mirror the strategies mentioned above in terms of targeting certain audiences, or even donors.

As demonstrated, the virtual pilgrimages strengthened the politics of belonging. However, while looking behind the scenes, and questioning the offline implications of these pilgrimages, the offline popularity of websites did not always correspond with virtual observations and online networks. Some of the websites present in the offline dynamic (mentioned in Palestinian internet cafes or during interviews) were rarely found on link pages. I consider these the 'virtual-present -absentees': present in cyberspace but considered non-existent by cyberspace. These sources are often those that galvanise resistance and are considered 'radical', and in due course unveil the selective politics of representation in Palestinian cyberspace.

Conclusion

The mere fact that the Palestinian presence on the web made a huge leap around the Intifada, determined how the websites were to be classified. Here the re-humanising issue was a key impact of Palestinian web publishing. The launch of countless pro-Palestinian websites led to an enormous expansion. The circumstances shaped by the Intifada led to websites like *Dying2Live* and *I am a Palestinian,* and *Solidarity Design.* The military incursions in March and April 2002, the destruction of Jenin refugee camp in the same period, and the collective punishment by closure and curfew over the years, determined the intensity of internet activity. These ground-breaking developments were accompanied by growing Palestinian solidarity movements across Europe and the USA, and the many blogs and *.ps* websites that continued to appear.

Although it was anticipated, the *.ps* domain seemed to have had little real impact, because most websites at the time did not migrate to it; however, this was more practically than politically driven – the internet is often navigated by hyperlinks and search engines rather than by domain names. A better basis for classifying the growing number of websites was by the audience targeted and by territorial references. Differentiating between globalising and localising inclinations helped to explain the political agenda of a website, predominantly the aspiration to 'rehumanise' Palestinians. Many of the examples have shown the significance of being connected to an offline locality. In the Palestinian context, this is a focus shaped by a collective identity and shared future visions. While the internet represents both diversity and fragmentation, the general outcome at the time was mobilisation towards collective solidarity and political unity. The unique timing and consequential push-pull factors shaped by this evolution signified that the development and trajectories of websites are not static.

A further major breakthrough was the possibility for people in Lebanon, for instance, to come across a website about their original village in Palestine. Localising Palestine was like building a virtual highway through which the diaspora could travel to places in Palestine, making it possible to connect with people around the world without needing a visa or proof of citizenship. The internet hereby revitalised 'long-distance' nationalism. Palestinian websites, chatting and mailing lists were the vehicles that structured this correlation. Sometimes the online imagined communities were juxtaposed with everyday offline life. Although the experience was virtual and could not really make up for actual return, some internet users talked about it with such emotion it was as if they had literally travelled to Palestine. Scores of websites and internet initiatives continued to be launched. This maturing was greatly assisted by the Arabisation of internet infrastructure. Thus beside the production of websites another aspect of the internet explosion in Palestine concerns the *users* of Palestinian websites.

The Palestinian public is explicitly imagined through the production and consumption of local Palestinian websites. Internet participants like Mohammed, who constructed *Al Bareeq*, spent days and nights developing and improving their sites, with the help of their friends in such places as Nahr al-Bared or the Gulf. Such bottom-up visions helped to demarcate the materiality of ICT and how this shapes face-to-face and on-the-ground experiences. The offline conditions and everyday power relations underlying these virtual traversals will be analysed in the next, final, chapter.

6

AT THE CROSSROADS: INTERNET CAFES

> Long after the night has descended and the shops are closed, their shopkeepers gone home, and the sizzle of the city turned cold, a few neon lights begin to appear.[1]

> How cyberspace will affect us, is not directly inscribed into its technological properties: it rather hinges on the network of socio-symbolic relations (e.g. of power and domination), which always and already over-determines the way cyberspace affects us (Žižek 1998: 511).

In the above quotation, Žižek articulates his discontent with a technological, determinist view on the social implications of the internet. A decade ago, when he wrote this, absolutist (whether dystopian or utopian) claims about cyberspace were still part of the debate. However calling attention to the dynamics of power and domination remains important, especially with regards to internet cafes (ICs).[2] First, power and domination are striking categories because, rather than being technological properties of the internet, they bring to our attention how the internet is 'embedded'. These categories in turn generate their own boomerang effects: struggle and agency. Secondly, the categories, together with these boomerang effects, allude to the offline, quotdian spheres of the internet.

ICs are places where the offline and the online are juxtaposed. More than any other setting related to the internet, the IC lies at the intersection between politics, technology and society. ICs, particularly those operating in extremely challenging conditions, capture important aspects of the relationship between virtual and everyday life. ICs, via the low-cost internet access they make possible, offer virtual mobility and virtual escapism to the community. Previous chapters describe the workings of Palestinian communities online and how the imagined Palestinian nation and deliberations about the state are mediated through the internet, and given a face on websites. This chapter, built on the above themes, is informed by an urge to study internet practices as they have evolved *on the ground*.

This approach, as part of the general *situated analyses,* will uncover how communities are seduced into entering and then embracing an IC, and which opportunities and limitations of the internet contribute to (de)legitimising the presence of ICs. What are the underlying issues and practices of the internet in everyday Palestinian life? Is the internet accessed at home or in an IC? Does the IC as a new public place enable the presence of people otherwise absent from the public sphere? How does internet use and going to ICs relate to collectively shared, if not dominant, notions of 'moral' and 'good' behaviour? Can people go to an IC during curfews? Addressing these questions will show, beside the impact of technology on society, how communities affect technology.

As formulated at the outset of this study, internet users are present online through chat rooms, via email or by surfing cultural or political websites and they are present offline as internet users when sitting next to one another in an IC, or when meeting someone face-to-face after establishing online contact. While new relations can be formed online, the focus here will be on the offline formations. The commercial ICs and the local NGO centres with internet access points are the experimental spaces – the particular hubs where the social implications of internet usage is sowed. One of the, perhaps inevitable, outcomes is that these offline internet places are *contested* spaces, similar to the Habermasian 'coffee houses' with regard to the public sphere. Interestingly, critical debates about the 'public sphere', (the contrast between reality and the idealised concept in particular) resemble discussions about ICs during fieldwork. Like a coffee house, the IC is neither neutral and open to all, nor closed and exclusively for the lucky few; the notion of ICs in this chapter is closer to how Oldenburg (1999) positions public cafes: as 'third places'.

ICs also represent public places where people assemble for pleasure, good company and lively conversation. Thus besides functional access points, ICs are at once technological and social spaces (Lægran and Stewart 2003); not only do they differ from public access points such as libraries and bars, there are contexts where such access points are not even attainable. Some may fail to create a 'cafe' environment, while some community centres may succeed (ibid: 307). The next question this immediately raises is which conditions generate these failures or successes.

In the second section the transformation of ICs is traced in a two-fold manner, through techno-practical and social-cultural prisms. Gender differences crystallise the disputed context of these new public spaces. This chapter will assess how particular conditions shape these new online and offline spaces which in turn evoke charged values, and which moral associations do IC users (or owners) refer to? To examine the local context fully requires being in the field during military occupation, visiting secretly opened curfew ICs, and spending time in remote refugee camp ICs to understand their challenges.

While unravelling these different layers it becomes clear that public internet spaces are not only centres of power and domination. Everyday internet utilisation also manifests struggle and agency. The third and fourth sections zoom in on IC users and on owners of these contested places. Two telling examples will be discussed at the end of the chapter. One is a direct example of a 'contested' space, namely where the public ICs defy curfews and offer access to the internet under extreme conditions. The other is an indirect example, about the fascinating formations of new friendships and romances via the internet. However, the chapter starts by illustrating how ICs attracted Palestinians to the internet, and how their motivation to use the internet in turn demanded more ICs. The encounters in Palestine, Jordan and Lebanon called for a deconstruction of the multiple faces and phases of the internet. To understand the transformation of ICs, the context of a community-based perspective of ICT developments had to be taken into account.

Situating internet cafes

> It's funny to hear elderly people sometimes ask 'Did anyone call us on the Antirnet today?'
>
> *Shaker, Beirut–Lebanon, 2003.*

The enthusiasm about the novel advances of the internet at the time were expressed in different ways. In the quotation above, 15-year-old Shaker captures this enthusiasm in his reference to the curiosity of elderly people. This example is also a marker of the internet becoming an integral part of society, whether through direct or indirect use. People's first introduction to the internet was mostly through school, work and community projects. Another commonly mentioned reason for internet use was the need to stay in touch with people abroad. Kholoud, a mother of two teenagers living in a Beirut refugee camp, gave in when her friend was about to return to Canada: 'Becca took me to the IC to show me how to use the internet so we could at least stay in touch by email.' And 17-year-old Samah, also from Bourj al-Barajna, used the internet to keep in touch with her father and brothers – all working in the Gulf.

ICs are dynamic spaces, in a constant state of change: some transmute from being a small local cafe to an internet cafe, some expand, and some cease to exist. The Palestinian IC presents a *fluid* space – sometimes the IC is even an extension of the home. Reading between the lines, ICs appear as products of social, political and technological factors. To understand the different faces and phases of ICs, the internet itself needs to be demarcated according to the values it represents. As argued in Chapter Two, this requires a study of the technological infrastructures at stake in different offline settings that shape internet use. This chapter looks further at how people actually use the internet in these different conditions and contexts.

This section explores how the intentions of IC owners and the practices of IC users intertwine, and how this in due course makes visible the similarities and differences between ICs. The birth and transformation of ICs are related to local power dynamics and the recurring impact of the Intifada. Two ways to map ICs are discerned: a focus on audience and on location. Considering conditions of poverty, occupation and population density, looking for (home) individual usage at the time was inadequate. Rather, a *community-based* approach of ICs is the most appropriate methodology in these contexts.

Community-based internet

A bottom-up perspective was particularly helpful during fieldwork because individual statistics, or even household data, did not serve as satisfactory methods to measure internet penetration. For Palestinians ICs were the most significant ways of entering cyberspace between 2001 and 2004.

The statistics of ISP subscriptions (the percentage of private/home access was estimated between 3 and 5 per cent in 2001–02) are primary indicators. The IC adds an important level to analyses about the internet and shows a broader penetration rate than initially expected as outlined in Chapter Two. There are many indirect home users (friends, extended family and neighbours), or friends gathering in an IC together using the same computer to chat and surf. Several additional reasons increased the importance of the internet, educational benefits and the 'post-office' services being the most relevant.

School projects and examinations more and more required a PC, and students could be expected to search online, and then deliver a typed and printed paper, sometimes even including images. During fieldwork in an IC in Bourj al-Barajna the supervisor was searching for images of dolphins on the internet for a young customer. She sometimes does this for her young clients and often teaches them how to use Google Search or to download images. She said she feels sorry for them because many children in the camp cannot do what they are asked to do by their school: not only did many pupils simply not know how to use Microsoft Office or Explorer, many families could not afford the LL 3000 (US$2) it might cost for internet access and then printing. Nevertheless, the fusion of educational demands with ICs further normalised the latter. Telephone *centrals* were of great importance in normalising the presence of ICs, especially inside the camps. ICs offered extra services such as printing and scanning, web cams, Net2Phone cards and a local telephone-switchboard system. In Bourj al-Shamali the system was sophisticated to the extent that there was a corner in the community centre with clocks pointing at the local times in different countries which could be called up.

The first fieldwork visits in Ein al-Hilwe refugee camp in 2002 illustrate very well the mobilising impact of the internet. While waiting for a friend's cousin to pick me up at the local central, I asked the owner how he had started the business, and (not knowing the real situation on the ground) what he thought of the fact that telephoning from Lebanon to Palestine was impossible. He laughed and said: 'You don't know how creative Palestinians are.' Pointing with his chin at his computer, he said: 'We use the internet to call Palestine, my dear.' He offered me the opportunity of trying it myself, and within ten minutes I was talking with friends in Palestine. One of them, surprised, asked me twice, 'Are you really in Lebanon? In Ein al-Hilwe?' he was moved and added 'You must send my greetings to the brothers and sisters in the camps.'[3]

Deciphering Palestinian internet penetration from a community perspective shifts attention to the IC as a *host* rather than merely a functional place. Some parents find the IC convenient, according to several of its employees: during the day it is like a crèche where the children are entertained and watched over. In the over-populated camps, the schools have to divide students into three shifts: early morning, noon and afternoon. The children play games in the IC while they wait for their shift; and many return after school, staying until their mothers or older siblings have to drag them home. Many of the ICs were noisy and overcrowded and indeed at times look more like a children's centres. But it soon appeared that the day is divided according to the age and gender of customers. After the supervisor of the IC sends the children away, around seven pm, the atmosphere changes: now is the time for young people and adults returning from high school, university or jobs to occupy the place. By around nine pm those left in the IC will be mostly youths and men.

Having nowhere to play in the overcrowded camps, bored children and young people become experts in computer games. These games sometimes became real battles; one of the supervisors at an IC in Im-Sharayet, a distant suburb of Ramallah, said: 'When they enter Israeli or American chat rooms it's like a war in the IC. They are so involved, and curse and fight on the internet ... It comes from deep inside, it's what they really feel.' For isolated and poor societies, an IC becomes a new form of amusement as well, and the IC itself a mixture of crèche, youth club, office space and entertainment area. Tracing the development of ICs from a multi-sited perspective is a challenge; they therefore need to be situated in the different Palestinian settings.

Contextualising the internet: cyber Intifada

ICs can be mapped in several ways, for instance through a focus on its customers (refugees/poor/middle class/elite), or by studying their specific location (inside/outside a camp). When considering audience or location as important demarcations, the internal dynamics of different national settings come to the fore (Table 7 shows the locations and the demographic data of the settings researched). The internal and external differences need to be analysed since distance and location matter greatly.

While Palestinians from camps in Amman or Beirut can walk within 15 minutes to an IC in Haret Hreik or downtown Amman respectively – also saving the cost of a taxi trip, which is often worth an hour on the internet – in other parts of Lebanon or Jordan they are more dependent on ICs *inside* the camp. Internet access in refugee camps is therefore important in two ways: it is *less expensive* and *less distant*. Thinking about a more comfortable and private place to chat or email outside the camp is a possibility, but it requires planning, mobility and at times family support. In Lebanon the remoteness of Sour's city centre from Bourj al-Shamali camp, or of Tripoli from Nahr al-Bared camp, was particularly problematic for girls and younger women. As I experienced returning from Sour to Bourj al-Shamali with friends, passing two military checkpoints on the long isolated road, and finally being dropped at the main entrance of the camp, a group of men sitting at the entrance stared at us as we stepped out and walked home. Sometimes, even when it is possible to go to an IC inside the camp, this is not an appropriate alternative if no special women-only hours are offered.

The internal dynamics also relate to the wider power relations to which refugee camps are subjected. Depending on their geographical context, camps can be a state-within-a-state, or effectively powerless.[4] The size and location of a camp matters too: Whether Irbid or Beqaa' camp in Jordan or Bourj al-Shamali in the south and Nahr al-Bared in the north, these camps are remote, and thus more socially isolated. This isolation can make the internet or IC popular, but also notorious.

As for Palestine, finally, it was the outbreak of the Intifada, and the consequent attractive force of the internet, that most strongly influenced the development of ICs. Zaina, a student from Bethlehem at Birzeit University, experienced the effect of the Intifada first-hand:

> The meaning of place and time changed for me; I am from Bethlehem, which is in reality not far from Ramallah. I could easily visit my family. But now with the curfews and closures it's almost impossible. If I want to know how they are or if I need to assure them that I'm all right, I email them. When they attacked and reoccupied Ramallah, I checked many websites and news sources on the net for information and pictures.

Many people who work or study in Ramallah live in the outskirts of the city or, like Zaina, in other cities. ICs have also been mushrooming in remote areas. ICs in areas outside the cities were doing well because closures (i.e. army blockades) and curfews prevented people from commuting to the cities. The high demand for computer use and internet services in order to continue their work, or for school pupils to complete their homework, secured an extra income for the ICs. However, this could not halt the devastating economic impact of the Intifada for the smaller ICs in Palestine. No compensation for the losses, of course, was available. As Abu Samer of the *Sadaqa* IC in Im-Sharayet on the outskirts of Ramallah said, during an interview in 2002: 'We don't get any compensation from the PA or Israel. We won't see a penny. I haven't seen green money [US$] since the Intifada started. Nobody cares.' Some ICs gave up because they were continually threatened. *Sadaqa* is one of these, a small IC which not only had less capital but was cursed by being situated on the military route taken by the IDF when they entered Ramallah. The sieges and reoccupation took many Palestinians by surprise. According to Abu Samer:

> This IC started as a joke. But we didn't expect the situation to become like this. We don't have any hope left for the future, we don't even know if we will live tomorrow. They even killed children walking in the streets, so what does that say about me?

Israeli soldiers often crossed the city, spreading fear and shooting at people in the streets. Thus, beside ICs with less capital like *Sadaqa*, better-off ICs situated in the line of fire were also sacrificed. Some of these hitherto successful ICs gave up after the IDF turned them into military posts or simply bombed them. The location of an IC is therefore extremely important in Palestine.

Situated on the top floor of the Lou' Loua building, with a view of Ramallah's main Manara square, was the popular and busy *al-Carma* IC. During the 'Operation Defence Shield' military siege in March 2002, aimed at crushing the uprising, extreme violence disrupted everyday life. Visiting *al-Carma* – which the IDF had occupied – right after the invasion, I could either enter through the door, or through a big hole next to it caused by explosives; this measure was sometimes used in case Palestinian resistance fighters had booby-trapped the door. The place was in chaos. The garbage and the huge gap in the wall were cynically introduced by Hisham, the owner, as the 'new interior design'. Pictures of the IC and its clients, spread all over the floor, reflected happier days. The interview took place as we were walking through what had been the cafe – covered in dust, broken computer screens, hard drives, floppy discs and debris from the explosions. The interviews in 2002, also quoted in Chapter Four, are a remarkable testimony of the Intifada context and provide crucial information about the trajectory of Palestinian ICs:

> During the first siege [February 2002] I was trapped inside the office for one week; nobody was allowed to leave Ramallah. I

> didn't want to put my customers at risk, so I closed the place. I stayed to protect it from burglars. I heard gunfire and explosions day and night. We could see the clashes between soldiers and the resistance on the streets from the roof windows. During the second siege [March/April 2002] I wasn't here; the soldiers got as far as the Manara and they occupied our building. They didn't use the door, they entered through the walls.
>
> They stayed for 23 days ... The building became an important military post because it overlooks the city from different angles. But there was no reason for them to do all this. It seemed they enjoyed it. They threw my PC files and data equipment out of the windows, they stole software I had been developing, they stripped all my computers. When the curfew was lifted for a few hours and people went out to buy food, some of the soldiers threw cans of urine at the people on the street from my window.
>
> When I finally managed to return after the siege I was shocked, I felt like a victim of rape; namely a violent violation of my whole being, my privacy, while I was helpless. Everything was done deliberately. They filled the toilets with sand after they had defecated, so as to clog them. Before they left, they collected all their rubbish and filth and smeared it round the place, even their shit. An American reporter came for an interview, and asked if all this made me feel like becoming a suicide bomber too; I threw her out.

Thus the context of the Intifada and of occupation also led to disempowerment and destruction. The sad irony was that the Intifada, which had led to the explosive growth in *Al Carma*'s customer base, also meant the ICs' destruction by Israeli explosives. Hisham's direct experiences with the military (re)occupation of the West Bank bring us to the differences between Gaza and the West Bank.

The towns and camps in Gaza did not have West Bank-type curfews to endure, and were not invaded in similar ways. The main reason was that IDF soldiers could not operate effectively inside the dense areas of the countless camps; for ground troops, Gaza was like a gigantic booby trap. Another reason was that Gaza had simply been turned into an open prison. The fate of the ICs in Gaza was directly affected by economic devastation and extreme isolation. Therefore both despite and because of the isolation and poverty, in 2002 the number of ICs in Gaza City went from a handful to approximately 150.

The Intifada also affected ICs in the diaspora. *Inner Space* began in 2000 as one of the first ICs in a Lebanese refugee camp. The launching of this new business coincided with the outbreak of the Intifada, and the newly politicised context played an important role in accelerating the start-up process. Politics was a key factor for the initiators: the hunger for information increased the ICs' customer base, especially around key events such as the siege of the Nativity Church in Bethelhem, the invasion of Ramallah and most notably the destruction of Jenin. In the ICs people were verifying the news, and often discussing developments with each other on the spot. Rather than being used only for entertainment and education, the internet became a valuable asset for the exiled, isolated and immobile Palestinians. The IC in this context therefore attracted a greater diversity of customers. These (internal and external) differences between ICs will be explored further in the next section, by looking at the birth and transformation of ICs and their prospect as public spaces.

The evolution of internet cafes

> [ICs] are de facto outlets for a sometimes bored and other times repressed youth who now spend hours playing computer games, browsing triple X sites chatting, and discovering the world 'out there' through a flat screen interaction with cyber reality.[5]

> In the beginning customers used to wait outside the IC for a free spot; it was a new thing, and there was a huge incentive because of the Intifada. The first thing many would ask when they came was: 'Can I chat with Palestine?'
>
> *IC owner, Beirut–Lebanon, 2003.*

The research into ICs brought up different, at times contradicting, findings. It was claimed that Jordan had the highest number of ICs in one street in the world. Walking through and around Shafaik Street in Irbid and across the Yarmouk University campus, I lost count; but it was claimed that there were 130 ICs. The development of ICs in Jordan underwent different phases. The initial trial-and-error phase was first-hand experienced by *Books@Cafe,* aka *Books*, in Amman, as will be illustrated. The mushrooming of ICs was at that time unregulated, because there was simply no government policy. At the end of 2000, however, the Communication Organising Authority began to create regulations, requiring for example that entrepreneurs apply for a special licence to open a new IC. They also had to register the names of users and produce a monthly record of websites browsed when this was required.

The ICs were somewhat naively expected to install censorship programs and official regulations also stipulated that internet computers be sited an open space, as opposed to more secluded arrangements.[6] It was general knowledge that the *mukhabarat* randomly visited ICs to uncover suspicious behaviour. The government later loosened these measures, partly encouraged by financial interests in the ICT sector. Similar developments were taking place in Lebanon, and initial restrictions were loosened there too. Developments in Lebanon, described in the quotations above, symbolise the meaning of ICs for the young and deprived sections of society, and for exiled refugees craving a way of communicating with Palestine.

This section lays out the different social and political Palestinian settings of ICs, and hereafter will take a closer look at the (infra-structural) challenges. The transformation of ICs can be unravelled in roughly two ways: in a techno-practical way and in a socio-cultural way. Several transformations can be discerned: from the IC as a functional and *technical* space, to the IC as a 'cool' place; or from a male-dominated environment to a contested, mixed, social setting.

At the start, around 1998, ICs in Palestine were uncommon and very expensive. Most internet users were students – universities were the first public institutions to introduce the internet to the wider public. When I returned, not more than three years later, cities like Ramallah, Nablus and Gaza were full of ICs. One of the ICs I regularly attended in Ramallah is *Future Net,* started by 27-year-old Ali when he returned from the Gulf with his family. Situated in the centre of Ramallah, on the always busy Rukab Street, it was probably one of the most successful ICs. It had opened its doors in the summer of 2001, ten months after the start of the Intifada. Most customers were students and young professionals from Ramallah or surrounding towns, and foreigners (exchange students, journalists, volunteers etc.) *Future Net* had 80 computers, of which 17 were kept in a separate room for games only, and was in the process of expanding with a coffee shop and family room.[7]

Waiting in the IC for a planned interview, there was a sudden panic: soldiers entered the street shooting percussion grenades (sound bombs) and tear gas. Clients were calmed down by the employees and asked to leave the IC before a curfew was imposed, trapping us in the building, as had happened before with such incidents. I had been waiting to start the interview, and was looking through a window; now the soldiers came nearer and nearer to our building. The clashes on Manara Square looked like a cat-and-mouse chase between soldiers and youths. The soldiers were criss-crossing in their jeeps while firing tear gas and rubber (but steel-coated) bullets. The streets were crowded with people doing their shopping, and parents with children coming home from school grabbed them and ran off. It was uncommon for the soldiers to come so close to the middle of the city. Watching how young boys tried to escape by running through alleys or hiding in buildings and shops had a paralysing effect on me. One part of me wanted to run away, as joining the crowd seemed the only thing that made sense; another part was appalled and wanted to join the stone-throwers.

Transformation of internet cafes

Later in that summer of 2002, Ali and I met in *Future Net* and recalled the events when we were supposed to meet for an interview. He explained that:

> [W]hen curfew is lifted, this place is packed with people who check the latest news or send emails about the events or assure their family or friends elsewhere. People chat or email about what they endured with the soldiers and tanks rolling through their streets, or clashes between youths and the army ... the day you were here the soldiers came to provoke. People protest this by throwing vegetables or stones at them. Everybody starts to run in panic when the army jeeps drive by fast. People can get injured or killed in such incidents, so shops were closing immediately. We also had to urge people to leave. Many people were still in the middle of their internet activities – some of them were angry, but we had no choice.

Despite the devastated economy and the dangerous circumstances *Future Net* enjoyed great success. Journalists came to work because the internet's speed and the services were good, and the IC itself was located in a central place, and as was shown by the incident described above, is sometimes at the centre of action. One of the journalists at *Future Net* was tragically to be well known as the first foreign journalist casualty of the Intifada.[8] Ali recalled: 'The night before they killed him he was working here until we closed. We knew him as a nice guy.' All this was clearly not what Ali envisioned when he returned to Palestine.

Palestinian returnees also played a crucial role in establishing ICs in Jordan. Median is one of the Palestinian entrepreneurs in Jordan who, like many Palestinians in Kuwait, left after the Gulf War and eventually settled in Jordan. 'Palestinians in Kuwait faced a lot of discrimination – they use to call us *humousy*,' he recalls. During several interviews in 2003 he explained that his own personal context shaped his motivations and the relevance of the internet:

> It was a great means of communication because [...] many of us are spread around the world. I have brothers and sisters in five different places in the world. The phone was horribly bad, and very expensive.

People were soon lingering in his IC, waiting for an available computer. The impact of the ongoing Intifada, and after 9/11 of Jordan's warm relations with the USA, meant that, besides the influx of Palestinian 'returnees' such as Median, Amman attracted increasing numbers of British army personnel, Arab businessmen, human-rights consultants and activists deported from Palestine. This amalgam of people prompted more internet usage. In March and April 2002, when the conflict in Palestine escalated, the entrance of *Books* was used for political mobilisation. One announcement on the message board read: 'All Palestinian women meet outside American embassy'. Later these announcements were removed, and Median said: 'That started to worry me; we knew the *mokhabarat* [secret police] did it.' Besides the political incentive, the materiality of the internet, and also the technological benefits themselves, played a crucial part in boosting the internet. Median said: 'Not really knowing what the internet and computers were, poor Iraqi refugees or Palestinian *hajjiyyat* [older ladies] also came ... People who wouldn't have used it otherwise, now do.'

How internet users were acquainted with the new technology for the first time is a fascinating marker in the evolution of the internet. Nuhad from Shatila camp in Lebanon recalls how she started using the internet: 'Because everybody was talking about it, I went to the IC to see what they were doing. Soon I asked others to help me and started to chat as well – I really liked it.'

Sana' from Lebanon started experimenting with the internet when she lived in Canada, to contact her much-missed family and friends in Bourj al-Barajne camp. Once, the opportunity to go to a concert by a famous Arab singer, her first-ever such experience, overwhelmed her. She had to share her excitement and the internet was the best possibility:

> I would mostly email with my brother in Bourj al-Barajne or sister in Holland; I shared everything with them. The best experience was when I went to the concert of Fadil Shaker; I managed to meet the singer and take pictures ...
>
> The concert finished at four in the morning. I waited in the streets until the photo-lab opened, when I developed the pictures I went straight to the IC to scan them and send them to every single person I knew!

Sana' shows the importance of the IC's multifunctional uses – scanning, uploading, sending, receiving. But the additional telephone services, the 'centrals' in particular, transformed ICs. Akram in Beirut's Bourj al-Barajne understood the need for telephone contact very well, and invested his savings to start an IC central. He acquired access by extending a telephone cable inside the camp from a friend on the outside. He brought his own computer, and soon added a second one; this was the beginning of his IC. The central made a great difference for people in Bourj al-Barajne. People could connect to each other inside the camp via the switchboard – best compared to an advanced walky-talky – for less than the cost using mobile phones. Akram explained the variety of his clientele: 'A mother can call her married daughters for long chats, and our whole football team is connected so they can plan training schedules on the telephone.'

Besides making calls inside the camps or to Lebanese landlines, Akram's clients could also make international calls with VoIP (Voice over Internet Protocol) internet telephony by logging on for instance to *net2phone* cards or Skype and using the headphone and a microphone. After five decades without a telephone or fax in the camp, this is an impressive phenomenon.[9] Telephone calls via the internet cost less than on official landlines. Uploading, scanning, and downloading shaped the face of ICs. Sahaar, at *Sirhaan Net* IC in Bourj al-Barajne, managed to complete the application procedure for a travel visa to the UAE for one of her clients. It had previously cost US$30 to send a copy of the ticket by DHL, and it would take at least a week before a reply could be expected; here the same process took half a day. Sahar scanned and then emailed the return ticket, which the client's friend in the UAE needed in order to obtain an application from the consul. When the client received the application form by email, Sahar printed it and helped her with the questionnaire. They then scanned it and returned it by email as an attachment.

WEST BANK	
name of the camp	number of refugees
Aqabat jabr	6,264
Ein el Sultan	1,828
Shu'fat	10,717
• **Am'ari**	**10,377**
Kalandia	10,759
Deir Ammar	2,335
• **Jalazone**	**10,966**
Fawwar	7,912
Arroub	10,246
• **Dheisheh**	**12,804**
Aida	4,715
Beit Jibrin	2,054
Far'a	7,540
Camp No 1	6,683
Askar	15,591
Balata	22,855
Tulkam	17,981
Nur Shams	8,998
Jenin	15,854

GAZA	
name of the camp	number of refugees
• **Jabalia**	**106,846**
Rafah	97,412
Beach	80,567
Nuseriat	58,727
• **Khan Younis**	**61,539**
Bureij	29,805
Maghazi	23,161
Deir elBalah	20,215

JORDAN	
name of the camp	number of refugees
• **Baq'a**	**90,515**
• **Amman New Camp**	**50,609**
Marka	44,198
Jaba el-Hussein	29,520
• **Irbid**	**24,758**
Husn	21,441
Zarqa	18,335
Souf	19,429
Jerash	23,034
Talbieh	6,107

LEBANON	
name of the camp	number of refugees
Mar Elieas	616
• **Burj el-Barajneh**	**15,718**
Dbayeh	4,025
• **Shatila**	**8,370**
• **Ein el-Hilweh**	**45,967**
Mieh Mieh	4,569
El-Buss	9,508
Rashidieh	29,361
• **Burj el-Shemali**	**19,074**
• **Nahr el-Bared**	**31,303**
Beddawi	15,947
Wavel	7,668
Dikwaneh & Nabatieh (destroyed camps)	16,518

Table 7 Demographic information on OPT and the diaspora [10]

A similar situation was noticeable during observation in ICs in Jordan. In Wihdaat refugee camp in Amman, I was shown how letters and application forms were processed, and pictures scanned and sent off. The *Firaaz* IC had a fax machine, and for the other IC in the camp, *Al Quds,* it was not even necessary to have an email address because people could use the IC's own address. Faxing, scanning and sending/receiving documents and messages via email make such ICs look more like local post offices. Since the IC benefits people in multiple ways, the inquiry into how ICs are set up in the first place becomes an additional query. This task was for the most part investigated in detail in Beirut.

It was particularly challenging to trace how ICs in Lebanon were connected, because communication infrastructures were prohibited in the camps. On top of this, the camps became overpopulated and building construction was prohibited. It was easy to pass an IC without noticing it because it often took up a very small space and sometimes was part of a house. ICs with extra capital could develop and expand their business. Small ICs, those that illegally tapped into other cable connections, sometimes closed or turned into video/game shops for boys seven to 12 years old. As Akram's experience showed, at first an internet connection was only available via telephone lines, later also through a broadband connection, and then in some cases even by a satellite connection. So what are concurrently the different ways of obtaining internet access in Palestinian camps?

One has to turn to a 'friend of a friend' or to a relative with a Lebanese ID, because refugees in the camps are not entitled to apply for a telephone or internet licence. The new IC connects the camp to the internet via a telephone or cable line from a home just outside the camp. After a licensed ISP line is arranged, it becomes easy to tap from this legal owner outside the camp and reconnect/re-sell to others inside the camp. However, sometimes the outside liaison is using an illegal connection, which the authorities disable as soon as it is discovered, and with it goes the illegal connection to the camp and thus also to any other sub-user in the camp. Wireless infrastructure would have been an option, but at the time it had not yet been fully developed, and was expensive: a simple receiver for instance cost US$75–150 at the time. Thus the ICs themselves had different characteristics, depending on the means, options and aims of the entrepreneur.

Scorpio Net and *Shatila Net,* the two ICs studied in Shatila camp, offered an insider's view with regard to how the local internet had started up. Despite a limited amount of capital to cover the basic costs of a phone line, a few computers and a room, the young men in Shatila started their collective undertaking with enthusiasm. Some of them had only recently experimented with internet and computers, and the initial setting-up was mostly done by people not professionally trained in ICT. The new owner of *Shatila Net* did not know much about computers or the internet, so he got his friends and cousins involved. One of these friends was Nehad, who in fact helped both ICs with the technical work. He could build computers from old parts that he brought from his work or that others gave him.

For *Scorpio Net* the situation was similar; the description of 21-year-old Rafiq during an interview in 2004 summarises the methods mentioned above:

> I am actually a carpenter. There were no cyber cafes in the camp and my father came up with this idea. My cousins helped me because they had some experience with the internet; one had taken computer-science courses. We used part of the ground floor of our house; first I had to make some modifications – a different door, tiles etc. When I first opened I only had games; I tried to get a phone line but I couldn't, so I looked for someone outside the camp to connect me. After two months the authorities cut it, then I finally found someone with a legal line. The authorities can't cut the [redistributed/diverted] line inside the camp because they have no control in our camps.

With additional internet connections, more cables were running through the already overcrowded and overprovided camp. Each cable connected to another, producing a creative system of tapping though some, fed up with the obstructing of their power supply, cut the cables (Figure 16). This would eventually form a web of cables between buildings. Since Shatila camp is one of the most densely populated camps it cannot meet the demand for electricity, resulting in an average of four power cuts a day. Power-supply capacity in Shatila had been fixed at 1,000 KW for a maximum of 1,000 families, but the camp hosted 4,500 houses and shops. Alternatively, a good generator could last up to ten hours, but can cost up to US$1,500. A UPS (Uninterrupted Power Supply) box for the computers was also possible, but also expensive, making these options affordable for only a few ICs.

Fig. 16 Shatila camp: A web of cables covers narrow streets.

Fig. 17 Electricity cuts in Sirhaan Net IC. UPS usage.

The two ICs researched in Bourj al-Barajne camp had different connection systems: *Sirhaan Net* had ADSL and *Inner Space* a telephone line. Both suffered from the usual power cuts, but were better equipped because they had UPSs to supply them with a few more hours of power. Thus it could be dark in and around the IC but the computers would still be on. During powercuts sometimes *Inner Space* has to close its doors in order to save the remaining power fuel, although exceptions for *ajaneb* (foreigners), mostly journalists, researchers or volunteers in the camp, were often made. Akram explained: 'It is because *ajaneb* usually do important work that benefits the camp', though after further inquiry he added, 'If a Palestinian is working on an important essay, he or she would also be allowed to stay.'

As illustrated before, economic differences influence how certain ICs are transformed. *Books* in Jordan is an excellent representation of such transformation. It went from a bookshop that also served coffee to a popular IC that also sold books and served coffee and snacks, to mainly a trendy cafe/restaurant with books and the internet. Unlike many of the ICs mentioned above, *Books* represented an urban hang-out space where boys and girls could mix. Median, the entrepreneur behind *Books*, was inspired by ICs in the US, and especially by their multifunctional characteristics. However, setting up *Books* was not easy. As the first one to open an IC in Amman, there was no existing bureaucratic framework for dealing with this sort of development as explained before. And it was thus difficult to get a licence. During an interview in 2003 he said:

> We labelled the place a 'cultural centre' and had to be creative with the Ministry of Trade. The policy was partly to 'go with the flow'. We were hot, and flaunted by the media as the first IC in Jordan, or even the Middle East.

Books invested its profits, but its customers also generated more money: the internet cost twice that of ordinary ICs in Amman – two Jordanian dinars (about US$3) per hour, triple the cost in refugee-camp ICs. This IC was clearly a place for Jordanian and Palestinian expatriates, middle-class young people, students and the elite. *Books* was an example of a class-based IC. Moreover, alcohol was served, and the bar-style interior created a certain atmosphere of exclusiveness. It was a safe space for gays and lesbians, *argila*-smoking women, students and foreigners. *Books* did not monitor its clients, and the PCs were in a separate area of the cafe which provided more privacy. Sometimes employees would find triple-X websites in the history pages.

After less than a year, *Books* was the coffee shop in town, and it was its bar and cafe rather than its computers that attracted the customers, as most already had internet access at home. When I visited in 2005, customers were bringing their own laptops because *Books* had a wireless connection. This combination meant that for those who could afford it, work or study could be combined with a latte, and chatting could be done simultaneously online and offline. This was a recent phenomenon in the region, emerging particularly in urban (and cosmopolitan) places such as in Cairo (De Koning 2009) but certainly also in Amman and Beirut.

The transformation of ICs was also related to the type of audience, and the different motives and strategies which inclined them towards a particular IC. The transformation of ICs is therefore also a matter of how they manage to attract and host different groups. The more liberal codes of conduct meant that Median had to overcome existing social barriers when he opened *Books:* 'It was at times used against me. Besides being targeted for my own personality, it was also said I promoted sexual behaviour ... in a way we had to fight for *Books*.' In other words, the IC is not a neutral public space: contesting the (implicit) rules is a way to operate such spaces and access to such offline public spaces sometimes needs to be negotiated.

Internet cafes as contested spaces

> Palestinian society is still a male-dominated society. Gaza is one of the most conservative places in Palestine. Some here consider the internet taboo. People in villages and deprived communities do not feel confident in sending their daughters, and often not their sons either, to internet cafes.
>
> *Sabri Saidam, Gaza–Palestine, 2002.*

The poster commemoration of the Intifada on the wall of the small four-by-four metre *Inner Space* IC evokes a sense of excitement and rebellion. The poster depicts a wounded Palestinian teenager being carried away, the golden Dome of the Rock and al-Aqsa' mosque in the background of the image. The collage includes the shape of a boy swinging his catapult, the picture taken just before the stone shot out of it. Besides this poster, screensavers with images of Palestinian martyrs and Che Guevara contribute to the ambience of the place. These poignant images in *Inner Space*, the IC in Bourj al-Barajne in 2004, are significant in multiple ways. The walls were not only decorated with Intifada posters, but had lists of popular websites, news sources and chat rooms as well. Decorations have an impact on the atmosphere – they can make a place look more youthful, political, serious or romantic. The interior design of an IC can help to mobilise national unity, and they are spaces of contestation and rebellion.

In Nahr al-Bared the walls of the Somoud centre had hand-painted evocative murals of Palestine. In the al-Najde ABP centre on the other hand the lights were dimmed, with only the blue computer screens providing a soft light. When the coordinator smoked his *argila*, passing it around to others in the room, the intimate ambience was complete. Besides location of the IC, the interior of an IC was also a social issue. It sheds light on the IC as a physical meeting point; it shows the relevance of such a space beyond the material or technological functionality of the internet. How the computer tables are set up might for instance encourage more personal contact with other customers or alternatively offer greater anonymity. The lounge corner in Ramallah's *al-Carma,* the separate computer islands in *Chat Net*, the drinks and food in *Future Net*, the music in al-Najde: all, in their own way, were contributing to a sense of comfort and to encouraging interactivity.

The diversity of internet users is adequately demonstrated by the daily experiences in *Future Net.* As Ali illustrated during one of our meetings in the IC in 2002:

> We have different types of customers, some more exceptional than others, like that young guy there who looks like a Taliban. He doesn't email or surf ordinary sites, but is just interested in [radical] Islamic websites. He came with a CD-ROM about Chechnya and brought five people with him, who all looked like him ... There's also an older man in the corner – he comes here to chat with girls for hours.

Although Ali keeps an eye on 'proper' behaviour, the IC still provides a sense of anonymity and secrecy. Hence the IC can be a meeting point for groups seeking ideological inspiration through specific websites or software, as Ali's 'Taliban' customers show.

Pleasure and comfort was certainly prevalent also in many refugee camp ICs. In one of the Bourj al-Barajne ICs boys and girls were surfing the internet together for stories about the contestants in the Arab *Star Academy*; another group of young people were watching websites about Palestinian resistance, with images of clashes with Israeli soldiers or pictures of *shuhada'* (martyrs), which provoked angry comments. Physical, material markers also reflect class distinctions, as described in the previous section. ICs where middle- and upper-class young people could gather had other norms. In one of the ICs in Ramallah there were 'computer islands': three computers on separate tables facing one another, giving the users privacy or secrecy to chat with lovers or visit 'improper' websites.

Unsurprisingly, ICs were also specifically contested spaces in terms of gender. The exposure to new ideas and contacts with the outside world that brought about ICs in the first place somehow challenged ideas about the presence of women there. Obviously, mixed public places such as the ICs described above influences existing gender divisions. Saidam, the Palestinian representative of ISOC and an internet expert in Gaza, explained this tension between the sexes and male domination in the opening quotation above. Men often outnumber women in ICs, and this is why the university districts of Gaza had two women-only ICs. This was not only the case in Gaza: Bour al-Shamali camp saw a similar situation. Waleed, who runs an IC there, summarised it as follows: 'The main problem is me: a 23-year-old guy running the place with only other men as customers.' During an interview in 2002 the Women's Union coordinator of al-Bekaa camp in Jordan explained further:

> Only a few young women go to an IC [here], many feel uncomfortable. The men sometimes open porn sites, this is very embarrassing. Men somehow think that girls who go to the IC are less respectable.

Many ICs succeeded in establishing a positive image, and some built good relationships with parents, putting a great deal of effort into hosting a mixed IC that was also a pleasant and friendly place. Other ICs only cared about making some extra money, disregarding the customers' special needs; it was these institutions that would often contribute to negative perceptions about ICs, and offered inadequate access to female internet users.

This issue came up a number of times in group discussions and interviews. Open conversations resulted in humorous or sad stories about double standards and secret internet escapades. The following extracts from a group interview with young women in Lebanon's Nahr al-Bared camp in 2003 provide a good example:

> Due to the morals in our society a girl does not have a chance to use the internet as she pleases because the men are exploiting

> the situation by sticking like glue to their chairs, not making any space or time for a girl to use the internet in the internet cafe.

Young women thus faced constraints, and in some settings their presence was an exception. In several refugee camps young unmarried women preferred to visit one outside the camp, usually on their way to or from town for school or work. Some would confess to these visits, while others would conceal them from their parents.

However, many of the men I spoke with do not agree with the way (young) women are treated. In Bourj al-Shamali, Abu Basel said: 'The person who is afraid his daughter will be influenced by the internet might just as well lock her in a room ... it is unacceptable to ban anyone from using the internet or going to an internet cafe.' Finding ways for girls to participate, such as the ABP centres, are effective alternatives in countering the inequality. Accessibility for women was thus an important motive for NGOs setting up internet centres as part of their community projects, the more so because small (politico-religious) sectarian groups were increasingly causing problems – they sometimes targeted mixed (-gender) projects, including internet centres. Activities for women – something quite normal in most refugee camps – had to be defended again. Baha, director of Beit Atfal Sumoud in Ein al-Hilwe said: 'I can and want to resist the Lebanese and Israeli oppressors, but I can't accept the social oppression by radicals inside the camp. For the first time in my life I feel like I want to leave the camp.'

Internet projects were susceptible to power games inside the camp. With the rise of sectarian movements and a further deterioration of political and economic conditions in Lebanon, groups such as Usbat al-Ansar, Fath al-Islam or Jama'at al-Nour emerged, one with even stricter views than the other. An activist in Ein al-Hilwe in 2004 commented: 'Sometimes even the smallest group can make the loudest noise.' They did not have numerical dominance, but in this period their hard-line attitudes had a broad impact. When militants detonated a bomb in an IC in Ein al-Hilwe,[11] Salah from Ajial Centre described a similar case:

> We tried to open an internet project and then these so-called 'representatives of God' threaten us. They are against mixed places, and claimed people are watching sex sites. These groups are a worrying phenomenon. When my brother refused to remove posters of Che Guevara and George Habbash in his little centre, they tried to burn his place too.

Some militants referred to ICs as places of moral corruption. Sometimes it needed one-to-one meetings with parents to convince them that their daughters should be allowed to join. On the other hand, parents and brothers usually allowed girls and young women to go to ICs where smoking or access to pornography sites was banned, or which offered separate areas for men and women. *Inner Space* in Bourj al-Barajne, for example, created a 'women-friendly' area. Many girls and women trusted the manager and considered it a comfortable place, especially because one of its employees was a young woman. Female instructors and coordinators were also important gatekeepers in generating a more diverse audience. They functioned as role models and helped promote the project within their own immediate families and networks of friends.

It was an important demand of the initiators of ABP that the internet centres be co-educational and inclusive. In fact, gender and social equality were part of ABP's aspirations. From the way ABP operated in Gaza it is also clear that sometimes such demands could not be imposed top-down. Although the ABP training sessions were mixed, free internet use was offered at separate times or in separate rooms for men and women. This approach was not simply a compromise but a tactical choice to guarantee female participation. The women's union in al-Bekaa camp also introduced a women-only internet project, and gave special internet training to girls. This combination was necessary to overcome the barriers, and it did in fact increase female attendance. As opposed to being places simply for 'hanging out', ICs are also related to social mobility. The IC was often considered a safe place for young women because it was not considered a cafe, which is seen by many to have the negative connotations of a bar. Education was a potent justification for women and girls to access the internet, which is partly why going to an IC is more common among schoolgirls and unmarried women; however for married women with responsibilities to the family and the home it could be considered a 'waste of time'. The social fabric in which the IC is embedded thus needs to be considered in the same light as for challenges regarding coffee houses, which were initially, and incorrectly, considered neutral public spheres (Calhoun 1992).

During fieldwork in Gaza in 2002, the ICs in Jabalia camp were dominated by men, especially in the evenings or at night. There was one woman in the IC, and she was one of the forerunners who had claimed a seat in the IC whether the men present liked it or not. The fact that she was a lawyer from the camp and needed to use the IC - and its additional facilities such as printing and scanning - rather than sitting there for 'pleasure' helped her. Her presence was further legitimised by referring to the equality of men and women in Islam, often supplemented with a reference to Khadidja, the economically independent and courageous wife of the Prophet Mohammed. This kind of agency was also apparent when student and community activists demanded a women-only IC. Their message to men was: if you don't behave, we create our own space.

These struggles bring to the fore new interpretations, namely that Palestinian ICs are part of public *and* private spheres, neither neutral nor exclusive, and reminiscent of Oldenburg's (1999) view of cafes as 'third places': spaces in between and beyond home or work. The next section deconstructs the struggle over ICs, which – rather than as free spaces – resemble the classic public coffee houses yet as places that need to be *negotiated.*

The coffee-house factor

> If it was possible to make a report of the human feelings that went through this place, you would read a lot of sad and happy stories about new love affairs and new friendships ... many different human feelings developed, and perhaps ended here as well.
>
> *Hisham, al-Carma IC, Ramallah–Palestine, 2002.*

In time ICs became the most common internet access points for Palestinian communities. The quotation above powerfully sums up the dual character of ICs as both public and private spheres. Hisham's account of *al-Carma* resonates with the impression of many ICs as offline hubs where many types of internet users come across each other, sometimes embarking on additional (private) adventures. Hisham's description of an IC where people gathered, exchanged and discussed news, waited, drank coffee or ate, indeed recalls Habermas. Of course the ramshackle ICs in Palestinian refugee camps, crowded with energetic young Palestinians, are a far cry from Habermas' 19th-century coffee house packed with members of the bourgeoisie. In unexpected ways, however, the coffee house and the IC serve similar functions. Oldenburg's (1999) framework of cafes exhibits similar meanings yet goes further to propose a semi-public/semi-private perceptive. Both frameworks help clarify how the IC overlaps with, and differs from, traditional community cafes.

ICs are more than just physical spaces with tables and connected PCs. While cyberspace has become an online meeting space, the IC became an offline meeting place: a public space by virtue of the online, yet going beyond the online. Samah in Bourj al-Barajne explained why the IC is more than what it initially seemed:

> My favourite place is here [Inner Space] with Akram. I can ask him anything and it feels like home. The guys don't bother us because we all know each other. Sometimes I come and I find most of my friends; we sit and talk a bit, then take a computer to check the internet.

Samah's experiences thus suggest that the IC is embedded in the private and personal experiences for the user.

Habermas and Oldenburg have also started important debates that account for the configuration of ICs in terms of their actual accessibility. Gender disparities signify that internet spaces are not accessible to all, and certain practices are encouraged while others are discouraged, indeed often with regard to female presence. The social shaping of technology means that ICs are techno-social spaces, spaces where technology is translated into local public contexts (Lægran and Stewart 2003: 359). However, public spheres are not neutral but this is not unchallenged.

ICs provide leisure and strengthen social and face-to-face contact outside the home. ICs host different kinds of participants, who ascribe different meanings to these spaces. The IC, if not internet access as such, is associated with diverse cultural expectations: the different faces of ICs are considered differently. Various values are attached to everyday rules and behaviours, and these formal and informal rules are infused by present (dominant and alternative) moralities and ideologies. ICs initiate change in various ways and contexts, and create new social spaces both *for* and *by* different publics. Depending on the eye of the beholder, they can be considered good or bad, beautiful or ugly.

ICs: the good, the bad, the ugly

> For Kuwaitis and other Muslims alike [sic] one of the problems of cyberspace is that it interrupts traditional systems for awarding authority and authenticity to public discourse. This concern, however, has not slowed Muslim uses of cyberspace. Some have

> even gone as far as to argue that cyberspace has created a form of Muslim renaissance (Wheeler 2003: 12).

While in Nahr al-Bared the introduction of the internet was a controversial matter, in Bourj al-Barajne it was hardly an issue. This could have had to do with what people sometimes refer to as the difference between camps that are 'closed' and 'open', or conservative or progressive respectively. Ein al-Hilwe was perceived as 'closed', and Shatila or Bourj al-Barajne in Beirut as very 'open'. Comparing attitudes towards the internet in northern and southern Lebanon with those in the camps of Beirut does show interesting differences. But below the surface matters become more complicated. For instance 'closed' does not correlate with lack of internet development. Whereas Shatila camp did not have ICs in 2001, Ein al-Hilwe was already experimenting with different forms of internet access. Thus rather than a generalised depiction of the internet as being particularly problematic in Muslim societies, these societies themselves represent an amalgam of views that mirror a variety of attitudes about the internet.

The visits to refugee camps in Lebanon at different times (2001, 2003 and 2004) were vital to understanding that notions about the internet were very susceptible to change. The prospect of making a profit and at the same time the local competition, sometimes had more impact than moral conventions. So while in 2001 a mixed-gender public place by some was considered *haram* (forbidden) or *'aib* (disgraceful), by 2004 mixed ICs were much more common. The shift towards tolerating or even embracing ICs also had to do with the efforts and patience of local initiators.

Trust and confidence in the internet and ICs was not a given but at times had to be won. An IC initiator in Bourj al-Barajne camp explained:

> As male employees we have a rule about not flirting with female customers. We certainly don't allow boys to bother the girls; they can talk to a girl, but only if she wants ...we don't wish to risk losing girls at the IC just because some guys want to watch porn sites. Everybody should be able to use the internet and we must make that possible.

ICs where women were protected, as well as ICs known as 'modest' places with separate areas or different shifts for men and women, worked well. The shifts failed to work in all ICs because young men did not follow the rules: Rasha in Nahr al-Bared described them as 'sticking to their seats', which was why, at the time, many girls in Nahr al-Bared ignored the ICs and joined NGOs that were starting internet centres, or went outside the camp to an IC in the city. As Saida summed it up: 'I'd rather go to Tripoli: no eyes, no ears.' This explains also why many young women in Ain al-Hilwe's IC *al-Jaleel* felt more comfortable in the women section. The separating curtains there give a sense of security, but also a cover that made the IC more acceptable.

The objection towards young women using the ICs mostly comes from the foreboding that they will establish contacts with men; some parents complained that their daughters might 'go to an IC and meet boys'. There was also the suspicion that boys and girls organise blind dates through the internet, or that girls are seduced into agreeing to meet offline. Such objections often represent the fear of losing (male) control over women; the young women interviewed were very capable of looking after themselves and were more often the ones in control of the situation. However, several interviews with young men revealed how they pretended to be a girl just to get in touch with other girls. Sometimes they would do this as a prank with their male friends. But as Mahmoud's following narrative explains, not all suspicions were without justification:

> I have a Hotmail with the name '--- girl', when I pretend to be a girl on MSN. It's just to make fun of friends. I make other guys on MSN fall in love with me. Once I made a date with a guy. We chatted for about three or four days when I told him, 'I'm in love with you, I want to date you' and such things. He said, 'Where can we meet?' – we agreed the Arab University, I saw him waiting for me there! Sometimes they suspect something and ask for a picture. But I copy pictures from the [profile picture] MSN of other girls, or from websites with pictures of Lebanese girls.

Knowing what they and their friends do, unsurprisingly, some boys I interviewed were not very keen on their sisters using the internet.

The internet was not embraced by everyone when it was first introduced. A number of local internet pioneers were at first reluctant to provide facilities for everyone. The *Al-Jaleel* IC was the only internet provider in Ain al-Hilwe camp in 2001; the owner was able to provide internet connections to homes in the camps. He said he encouraged people to use the internet because of its empowering possibilities, but to allocate the internet was a dilemma. On the one hand it was tempting to sell more such connections, on the other he was not pleased about allowing people freedom to access the internet in their homes, out of his 'guidance' sight. He said during an interview in 2001:

> We have to be careful because the use of the internet at home can be harmful. The internet has negative characteristics and people might be seduced by some of these elements ... We don't want to limit people's freedom, but sometimes we have to be careful; we have to give guidance.

When we met again two years later I asked about the dilemmas he used to have; he was less worried about the issue. A factor of importance was that he no longer monopolised the distribution of the internet in the camp. Other ICs had opened up and even started offering private internet connection at home. The internet was a *fait accompli*: his moral persuasions had become irrelevant. But however the internet was looked at, there were always rules to consider. Wheeler's (2003) suggestion that the internet embodies a renaissance assumes some significant changes, and this calls into question certain 'rules' related to ICs.

As shown above, Samah does not face problems going to an IC in Bourj al-Barajne: she even used the internet before it was introduced in the camp. One of the Lebanese ICs in the suburb of Haret Hreik, Beirut, a few blocks away from the camp, used to be her meeting point. For those who have a choice, the explanation was that when only printing something or sending a quick email they stayed inside the camp. For more extensive work on computer, or when sending private emails, they preferred to go to a quieter and more comfortable IC outside the camp.

The physical encounters and eye contact between boys and girls in ICs caused excitement. In fact, ICs became places to meet one another. 16-year-old Hayaat from Bourj al-Barajne said:

> He came to meet me while I was in the IC helping my aunt open an email account. We didn't really talk, but we did exchange emails. Shortly after meeting online he said he loved me: I explained I just wanted to be friends.

Such meetings in ICs, especially when very explicity, were not always thought to be acceptable. Sahar, manager of *Sirhaan Net* in Bourj al-

Barajne, disliked the practice: 'There was this couple that used to agree to meet in my place. After a few times I refused because I have to think about my shop. I told them, "If you want to use the internet you're welcome, but go and meet somewhere else".' Sahar recalled another incident. A mother and daughter had heard about a woman who had married a nice man after chatting with him. They wanted to try too.

> Her daughter explained what one of the men was saying in the chat room. The mother practically dictated to her what to reply, as she really wanted her daughter to find a husband and leave the camp. This is very degrading; I mean it's wrong.

She felt such behavior risked her IC's reputation. But for the most part she was very accommodating to everyone in her own little IC. Another customer, a young man who was regularly came into the IC, was often online with his girlfriend from Sweden. He asked Sahar how to answer some of the 'girl stuff' that she was asking him. They joked about his love affair and gave him advice how to deal with a girl. Such a relaxed exchange could only take place there because, in the first place, men and women felt comfortable in this IC. Sahar and her sister, who were running the IC together, tried hard to make it pleasant. *Sirhaan Net* was a very lively and safe place, said Sahar:

> Sometimes it's like a family gathering. During Ramadan all our customers, old and new, continue to come, sometimes we made *iftar* [daily breaking of the fast] for the loyal customers, and during *Eid* [end of Ramadan] we had a small party.

I noticed that the personality of the IC supervisor makes a difference. Some were very outgoing and warm, others though present physically not involved with the place at all. In *Inner Space* in Bourj al-Barajne, the relaxed coexistence was striking as well: young women, macho boys, a mother, a carpenter, a young imam: none interfered with each other. The imam told me that he liked the IC, and while he criticised girls who chat with boys, he added it was not his business. A young female client sitting three computers away confessed she would sometimes go to an IC outside the camp to chat with a man in privacy, so as not to risk someone, like the imam in the same room, finding out that she had agreed to meet him. In fact, in Ain al-Hilwe camp, several of the women interviewed enjoyed *al-Jaleel* specifically because it gave them this extra privacy: the men do not see what they write. Thus, rather than interpreting the dividing curtain as a sign of oppression it offered legitimacy to visiting a public IC. However, as discussed in the previous section, the new ICs caused exceptionally tense situations in some places. In Nahr al-Bared the internet was initially labelled *haram* (prohibited by Islam) and the stories about ICs grew out of proportion. Yazan's father did not even allow him to visit them:

> I told my father to come with me, to see with his own eyes. But he said that people said it was bad. I argued that everyone uses the internet according to his own aims, bad or good. Eventually he allowed me to go.

The internet created numerous disputes in the camp and was several times discussed during Friday prayer *Gutba* [sermon], for instance in the mosque led by Sheikh Ahmad.

According to Ahmad, notions about the internet were dominated by fear: 'In the beginning people thought it was nothing more than a screen that displays pornography. Youngsters stormed the ICs even when many didn't have the slightest idea about computers: they saw it as a magic screen.' During a longer interview in 2004 Ahmed outlined how he came to terms with the internet:

> Islam is a religion that appreciates knowledge and science. Many people have ignored or missed this point, and instead depict Islam as anti-progressive. The first *aya* [verse] of the Qur'an, *Iqra'* ['read'], is clear evidence of the value of knowledge in Islam. The internet can be considered as part of science and the internet generates knowledge. Allah says, *Qul hal yastawi al-lathina ya'lamuna wa al-lathina la ya'lamun?* ['Are those who know and those who do not know equal?']. 'Only those who are educated will know.'

After he had enquired what the ICs offered and how they functioned, his views transformed, from discouraging the internet to experimenting with it and finally to sharing it in the mosque. His positive opinions on the internet meant that Sheikh Ahmad aimed to educate new internet users and give instructions on proper behaviour in ICs to its owners. This was often effective, but there were also those who were uninterested in his advice. Sheikh Ahmad continued:

> We contacted the IC owners and invited them for a meeting. Sometimes we visited their IC and explained how they could work better. It didn't happen at once, it took us a few months. One of the suggestions was to make a list of the best educational and religious websites for customers, and to show how to communicate with our brothers and sisters in Palestine. Most ICs cooperated but in a few cases there was no cooperation: they will allow anyone to use the internet in whatever way.

If these interviews confirm one thing in particular, it is that community views on the internet cannot be generalised. Hence, whilst reviewing the frameworks used to describe the good and bad aspects of the internet, acceptance or resistance related to certain conditions. One of the conditions being that the general, social disputes were infused by a sense of morality.

The rules of engagement: everyday internet ethics

> Fatima: Let's not beautify things that are ugly, please 'let's be frank: we're living in a really closed and strict society. Some of our traditions don't make any sense. I mean, where does this nonsense [about ICs] come from?' Ibtisam: 'Of course we must be frank about these conservative mentalities and the oppression. But we must also explain why this is so. You must understand the conditions, especially the remote location of our camp. Being far away is important for how people think. Many people in our camp came from rural areas in Palestine; it's still part of their way of life.' Hanane: 'They stick so much to their old traditions and habits.' Fatima: 'Yes, but the consequences are directly and always for the women, so we can't accept it'.
>
> *Group interview, Nahr al-Bared–Lebanon, 2004.*

The particular patterns of internet usage and the significance of internet access goes beyond mere technical questions as the previously discussed case studies have demonstrated. IC visitors engage with each other when they surf websites varying from sport and music to Palestinian prisoners and martyrs, and sometimes discussed the content with each other. From observations I noticed that young audiences, particularly in the camp, were engaging and escaping in the ICs, were politically minded and merely into leisure activities such as listening to music or surfing websites with the latest fashion or cars. Sometimes pleasure and politics collide when youths play the latest combat games. It is these multilayered and manifold activities that led me to note the different IC settings, or simply that some ICs are not as pleasant as others.

As mentioned, sometimes a girl going to an IC was considered to be *'aib*, and the gossip to come with her action was especially discouraging. As Mahmoud confessed in the first section, bragging about manipulating profile pictures of other girls fed these gossips. Some expressed their frustration during a group interview in Nahr al-Bared as in the opening quotation. It happened that girls and young women were hampered to use the internet in nearby camp IC even when their own families did not object. Hanane added during the group discussions:

> My brother encouraged me to use the internet, but the guys here are stupid ... Men are the ones with the best access; they're privileged in using the internet ... We're fighting on many fronts; we're poor, refugees and female.

Ibtisam, Hanane and Fatima continued to share their experiences. But the topic moved on to how the situation might be changed. Saida said, 'You won't be spared if you fall victim to the *awlad al-shawari*' [misbehaving young men]. On the question of what would happen if one if them rebelled and decided to go to an IC, Fatima said:

> Impossible: I'm not going to expose myself to them. My parents don't have a problem with me going to university or having a job, or going to the IC. But the IC is just considered a bad place and our reputation is still very important.

The way ICs dealt with the existing social realities was crucial for how they eventually formed accessible spaces for female customers and became accepted as exemplified in the previous section. However, these young women in Nahr al-Bared did not have such safe places, though another solution emerged when local organisations opened internet centres. They created practical opportunities for women and girls to participate in new public spaces. References to Islam were used either to encourage or to discourage internet use and female participation in ICs. Sheikh Ahmad in Nahr al-Bared explicitly encouraged internet use by employing religious and political arguments to legitimise it. Explaining how internet use should not be gender-biased, he said: 'The

Prophet's words are clear when he said that "seeking knowledge is a duty which every Muslim must fulfil". However:

> The good side of the internet is clear, but it is also harmful. Many dangers are present, and no one can avoid them. Also in politics there are sites that propagate certain ideas influenced by globalisation and the New World Order. They are a threat to our children's mentality and minds, especially because our religion and country is under attack.

The situation improved after Sheikh Ahmad had become involved and convinced ICs to behave according to Islamic values. The Shaikh also visited al-Najde Women's Centre and approved their mixed internet centre; he was for instance happy to see that the computer screens were all against the wall and thus visible to the ABP coordinators. During the following Friday *gutba*ʿ he referred to al-Najde as a 'safe' and 'clean' place; which seemed to mean no pornography and offering respectable (not too close to each other) spaces for men and women. In reality, however, these rules were not strictly applied, because, as even the Sheikh confirmed, the image and status of the IC were equally important: how others referred to it and talked about it was sometimes more important than what actual practice was. As Fatima and Saida from Nahr al-Bared described, gossip and damage to their reputation were important considerations. It is therefore imperative to look into the deeper social structures that lie beneath the question of access.

Sanaa, a divorced mother in Ein al-Hilwe, learned to use the internet via computer courses in local community organisations. She made many friends online and says she feels happy because 'people accept me for who I am', and that 'it was the first time I'd met people that were different from me'. More ICs had opened in Ein al-Hilwe, at least three ICs operated that I visited, one of which was mixed, even though people were still saying such a development did not exist in the camp. The most often-mentioned IC was still *al-Jaleel*.

The fact that in *al-Jaleel* all the computers had mirrors on the wall facing the screens and a separate space for female customers might be considered a restriction, but they were not only experienced as such. Officially, the thick curtains separating women from men, and the mirrors behind the computers, were for the manager to see what was being viewed online. But after spending time in *al-Jaleel* several scenes of distinctly unofficial practices were observed. When a group of boys and girls assembled at one computer, I asked whether this was allowed, and whether they should sit separately. One of them grinned, and another told me with a smile that they were doing a school project, so they really had to sit together. Again, when it came to school, matters were treated differently. Moreover, the owner would often leave the IC to run errands, leaving a very young nephew to watch the place. This meant that customers could open any website they wanted. Thus the image of a particular IC generates a certain status, but also the *potential* for control worked as a self-censor to prevent 'misbehaviour'. This 'potential' surveillance was also employed with regard to internet content.

Fig. 18 Monitoring the IC: Mirrors in Al Jaleel, Ain al-Hilwe camp.

Some ICs add firewalls to block pornographic sites; others cleaned PCs of such material after customers had left. If something improper was discovered and the customer was known, they were asked not to access the websites any longer. Another IC in Bourj al-Shamali in south Lebanon, *Al Karame,* randomly surveilled its clients, including the home users. Asking the owner about his motivation in prying into people's private internet activities, he answered:

> After getting the monitoring equipment it became easy for me. I don't monitor the ICs that connect through us because they should make their own policy. And home subscribers, yes,

> sometimes I monitor them too ... Before my clients knew they were being watched, many were surfing porn sites. I warn the user twice, if it continues I disconnect him – I just tell him so that he knows I know, to make him feel ashamed and think twice before doing it again.

> After getting the monitoring equipment it became easy for me. I don't monitor the ICs that connect through us because they should make their own policy. And home subscribers, yes, sometimes I monitor them too ... Before my clients knew they were being watched, many were surfing porn sites. I warn the user twice, if it continues I disconnect him – I just tell him so that he knows I know, to make him feel ashamed and think twice before doing it again.

ICs were set up by people with different intentions and abilities, and this was usually reflected in the sort of people it attracted. ICs that were catering to new styles of interaction played a role in transforming the way the internet was looked at. There were of course limits: overt public expression of anything from the private spehre is generally discouraged. Yet such 'rules of engagement' were continually challenged. The next and final section examines the everyday articulations of this agency by virtue of internet usage and IC access contributing to change.

Beyond contested

As mentioned above, the murals and interior designs of ICs in Lebanon and Jordan are an organic continuation of the Palestinian nation's reality, albeit through animation – the artistic representations in refugee camps outside were after all inspired by real life events inside Palestine. The re-occupation, the curfews and the military actions stripped Palestinians of their customary liveliness. Rukab Street, the main thoroughfare in Ramallah, once overflowed with life – cars and carts choked its intersections and pedestrians milled around its shops and stalls; now it was eerily silent. A few people were scattered around the dim lights of shops and homes, while a single car sped past the closed storefronts with the sound of its engine echoing through the nearly empty streets. Many walls were pock-marked by bullet scars, plastered with posters of martyrs and scrawled with graffiti. Rami and I cautiously avoided IDF patrols on a mission to find this particular IC I heard about.

Because the street was effectively empty, some of its details, normally hidden by the cars, stalls and people, became more noticeable. One image on the pavement was particularly striking: that of an Israeli tank crossed out and circled in red. International activists spray-painted this modest sign of protest. Through its simplicity the graffiti screams a clear message: that army jeeps and tanks should not pass through. Rami joked about the possible response of Israeli soldiers, and his cynical remarks were fed by the deafening reality. In the past five years, hundreds of tanks and bulldozers, bothered neither by international law nor by grassroots protest (and still less by graffiti), have ploughed through Palestinian towns and villages, levelling homes, buildings, schools and gardens. At the time this was commonplace in the OPT.

A few hours after Rami's and my labyrinthine journey, we had been breaking IDF rules, like the rest of the people in the illegally opened IC *Chat Net* in downtown Ramallah. We spent the evening in this secretly opened IC – secret because during curfew nobody was supposed to be on the streets, and everything had to remain shut. The collective punishment lasted either the whole day (24 hours) or from five pm to five am. Sometimes completely unexpectedly, Israeli jeeps would drive through announcing on their loudspeakers that a military curfew was being imposed.

Mahmoud's friends were smoking a joint in a space at the back of the IC; they went in and out, but the smell gave them away. Mahmoud, who runs the IC, was not making an issue of this. After all, it was *mani' tajawwul* (curfew), certainly not a normal work situation. After talking with some of the customers, I returned to Mahmoud at the counter. Not far from us, in a corner, sat one of the new customers, chatting excitedly and asking friends: 'She's asking me where I live. What do I reply?' The thought of Israeli jeeps patrolling the streets and death so nearby made everything inside seem unreal: their defiance was about reclaiming a part of their life.

The chatters demonstrate that online encounters and reconnections with part of the community generate another indirect level of agency. Chatting, a lot of which involves flirting, is one of the main activities in Palestinian ICs. The previous section showed that this activity, though influenced by the on-the-ground rules of engagement, is also popular amongst Palestinians outside. Exiled Palestinians chat with other Palestinians, who were sometimes no more than a stone's throw away.

For Palestinians inside, the importance of internet access was never as clear as during the crippling curfews. First, the story of Mahmoud's

IC: a remarkable fact is that he continued to provide many people with access to cyberspace despite the impediment of the curfews. Through their online connections, relationships are built between Palestinians inside and those outside. Second, this chapter's final part will consider how the different types of relationships, whether involving friendship or romance, represent self-activity and generate empowerment.

Curfew cafes

> People act like a family: customers offer each other cigarettes or give advice. And during curfew there is more solidarity. It's what we also feel in the neighbourhood or supermarket these days – in the Intifada people help each other to survive and to carry on.
>
> *Mahmoud, Chat Net, Ramallah–Lebanon, 2002.*

The main lights were switched off in *Chat Net*, but the dozen or so computer screens were illuminating the space; the blue-green colour actually created a cosy atmosphere. Sitting comfortably with the cup of tea that Mahmoud had made for me, and trying to take notes, my attention was drawn back to the man in the corner. When I later interviewed him he, Said, explained that he works in a restaurant kitchen and had never used the internet before. But there was nothing else one could do during curfew and this IC was situated near his work. Said had a friendly face, but from time to time his smile switched to a grimace, caused by his tensed body: face down, shoulders bowed, two fore-fingers waving anxiously above the keyboard while he searched for the right letter, then hitting the keys.

All this took some time, but after he had finished typing his reply in the online chat room, he would gaze at the screen awaiting a sign back from the girl. When he finally received an answer, he was delighted. By way of an update he said to his friends: 'She said she's fine,' adding, 'She asked me where I live.' A few friends joked with him, one man saying 'So now you're chatting too, huh, well well well ...' Amidst the laughter Mahmoud urged, 'Shhh – not so loud, the soldiers will hear us if they come by.' But Said declined to be bothered by their teasing; he was too thrilled by his new discovery. 'What more did she tell you? *Yallah* [come on], tell us,' his friends continued. He didn't answer because he was concentrating, repeating the same ritual: face down, shoulders bowed, his eyes scanning the keyboard for the right letter, two fingers pointing at it, then pouncing. More people gathered around him now, patting him on the shoulder and asking how she had replied. One of them teased him by claiming that now he had lost his 'internet virginity'. But despite their talk, they were supportive and the mood was amicable. After a while the men went to their own computers and began surfing the net, playing games, writing emails or chatting.

Walking around Ramallah with Rami during a curfew night highlighted an important element in the research on ICs in Palestine. The study of ICs in the context of occupation, whatever the level of analysis, cannot be divorced from its material location. *Chat Net*, or 'curfew cafe', as some called it, located in the centre of Ramallah, was the first to rebel, refusing to close its doors to customers, while the rest of the city was like a ghost town. During the day, before curfew was imposed, the IC was crowded, with loud music and noise, but now it was quiet and dim. Mahmoud was initially unsure about opening during curfew, but his friends and customers urged him to do so. He explained during an interview in the autumn of 2002:

> It started when I was cleaning up and preparing to close the IC before curfew started at five. A few customers came to check if we were staying open, some wanting to use the internet. We decided to give it a try. Now we earn almost the same as on a normal day. I don't find curfews boring: I'm using my time being with my people and making my money. They didn't manage to stop my life like they did with many others who are locked up.

His customers enjoyed the curfews, and it became clear that the IC was there for entertainment as well as for work. Perhaps people in *Chat Net* would have preferred to be in a restaurant, having a drink with friends in a cafe or strolling the streets. However, frequent internet users would have been there regardless, because at the time home internet connections were rare. Many came to *Chat Net* to overcome the boredom and loneliness typical of curfew days. Interestingly, another person two seats away actually had an internet connection at home, but would still come because, he said: 'It's lonely at home, but here I can meet and talk to my friends. During curfew a visit to the IC is my only activity.' Most of those who come to Mahmoud to finish their work (or homework) live nearby, in the vicinity of *Chat Net*. Yet some were willing to take more risks. One of the customers worked in a small music company, and was busy surfing the internet for pictures of celebrities as well as song titles or lyrics for the CD covers that he had to prepare.

The customers in the IC, while from a distance joined by those in the online forums, exchanged news about other West Bank cities where some of their common friends lived. 16-year-old Ali was chatting in a Palestinian forum, meeting his friends and introducing himself to new ones. They talked about personal things, but also about how the political situation affected them. 'Even though I'm here and trying to continue my normal life, I sometimes feel overpowered. It hurts to know that there are foreign soldiers in my city as we speak; this is the true meaning of being occupied.' 14-year-old Eid from al-Bireh, younger than the other boys, told me enthusiastically: 'I like to chat with anyone so that I can improve my English. I want to become a singer, you know.' He and his two friends had set up a band called *The Golden Three.* He was viewing all kinds of music websites, and checking the latest celebrity news: they were watching Justin Timberlake and the boy-band 'N Sync. He also collected information and ideas for a website about their band they planned to set up.

Going back all the way to al-Bireh (a town closely connected to Ramallah) during curfew seemed awkward, especially since Eid and the other boys were relatively young. Asked if they were ever afraid, he answered: 'I think Israelis want us to be in constant fear. Today I managed to get here. When there's a very tough curfew with jeeps in our own streets, I don't come. I ask a neighbour who has the internet if I can use it for a bit.' Asking further about their transport uncovered another example of how people deal with the curfew: Eid and some others from surrounding districts actually came and left by illegal 'curfew taxis' taking great risks – Israeli snipers had already killed several people who were trying to move around during curfew.

Most customers made sure they were in *Chat Net* just before the curfew hour, but they still had to find a way back home late at night. The curfew cafe filled an important gap, but could not completely overcome the dangers of life controlled by the IDF, during *Operation Defence Shield* in particular. Manoeuvring to avoid the military was part of the reason why there was only one female in the IC. Mahmoud explained:

> During curfew there will be fewer girls or children. The main reason is the danger. Also, if soldiers catch a boy they'll beat or arrest him. If they catch a girl this causes more problems for her because they might do other things. Only the girls that live very near sometimes come.

Mahmoud suggested that if a soldier sexually harasses a girl it would violate her reputation. Although actual examples were not quoted, this was not an uncommon argument to hear.

But even after making it into the IC, with everybody inside, and when the sound and lights were turned off, the IC was still not completely safe:

> We keep the lights down so that the [soldiers in their] tanks won't see us. The customers are less afraid; they've already got over their fear by coming here. I used to be the scared one. Once a tank passed by, it felt like the building was going to collapse, everything was shaking. I jumped to switch everything off – some customers laughed and said I was too scared!

Unlike Eid and his boy band, for instance, risking the journey to *Chat Net*, many customers lived or worked very near the IC. Some clients, such as restaurant workers like Said, were forced to spend the night in their workplace during curfew. They came out of curiosity and mainly to learn to use chat programs and were still inexperienced. Another local worker was Ahmed. He saw friends and colleagues enjoying their time during the futile curfews, and wanted to try it out too. 'I'm a very new user, I usually work a lot, so I never have time for the internet. Now I understand the basics and I want to learn more.'

During curfew the atmosphere in *Chat Net* was much more relaxed, cheerful and helpful compared to fieldwork visits during normal opening hours. One of the clients was in his *jilbab* (clothing worn at home), while Mahmoud was preparing some snacks for his friends, which were also offered to customers sitting nearby. This public place had the private atmosphere of a home. People were still there by the time Rami and I left to embark on our journey home around 10 pm.

People were experimenting with new internet encounters during the face-to-face meetings in the IC and during their online interactions. Whether in Palestine during the curfew episodes or in the isolated refugee camps of the diaspora, people managed to temporarily overcome the challenges of occupation or exile. Their reward was the joy and entertainment of making new friendships, especially the pleasure of flirting and engaging in love affairs.

Romancing the keyboard

> Pretty soon we will stop distinguishing between online and off, dating site or virtual community. The internet has become as

> ordinary as any church group, running club, or singles hangout when it comes to meeting a special someone or two ... We've finally accepted that it's the connection, not the connectivity that counts.[12]

The claims in the quotation above would probably apply to those who can jump on a train or plane waving their North American or EU passport when crossing from one border to the other – indeed, almost as easily as surfing from one website to another. It is not so much a problem of whether we finally accept that connectivity is a determinant. Stories about virtual love or sexuality like those referred to by Regina Lynn forget that most people cannot just take a plane and meet their future friend, spouse or lover after having found him or her online. Not only is the debate about right and wrong on the internet often reduced to issues of sexuality. The experiences of young Palestinians in exile, yearning for an internet lover in Palestine, are a world apart from Lynn's scenario. But this does not mean that online romance and friendship are for the privileged only.

Writing about her experiences in the Gulf, Wheeler comments that the 'most magnetic quality of internet which drives Kuwaiti youth to the net is the way in which it enables 'them to transgress gender lines ... interrupting traditional social rituals and giving young people new autonomy on how they run their lives' (2003: 13–14). The positive and negative effects of the internet have an impact on everyday face-to-face manifestations because they are partly conditioned by them. When digging a little deeper, the new social configurations in cyberspace become visible – even where they were not expected at first. According to Wheeler: 'The protection of the screen gives individuals the opportunity to overcome inhibitions and fears without violating the principles and values with which they were raised' (ibid). Given the aforementioned dominant rules of engagement about proper and modest behaviour in public, Safa's experiences in Lebanon's Ein al-Hilwe, narrated at length during interviews in 2004, explain how gender, social norms and cultural expectations are juxtaposed with the new public internet spaces.

> Many people behave as if chatting is only something between men and women. Girls sometimes don't like chatting with me, or some men don't continue when they know I'm 33 and have a child, which I don't like to hide. Some politely say, 'Sorry, you're not the person I'm looking to chat with.' But others don't have a problem, especially people in Palestine, who have become good

> friends. When we meet online they ask about my daughter, they know my story. I feel so happy when people accept me on the net, even though there will still be those who don't accept me as a divorced mother. I have friends that I meet here in the camp too, but my experiences with online friends are different. I've met people with a different mentality – a new world has opened.

Hala from a camp in north Lebanon had similar experiences with other women online: 'Sometimes I don't even get a chance to talk: she's gone before I even finished saying, 'Hi, I'm a woman from ...!' But Hala was disappointed in men as well: 'When guys ask where I'm from and I say Lebanon, they're often interested, but once I say I'm originally Palestinian and that I want to know about the situation in Palestine, they lose interest.'

Safa recalls the importance of friendship via the internet: chatting is not just meaningless time-wasting entertainment, as it is sometimes belittlingly called. Online adventures enrich people's social networks and often boost self-confidence. Like Safa, Hala was a divorced woman: her husband had taken away her children and left her without an income. She tells how marrying him meant she 'left the harsh life in a camp in Lebanon only to live in a cave in Canada', but could not bear to continue to live with her husband in that way, and returned to the camp alone. Feeling depressed and socially excluded and deprived of dignity, she found in the internet a comforting space in which she could escape. Hala's experiences with the internet show that a person's life can be affected.

The only time she could escape from her 'miserable' daily routine was with her new online friends. They accepted her for who she is. Things then evolved further when she met a man in a chat room with whom she developed a very open relationship. She explained how, slowly, her life online transformed her:

> I found lots of people through the internet, and even met some [face-to-face] here in Lebanon. I discovered what it means to talk to people about my feelings; I started doing it to help myself. I just wanted to have good times for a change. I was specifically interested in men from the Gulf. One guy, very rich and from the Gulf, was very nice to me; we talked about everything. Then something great happened: one day we were on the internet and the next day he was sitting next to me when he visited Lebanon

> on a business trip. He only stayed six days, but we met a few times in the afternoons. Before he went back, he encouraged me to go back to school. He also said I should fix my teeth, and to send him the dentist's bill, whatever it cost. I didn't do that of course, but it was very kind.

A search for intimacy, to be loved, is partly evidence of loneliness, abandonment and alienation. Something as banal yet generous as offering to pay for the dentist becomes something tangible and meaningful in an online and offline way. Thankfully, the IC in the camp was an accessible space for Hala and only five minutes from her house, a friend of the family was working there and her cousins were regular customers too.

New friendships and romantic experiences have become part of the blend of new social networks. There sometimes seems a thin line between being friends and being more than friends; Hala admitted that one of her aims was finding a good husband:

> I didn't share this with anyone, because it's different for me – I'm a divorced woman. No one would believe it, that I met a guy from the Gulf who was an online friend. But even if no one would believe I'm not a virgin any more, I couldn't prove that we didn't have sex ... Those times were so exciting – the best days of my life. Anyway, I stopped looking on the internet for a husband, it doesn't work that way; it was my aim but I didn't believe in it anymore.

Love is one of the most exciting topics in discussing the influence of internet use, and there were many stories about internet marriages. For Hala the internet was more about friendship, fun and daring to challenge the moral rules of engagement. But unlike the many legends it proved not to be the proper mediator to find a new husband. During a group interview in Shatila, three other young women shared their excitement: the internet and love provided rich anecdotes. Mary shared her excitement at her escapades with internet boyfriends:

> When I told my neighbour about meeting guys online she became very curious and started to chat with guys too. Now she's also making boyfriends and meeting them. It adds something to your life, a break from the daily life of school and home: you can meet new people and go out of the camp. But even in the IC you

> can meet new people: most of the employees are guys. It's really nice to have these new things in the camp now.

Meeting someone from the other sex online or in an IC means that people no longer have to meet in secret when they want to talk privately. As Mary continues:

> Once my mother went to the IC to fetch my sister because it was getting late. Mum sat beside her till she finished chatting. She was chatting with a guy, but my mum didn't notice because the romantic exchange was in English!

These 'nice new things' in the camps also reflect the way online dating has offered an alternative to traditional match-making between families. Some refugees were experimenting with online lovers or blind dates, meeting them offline, face-to-face. Mary said: 'It was so exciting. But then I met him at Verdun: he was so ugly!'

Most striking were the online romances between Palestinians in the diaspora and in Palestine. This was a first opportunity for romance between those in the diaspora and Palestinians on the inside on this scale. Most interviewees in Lebanon and Jordan agreed that being in love with someone in Palestine tops all. One of the unique examples of direct contact through the internet with a Palestinian man came from 25-year-old Palestinian Zainab, from Beirut:

> Ahmed was one of the *tanzim* [the Fatah resistance faction] during the siege of Bethlehem. He was interviewed on television. The siege was horrible; they were forced to eat grass because they were trapped inside the [Nativity] church for weeks. I asked a friend to help me trace him via the television broadcasters. When I got his email [address] I had to convince myself to write him because I was afraid it was not the same person. Two days later I received a reply; it was a short email, but I recognised the Palestinian dialect in his phonetic script. I emailed him a lot, even though he didn't answer back all the time. He asked me to email him as much as possible because he really appreciated it. I think he was lonely. He asked me about other Palestinians in Lebanon, and if people were still committed to the cause, and what we were doing in our daily lives. He didn't write much about himself, but so long as he was writing back, it was enough for me.

Zainab idealised Ahmed and his role in the resistance; she seemed in love, and wondered what he felt for her. But her hesitation was also fed by something else: a reluctance to invest in and express feelings of love, to do with the fact that the internet could not transform their exile. It is here that the spaceless context in the opening clash most directly. Although Zainab loved Ahmed from the West Bank, they were unsure whether they would ever be together.

Dali's experiences in a small IC in Shatila camp sadly confirmed the reality of being in love with someone in Palestine:

> You feel like drifting away, as if no one's around you – the only aim is to talk with him. But I want to see him too, something's missing. I feel I shouldn't make the mistake of talking about love, just politics and Palestine, because it's impossible for us to meet. It's hard.

Having to deal with heartache as a Palestinian refugee in Lebanon was even more complicated, as connection may end due to a power cut. But sometimes contact with online lovers or friends in Palestine stops for no apparent reason, only to find out later that the person in question was injured or arrested, or in a few cases even dead.

While online contact is often followed by offline contact in the form of blind dates, online relationships could also be the result of previous offline meetings. This was particularly the case in summer, when Palestinians have lots of gatherings and parties. Many Palestinian migrants return from Europe, the USA or the Gulf to visit their families. There are also plenty of foreign volunteers who join summer programmes in refugee camps and the international Arab Youth camps often taking place in Jordan and Lebanon. Every summer new love affairs are born. Without the internet, these new friendships and romances would have been difficult to maintain and in most cases would fade away.

Sometimes follow-up online communication involved different languages, but ways were invented to bypass linguistic problems. The internet allows this flexibility, and has become a major tool in overcoming linguistic barriers. 20-year-old construction worker Samir from Bourj al-Barajne met his girlfriend during the summer when she came with her parents from Denmark. Samir, like many others, created his *lou3at al internet* (internet language) writing in his phonetic style using numerical symbols to indicate specific Arabic pronunciations.[13]

Through increasing mobile text-messaging and internet chatting this 'cyber slang' became a common practice. This is an example of a poem received by one of the girls in Nahr al-bared:

a7 abeke gedan wa a3ref ene a3eish beman
Wa bayne wa baynek re7oun wa bardoun
Wa naroun wa a3ref en al wosoul
Ele 3eynayke wahmoun wa el wosoul ela
3eynakyk entra7ar wa ys3adone an
Amazzeqa nafsse la2aglek ayath al
Ghaleya wa law 5ayaroune la5tart
7aboke lel mara al thaneya

Samir now has extensive discussions with his girlfriend. The transcripts he gave me of his instant messages were fascinating, however difficult to unravel.

Besides emailing and chatting, many were also surfing to find jobs, scholarships, grants or information on how to obtain a visa. The summer affairs are also important for more a much more pragmatic reason: a ticket out of the hopeless refugee camp. Many young Palestinians were using the internet to emigrate. Online love is part of the purpose of emigrating. The following extract of a group interview in the winter of 2004 with young men between 18 and 25 from Shatila express what many of their peers feel. In this specific moment of the conversation A's bitterness grows while MD expresses his reservations:

> A: If she's abroad, like in Sweden or Denmark, she can help me to leave; I can get European citizenship later. You think with your mind now, not with your heart ... I could love a girl here for four or five years and then can't marry her in the end because I'm [financially] unable. It's worthless. I experienced that, just imagine: after loving someone for years, at the end someone else comes who has money and takes her, just like that. For everyone, whether educated or not, the most important thing now is to leave.
>
> MD: Yes, some guys only pretend there's romance, love, but some really do.

A: Well, there may be a romance even if it's only via the net, but not true love. How could someone love me via the net? It's not love, it's self-interest. I pretended that I loved my internet girlfriend, and when I asked for her hand, her family humiliated me. If you have money you don't have to think like this; then I would have married a girl from the refugee camp who I at least know personally.

MD: I don't think about leaving the camp.

A: Well, maybe you don't, but most of us do.

This extract illustrates the juxtaposition of the internet, love and politics in the Palestinian refugee camps. But it also shows how, while offering a tremendous source of communication, cyberspace is no surrogate. The online experiences, however, while embedded in the struggle for offline mobility political justice, do empower its users.

Conclusion

ICs are the offline settings of *Palestine Online* that capture the interconnections between virtual and everyday life. This juxtaposition affects Palestinians living both inside the territorial boundaries of historic Palestine and outside in the diaspora. Palestinian ICs are spaces susceptible to political, technological and social change. The dialectical approach in this chapter creates the possibility of looking beyond materiality only and seeing through the obvious manifestations, to discover the latent dynamics that are involved in the evolution of Palestinian ICs. The *lou3at al internet* meanwhile has eased the everyday practice of the internet.

While walking through the camp and sitting around in its ICs, the view from within exposes the illegal cable networks running between the small houses, the UPS boxes under the tables and the creative tapping that would not have been noticeable otherwise. The public nature of the IC challenges dominant morality and the ruling powers. Looking at the everyday rules of engagement sheds light on different attitudes. Rather than generalising about using the internet, the analyses relate to economic relations and differences of social class. Applying a community-based approach with regard to ICs therefore proved enormously valuable.

Transgressing the boundaries of 'acceptable' (Muslim) behaviour was a recurring topic during interviews. Talking with ISPs and IC owners about the internet *vis-à-vis* Muslim ethics showed that, besides objections to gambling and pornography, Islam does not discourage internet use. With Muslims actively using the internet to disseminate and attain religious messages, the opposite can be true. Sheikh Ahmad in Nahr al-Bared showed the importance of unity when he defended internet use in the Women's Centre. Despite radical groups' propaganda about the dangers of the internet, it triumphed.

The mushrooming of ICs offers internet access to marginal and excluded communities – an affordable means of facilitating the exchange of news and ideas and of forming relationships, even when people could not afford the internet at home. The social effect of such public spaces, such as flirting online and, where possible, dating offline, became popular. Yet, Dali and Mary in Shatila remind one that online relationships still need to be *verified* in everyday life, whether the desire to physically touch the other or to check out if someone is attractive during a secret rendezvous.

The story of the curfew cafe, and of how Mahmoud's IC continued to provide internet access in the dangerous context of OPT curfews, was a forceful example. Not only that ICs are both a means and an end – meeting others in the IC and online. But also of how agency and empowerment become crucial: first, sharing ideas and feelings helps overcome existential and social experiences of isolation; and secondly, through access to information (jobs, grants) and taboo topics (often sex or politics) previously unavailable on this scale, speed and this anonymity became possible. Other examples of male and female agency also proved that participation in internet activities was high among female students and workers, in particular galvanising new friendships and romances.

7

EPILOGUE

This research evolved at several extraordinary crossroads. First, the return of post-Oslo expatriates to the OPT in the mid-1990s marked the birth of a professionalised ICT sector in Palestine. Their investments, joined by a new generation of IT graduates, would have an enormous impact. Determined by the major barriers to direct communication between Palestinians, and by one-sided representations about the Palestinian-Israeli conflict, the birth of the internet entailed a major transformation of information and communication processes. Secondly, when the al-Aqsa Intifada broke out in 2000, Palestinian internet developments made a leap forward. The Intifada roused the Palestinian diaspora, and in contrast to the previous Intifada Palestinians could now communicate directly with each other: Palestinians inside and outside grabbed this opportunity with both hands. Immobility and censorship were partly overcome by grassroots internet utilisation.

Technology and politics fused even further in the aftermath of 9/11, of Arafat's death in 2004 and of Hamas' election victory in 2006 when the internal Palestinian political landscape was in great turmoil. The evolution of the Palestinian internet between 1996 and 2006 was important but overall, the internet in Palestine is embedded in a colonial reality. Despite the Oslo agreement and many other promises, Israel continued to stifle the flow of information, people and goods. Necessary material support was prevented by checkpoints, closures and curfews, and equipment for the ICT sector was often withheld at the borders, in clear violation of the Paris agreements. Internet development requires economic and political independence. For a community wedged between the hammer of neoliberalism and the anvil of occupation, a positivist methodology is an unrealistic exercise. Identifying the level of internet penetration through absolute and statistical data to arrive at an objective measure of the internet's socio-economic effect becomes a meaningless exercise. Nevertheless, the persistent efforts of the Palestinian Bureau of Statistics and the Palestinian ISPs and studies by Zureik (2005) to record Palestinian ICT developments have provided an empirical basis for this ethnographic study about the social and political implications of the internet.

The internet has become fairly normalised. But the narratives from Lebanon, Jordan and Palestine in this book capture the first reactions, and the case studies signify the novelty of the internet when it commenced. These studies do not speak only for Palestinians: they show the importance of the internet in the struggle for self-determination and for exiled diaspora communities in general. The internet influences the process of nation-state formation and shapes collective identity, because it stirs the imaginings of a national community. Two related processes are important here: first, the communicative act itself – connecting Palestinians to each other for the first time on this scale since 1948 – is imperative. Second, the content – through online discussions and exchange of images – led to new ways of imagining and identifying with the nation. The contradictory processes involved in the creation of transnational Palestinian linkages, and the diversity of interpretations in the formation of national imageries, were structured around the tensions of mobility/immobility and space/place.

Virtual mobility

For Palestinians the meaning of the term 'mobility' has been turned on its head. Black-and-white photos of the long trails of people staggering towards the borders of Jordan, Syria and Lebanon – the massive Palestinian exodus of the 1948 Nakba and the 1967 Naksa– left a deep imprint on the Palestinian psyche. These traversals, as well as the flights in 1956, 1982 and at other times, transformed mobility: a notion signifying free movement became a notion signifying force. Leaving the expatriate exceptions aside, the Palestinian diaspora is formed by forced displacement and consists of a diaspora in *ghurba:* fragmented, far off, and unable to return. Besides this immobile ghurba, the movement of people in the OPT is tightly curtailed, by curfews and closures, by cities, towns and refugee camps cut off by the wall and checkpoints, and by the thousands of Palestinians in Israeli prisons. In other words, mobility is naturally the adjunct of immobility.

Although only partially and temporarily, the Palestinian internet helps to overcome this immobility and isolation. The fragmented

Palestinian nation, the 'divided body', as a refugee from Nahr al-Bared camp described it, has started to reunite. Through websites, chatting and emailing, Palestinian internet users outside, especially in the refugee camps, were back in touch with long-lost Palestinians inside. These traversals have had a tremendous impact in overcoming a sense of alienation. The internet made it possible to engage politically and provide urgently needed forms of entertainment; both forms of participation allowed for 'virtual escapism'.

Alternative linguistic styles and 'cyber slang' helped increase grassroots communication. Direct connections also enhanced refugees' self-confidence: it helped to 'reinsert' the refugees at the centre of Palestinian politics, as a refugee from Bourj al-Shamali camp formulated it. Diasporic traversals in cyberspace are grounded in imaginations about (the return to) the homeland. Rather than understanding online mobility as seeking virtual reality to avoid territorial reality, it was often about drifting in space in search of place. But the internet is not only about the online: internet cafes as public places are new sites of contestations that may provoke and promote social change. Studying the dynamics of everyday life has shown that these cafes are contested spaces; by flirting online or arranging offline meetings, social boundaries were by-passed.

The outbreak of the al-Aqsa Intifada not only spearheaded internet consumption, but interactions between and about Palestinians in cyberspace nurtured sentiments of unity and solidarity. Nevertheless, promoting or supporting the collective national identity does not do away with internal differences: the construction of an imagined community online is not a linear process, and is vulnerable to challenges. Looking through the prism of class and gender in several case studies has prompted a re-examination of the ideal (online) public sphere. Online debates between Palestinians from disparate socio-economic groups led to small scratches on the idealised picture. The disappointment amongst refugees in Lebanon when realising that not all Palestinians cared about the plight and rights of refugees in exile is exemplary. The discourse on virtual mobility, cyberspace and online networks corresponds with new conceptual interpretations.

The nation and the net

The new interpretations, most prominently the weakening of nation-states and of collective national identities, were inspired by postmodern discourses and illustrated through novel terms such as 'placeless', 'multitude', and 'de-territorial'. The creativity of this vocabulary notwithstanding, the importance of nation-states, locality and political independence were not fading away. As debated, the paradox is that by the logic of global capitalism technologies are not autonomous forces but part of it; moreover: nation-states serve as the protectors in the global competition over territorial and politico-economic interests.

The collapse of the IT bubble had already damaged the neoliberal free market mantra, but the real collision came a few years later. The 9/11 attacks and the military response, followed by the global economic crisis that began in 2008, have rigorously debunked the 1990s myth of the 'retreat of the state'. The unveiling of such myths embodies the deep crisis, and also shows that collective and national identities do not depend on territorial location. It is true that ICT developments and increasing global migration play an important role in the amalgamation of time and space, and what can be seen as an increasingly de-territorialised network community. However, as argued throughout the chapters, mobility or territorial fragmentation modify into long-distance nationalism rather than causing its decline.

As discussed in Chapter Four, rather than national identity as a reactionary mobilisation, anti-colonial nationalism is the dominant factor in Palestinians' online presence and in their interaction. The Intifada politicised everyone, including Palestinian entrepreneurs who referred to the Israeli closures and occupation on their commercial websites and people from the elite who initiated websites. Palestinian commercial projects capitalised on the possibilities the internet offered, and this combination resulted in the commodification of Palestinian identity, with such slogans as 'Made in Palestine' and 'Palestine Online Store'. Collective identity and the internet strengthened each another when a long-desired meeting point was found online.

In the inside, the internet is an outlet for expressing what takes place in the OPT, while on the outside the internet offers direct information about the homeland. Participants in the Across Borders Project in Lebanon and Palestine show how the internet helped shape a virtually imagined community and generate knowledge about the present to recover the past. Destroyed villages displayed online revived and reconfigured Palestinian memories. Dali in Shatila camp emailed a collage of images of Palestine to a list of people with the message: 'Here is our past, present and future', adding, 'I want to jump in the computer and run in the fields'. This and the many Messenger meetings between Palestine and Lebanon are examples of the emotional and political impacts experienced by people in exile finally coming across a site about their original village in Palestine or meeting those actually living there.

If emailing and chatting are the vehicles that restructured the diaspora, then Palestinian websites provided the frame for imagining the Palestinian nation. Palestinian websites not only became mediating spaces; eminent public-relations strategies after the outbreak of the Intifada set the tone. An amalgam of websites aimed to 'rehumanise' Palestinians. Groundbreaking developments continued with the 'Arabisation' of the interface and a much easier system for setting up one's own web-page. As traced in Chapter Five, the territorialisation of Palestinian cyberspace further marked a *Palestine Online* when *.ps* saw the light of day.

Virtual participation is nevertheless embedded in everyday political and economic realities. Deconstructing the materiality of the internet from an anthropological point of view instigates to investigate its *mode of operation*: to see how websites are grounded, and to introduce the people behind the projects. This approach enthused me to discover the illegal infrastructures and networks and the creative tapping of satellite connections, and to uncover inspiring forms of agency. From this perspective internet cafes are not just technological access points but places where the offline and the online meet. They harbour the face-to-face participation of internet users: male and female, young and old. As described in Chapter Six, they sometimes open their doors secretly, defying curfews and taking risks, in order for eager customers to stay online.

Palestine online

Indeed, internet cafes capture important aspects of the connections between virtual and everyday life practices. The accompanying opinions remind one of the classic 'coffee houses', which like internet cafes, are neither open and solely public nor closed and solely private spaces. Thus cyberspace and internet cafes alike impose new interpretations of place, time and space.

However, one of the crucial reminders of offline ethnography is that the virtual does not in effect replace the territorial. Online romances between Palestinians sometimes even increased the longing for physical contact. Some of the girls interviewed were yearning for a caress by an online lover in Palestine, and wanted to 'break through the glass wall'. The internet does not replace the desire for a state, for justice, or for an account of the past.

The internet does, however, present a platform for belated memoirs to be told. In the past many reasons prevented Palestinians from telling their stories. Besides the traumatic consequences of becoming stateless there was also simply no interest in Palestinian narratives. 'How can those without lips whistle?' was the answer of a refugee (in Sa'di and Abu-Lughod 2007: 10). This research showed one of the new and exciting ways of breaking the silence. After half a century of being ignored by the dominant media and terrorised by their occupiers, Palestinians were engaged in narrating the present through the past, and the future through the present. The advent of the 50th Nakba commemoration in 1998 stirred awareness and helped dust off the past. This renewed alertness found an accessible medium for disseminating memories, but also, and in particular, Palestinian demands for justice. At the conjunction of these delayed testimonies, coming out via books, films and oral histories, Palestinian messages are now disseminated more loudly and more widely then ever because the grassroots proliferation of Palestinian narratives and politics merged and consolidated with the internet. A voice was found through internet projects, mushrooming internet cafes, and websites such as *Palestine Remembered* and *alnakba.org*. Palestine Online was born, speaking though the keyboard and the mouse.

APPENDIX

	Gaza			West Bank			Palestinian Territories		
	1999	2004	Growth	1999	2004	Growth	1999	2004	Growth
Computer Ownership (Households)	9.6	22.5	134%	11.4	28.4	149%	10.8	26.4	144%
Satellite TV as % of TVs (Households)	29.7	77.3	160%	31.4	72.9	132%	30.9	74.4	141%
Internet at home (Households)	4.7	7.8	66%	5.7	9.8	72%	5.4	9.2	70%
Availability Mobile Phone (Households)	29.8	64.1	115%	51	77.6	52%	43.7	72.8	67%
TV (Household)	82.8	91.2	10%	92.3	94.6	2%	89.2	93.4	5%
Telephoneline (Households)	36.5	36.5	0%	45	42.9	-5%	42.1	40.8	-3%

1. Data from PCBS surveys for 1999 and 2004, analysed by Waked (2005). [1]

Content Markers		Owner or alignment	Location (where is the owner located?)	Issue orientation (if applicable that exist for one issue)	Focus (is it purely Palestinian focused site or not in according to the material it presents?)	Intended audience		Primary Language usage
Primary Content Marker	Secondary Content Marker					Age group	Target audience	
Government International Org Embassy Political Social (NGO) Educational Business Religious New Media (blog,forum) Entertainment News (formal)	Political Social (NGO) Educational Religious Business New media (blog, forum) Entertainment News (formal)	Secular aligned Religious Political NGO (name) Company (name) Media (name) New Media (say alignment or tendency - liberal, conservative, or open)	Country, town camp	Single issue: [name issue] the Wall Gender, Right of return. Multiple issues [list issues in order, using comma as separator]	Palestinian - WB/G Palestinian - refugee Palestinian - diaspora Arab Islamic International Other: [state which]	Children (up to 12) Youth (up to teenage) Student Adult Older Adult	Domestic [wb/GZ Refugee Diaspora] Foreign [Int. com, Israeli Arab Islamic] Other: [state which]	English Arabic Hebrew French Russian Other [which] Multilingual [which] using hyphen in alphabetical order

2. Qualitative classification of Palestinian websites during P@IP analysis [2]

NOTES

Chapter 1

1 The internet is considered a medium, like radio and television; this also implies that the internet does not need to be written with a capital I.

2 Israel confiscated land and built settlements on a larger scale than before Oslo. See Said (1996) for a critical analysis of the Oslo agreement.

3 Sharon is often remembered for his role in the Qibia massacre in 1953 and the Sabra and Shatilla massacres in 1982.

4 Not much later, Israel embarked on an even greater plan for closure: the Wall along and within the West Bank. This finalised an immense entrapment and caused the Palestinian economy to suffer severely.

5 The title *Palestine Online* is inspired by one of the first internet providers, starting in the late 1990s and called *Palestine.On.Line*, and by *Ramallah Online*, a popular website at the time. But the title is particularly chosen for the simple subtext it captures: a Palestine shaped by and located in cyberspace.

6 Despite the catastrophic consequences of Israel's actions in Gaza, the general suffering of the Palestinian is worsened by Israeli house demolition and by new settlements, referred to by Hilary Clinton as 'unhelpful'. Available from :<*http://www.huffintonpost.com/2009/03/04/hillary-clinton-in-west-b_n_171700/html*> (Accessed 4 March 2009).

7 The USA is the major voice in the UN, especially under the Bush government, and it regards the Palestinian case through its own interests. De Soto (2007) shows that American pressure has pummelled the UN's role as impartial negotiator. Available from: <*http://www.guardian.co.uk/world/2007/jun/13/usa.israel*> (Accessed 13 June 2007).

8 Al-Bekaa camp was once literally closed off during protests in support of the Intifada.

9 For a history of the impact of Zionist ideology and the symbolism of Herzl and Meir, see Nur Masalha (1992) and John Rose (2004).

10 This led to the first televised pictures of Israeli oppression, showing soldiers breaking the arms and legs of young Palestinians with rocks

and rifles. Though the 'carrot' metaphor implies being bribed into submission, for most Palestinians at the time this approach was not like being bribed but about being violently beaten up. Kimmerling's 2003 description of Israeli policy as 'politicide' is much closer to reality.

11 The 'Seattle protest', where thousands demonstrated against the WTO meeting in November 1999, marks the birth of the new anti-capitalist movement. Prague 2000 was the first major follow-up, when 25,000 people from across the world gathered to demonstrate against the IMF and the World Bank.

12 Since the postmodern 'end of history' paradigm, capitalism has consolidated its hegemonic force even further; according to Kellner, unrestrained capitalism continues to dominate production, distribution and consumption. With the 2008 collapse of the financial sector, the dramatic 'credit crunch' and the economic crisis that followed, the critique of capitalism returned with a vengeance.

13 Marxist scholars in particular offered some of the crucial critiques; a useful overview can be found in Stevenson (1995), and see also Sparks (2007).

14 This characteristic reminds us also of the internet's limits. While putting up a blog is possible for anyone with access to a computer and internet connection, the blogger cannot generally change how radio or television programmes are controlled, nor can a personal website reach the same mass audiences.

15 Available from: <*http://www/jofreeman.com/joreen/tyranny.htm*>(Accessed January 2008).

16 A 2006 report by CPJ showed that one in three jailed journalists worldwide had been an internet blogger. Several well-know bloggers in Egypt were arrested and imprisoned; the cases led to international uproar. More from: <*http://www.guardian.co.uk/egypt/story/0,,2019064,00.html*> (Accessed 22 February 2007) and: <*http://www.dailystaregypt.com/article.aspx?ArticleID=1456*> (11 May 2006).

17 These are rough estimates because community (shared) access often occurs. These and a general overview of internet penetration and growth rates are available from: <*www.internetworldstats.com/me/reports.htm*> (Accessed February 2008).

18 Available from: <*http://www.btselem.org/English/Statistics/Casualties.asp* and *http://www.palestinercs.org/crisistables/jan_2003_table.htm*> (Accessed February 2008).

19 In addition, Hezbollah's success in forcing Israel to withdraw from South Lebanon in May 2000 added legitimacy to armed resistance. Hamas won the Palestinian elections in 2006, which showed strong and widespread criticism of Fatah, but the Palestinians were met by unprecedented punishment on the part of the international community.

The USA and EU froze all financial support, causing a catastrophic degeneration of living conditions. In particular, this was worsened by the explicit favouritism shown to Fatah and by a boycott of democratically elected parliamentarians, which eventually led to a rise in tension and a constant fear of civil war. The suffering of Palestinians could now be blamed on Hamas by its rival Fatah, and this narrative was repeated by the latter's US and Israeli allies and funders.

20 Benschop's study refers to specific (unidentifiable) online examples, yet it propagates larger assumptions about Moroccan culture and Muslim identities. A person 'shouting "Jihad"' on the internet is represented as effectively acting in the same way as when organising violent attacks offline; the predictable consequence is that this should be punished in the same way. This is not without consequence in the post-9/11 context, with right-wing politicians proposing new laws that degrade former codes of democratic transparency or by increasing prison sentences.

21 Because after-school and work hours coincide with the temporary lifting of the curfew, once out of the office it is the time for buying groceries and other necessary tasks before the curfew is reimposed, and this leaves very little time for interviews.

22 The immobility in Palestine also confronted me with how researchers with a disability are particularly limited in their research.

23 Vol. 40, No. 3 (June 2008), pp. 345–497.

24 Groups like *Campus Watch* attack and vilify academics critical of Israel. Initiatives such as *Academics for Justice* try to challenge such post-9/11 McCarthyism. See: <*www.academicsforjustice.org*> (Accessed February 2008).

25 During one of the first academic conferences I attended as a junior researcher, I was confused as to why participants repeatedly objected to my use of the term 'Palestine' and 'Palestinian'.

26 Ascherman, A.W. (2009) 'Rabbis for Human Rights and the Current Violence: We Never Know What Little Act Will Tip the Scales'. Available from: <*http://www.rhr.org.il*> (Accessed February 2009).

Chapter 2

1 This observation was the more relevant because then internet access required a telephone connection.

2 Palestinians with EU or US passports can enter Palestine on a tourist visa. Nonetheless, many Palestinians have been refused entry. See for instance Bahour, *We Can't Go Home Again*. AMIN, 9 October 2006. Available from: <*http://www.amin.org/look/amin/en.tpl?IdLanguage=1&IdPublication=7&NrArticle=37435&NrIssue=1&NrSection=3*> (Accessed February 2008).

3 This was to be a prologue to what would happen in 2008, when

the housing market collapsed. This market was built on similarly irresponsible, even fraudulent behaviour, but with deeper consequences for the world financial system because the banking sector was itself deeply entangled in the fraudulent deals.

4 At the time, Area A contained 95 per cent of the Palestinian population and represented approximately 3 per cent of the land area of the Gaza strip and West Bank. Areas A and B (shared control) were geographically fragmented by the larger area C under full Israeli control; thus Palestinian telephone networks still remained an integral part of the Israeli telephone network. Since the Al-Aqsa Intifada these area divisions have really meant very little, since everything is now under military control.

5 Though some Palestinian cities were still interlinked via Israeli connections, mainly because of the Israeli settlements in the OPT.

6 Report on Palestine, World Summit for Information Community. Tunis, 2003. Available from: <*www.itu.int/dms_pub/itu-s/md/03/wsis/c/S03-WSIS-C-0007!!MSW-A.doc*>(Accessed February 2008).

7 Reports on the West Bank and Gaza between 2002 and 2004 can be accessed at <*http://www.worldbank.org/*>.

8 The PalTel monopoly eventually ended: in 2006 the Minister for Telecoms, Jamal El Khodary, granted another license for mobile-phone services to the Kuwaiti Al Watania company.

9 This estimate was probably larger in reality, because extended families and neighbours often share a house line, increasing the average number.

10 The other ISPs I asked generally agreed with the outcome of these calculations. The PCBS was not able to conduct extensive research at the time due to the military occupation.

11 El Haddad, Laila (2003) 'Free Internet in Palestine could have negative impact on local ISPs'. *Daily* Star, 16 December. In a joint statement Palestinian ISPs protested PalTel's unfair monopoly.

12 PCBS survey for 2004 in Waked (2005:20).

13 Arnon, A. 2002. The implication of economic borders between Israel and Palestine'. The Palestine Israel-Journal, Vol. 9, No. 3. Availble at: <*http://www.pij.org/details.php?id=122*>.

14 Int@j report of 20 February 2002, available at <*www.intaj.net/news/readnews.cfm?id=335*>.

15 For further information on Int@j and Reach, see at <*http://www.reach.com.jo/about_reach.htm*>.

16 Palestinians also played a prominent role: some of those skilled and successful Palestinians who returned after the 1991 Gulf War were to become Jordan's ICT pioneers.

17 This was discussed in the press because Irbid made it into the Guinness Book of Records as the centre hosting the highest number of internet cafes worldwide.

18 It was not clear whether the fact that JITCC could (via a remote device) monitor the websites accessed by its participants had any negative effect.

19 Saadi, Dania. (2004) 'Lebanon tops Levant PC sales'. Daily Star, 16 January 2004.

20 Data from PCBS surveys for 1999 and 2004 are here merged into a new graph. The original statistics appear in Appendix 1.

21 The Information Revolution in the Middle East and North Africa (2003: xii). A review of the Rand findings on the internet shows that they are politically charged. It is daunting that while being presented as an academic study, the report does not question 'what the US considers': more importantly, it refers to how Israel was installed with no reference to Palestine being sacrificed as a prerequisite of this action. It has become clear following the US boycott of Hamas that democratically elected states are only accepted when the winning party fits US foreign-policy strategy. Strong leaders, such as in Egypt or Saudi Arabia, are presented as cultural preferences, but rather are maintained through US backing.

22 Apart from the fact that it is not possible to retrieve data from refugees in exile, in the OPT the curfews and closures made sampling and face-to-face methodologies extremely difficult.

23 See Appendix 1 for the separate sets of data, part of Zureik's (2005) study on Palestinian ICT including Waked's analyses referred to here. It must be noted that measures of internet penetration itself are the subject of debate. It makes sense to measure internet connection in a home that actually offers internet connection to more than five direct family members, friends or neighbours; in other words the figures are fairly conservative.

Chapter 3

1 As discussed in Chapter One, many of the postmodern redefinitions disregarded the importance of nation state, territory and collective national identity as 'outdated' – a comfortable position to take, especially when rights to land, a constitution and travel documents, or means to resist injustice, are at hand. This contradiction will be further studied in Chapter Four.

2 See Takkenberg (1998: 133–70) for a discussion on the status of Palestinian refugees in the Arab world.

3 The citizenship status of West and East Bank Palestinians was well defined until the First Intifada (1987). In 1988, however, King Hussain renounced his country's claim over the West Bank, acknowledging Palestinian sovereignty. The effect of this was that West Bank Palestinians lost their Jordanian citizenship, though they were allowed to keep their Jordanian passport until it was replaced by one issued by the Palestinian state; but since in 1988 these Jordanian passports were only temporarily

valid, holders could only reside in Jordan for a maximum of 30 days. For more on Palestinian-Jordanian history see Takkenberg (1998: 158).

4 Journalists and researchers require special permission from the DPA to talk to people in the camps. Permission was difficult to obtain at the time, and I was even asked to stop the interview on one occasion.

5 The status of Palestinians was also an issue of class: the upper-class and wealthy Palestinians who had left Palestine before the great exodus and settled in Lebanon were given Lebanese nationality.

6 Available from: *<http://groups.yahoo.com/phrase/free-palestine> (Accessed February 2008).*

7 Available from: *<http://www.palestinemonitor.org/spip/>* and *<http://www.hearpalestine.org/>* (Accessed June 2005).

8 Available from: *<https://ritaj.birzeit.edu/>* (Last accessed June 2005).

9 Available from: *<http://ramallahonline.com/>* (Last accessed June 2005).

10 Available from: *<http://www.palvoice.com/forums/, http://palvoice.8k.com/, http://www.mirc.com/, http://www.zorona.com,http://, www.arabia.com, http://www.alburaq.net/, and http://www.3oyoon.com/>*. (Last accessed June 2005).

11 Some of the stories described here by the children interviewed can also be seen in a 2001 documentary by Lebanese film-maker May Masri: *Frontiers of Dreams and Fears*. This crossing-borders project and the children's experiences will be further analysed in Chapter Four.

Chapter 4

1 Oddly, in Eriksen's later work about pre-independence nationalism, he does not mention Palestinians; yet it is actually from his earlier work (1993) that I derive the notion of Palestinians as 'proto-nations', to be discussed later in this chapter.

2 Up until 1988 'Jews Only' job advertisements were allowed. The Israeli economy has survived the impact of ethnic segregation and apartheid policies in its labour force by importing large numbers of 'guest workers' as cheap labour (cf. Kalir, 2006). Looking outside Palestine we see similar cases, but in South Africa (for instance) blacks outnumbered whites and their key role for the white economy as a working class implied other (potential) means of resistance. Though colonial occupation is often regarded as something of the past Gregory (2004) offers a critical review of contemporary colonialism.

3 *Al qawmiyy al-arabiya* was popular during the 1950s and 1960s, when the Egyptian president Gamal Abdel Nasser attempted to mobilise anti-imperialist and unified Arab coexistence. Both Arab nationalism and Palestinian nationalism refer to a form of patriotism rather than nationalism as known in Europe.

4 Saloul studies the issue of the denial and remembrance of *al-nakba*,

especially in Chapters 2 (Out of Home: On the Balconies of Our Houses in Exile) and 4 (Performative Narrativity and Identity in 1948).

5 According to Gonzales, the Israeli withdrawal from Lebanon in May 2000 increased internet usage by 60 per cent in Lebanon. This timing coincided with the post-war reconstruction and the maturation of the ICT sector in Lebanon. In other words, the overlap between the Intifada boost and ICT development in Palestine is very similar to the overlap between the withdrawal/resistance boost and ICT developments in Lebanon.

6 mIRC, Internet Relay Chat (IRC) was developed by Khaled Mardam-Bey in 1995 from dissatisfaction with the initial IRC Windows (WinIRC). He turned it into a very adaptable method because of its integrated scripting language. It became the most popular chat programme, downloaded over 20 million times from www.download.com service, and ranked by NetRatings among the top ten most popular internet applications in 2003.

7 The first slogan refers to a speech by Patrick Henry in 1775 on the American War of Independence; the second is a reference to Descartes' 'Cogito ergo sum' ('I think therefore I am').

8 The importance of the visual representation of Mohamed al-Durrah is understood when addressing the highly controversial context of the Israeli propaganda machinations after the powerful image had begun to be an icon of Palestinian suffering. Pro-Israeli pundits started a massive campaign to raise suspicion of what happened and there have been numerous video analyses on the internet. See for instance 'Mohammed al-Durrah was not killed': Available from: <*http://www.youtube.com/watch?v=DzsCBFhCsyY*> (Accessed March 2010).

9 Rim Banna on Faris Odeh available from: <http://www.youtube.com/watch?v=BEpSOpfYaaQ>and Mahmoud Darwish on Mohammed al-Durrah from: <http://video.google.com/videoplay?docid=-6816147079262871882#docid=5262239575623517971>(Accessed January 2008).

10 *Maktoob* started as a basic website in 2000, and grew into a complete portal in 2003.

11 *Palestine Monitor* is a joint website project of Palestinian NGOs; see also Chapter Five.

12 Available from: <*http://www.al-carma.com/*> (Last accessed June 2004).

13 Available from: <*http://www.palestineremembered.com/*> (Accessed February 2008).

14 It is important to remember that satellite television has much wider accessibility, and probably a stronger impact of image and sound. For instance, even though the Palestinian Broadcast Centre (PBC) is not as specialised or widely watched as *Al Jazeera* or *Al Manar,* many

Palestinians in Lebanon watched it at the time. The television was often left on also while talking or engaging in other things, which meant President Arafat was often 'present' in the living rooms, while news from Palestinian was being aired, frequently causing praise or denigration from the people. However, it is not the aim here to compare the potential effects of different (cultural) media on transnational communities.

15 Abdoun is an upper-class area in Amman, Wehdat a refugee camp in Amman's outskirts.

16 The *kufiya* became part of urban street-fashion, not necessarily connected to Palestinian politics. A modified kufiya soon appeared – smaller and available in many colours.

17 Available from: < *http://www.paltime.com*> and <*http://www.palestineonlinestore.com/.*> (Accessed February 2008).

18 Available from: <*http://www.palestinecostumearchive.org*>. (Accessed June 2005).

19 After access to Palestine was denied, the interviews were conducted by telephone at the University of Amsterdam partly with research assistant Donya Alineyad at the time.

20 Available from: <*http://www.nakba-archive.org*>. (Accessed June 2005).

21 She was the first person to put entries of her personal journal on the internet, reflecting on events and lived experiences during the first weeks of the Intifada and was one of the inspirators of ABP. See also Hamzeh (2001).

22 Available from: <*http://www.accrossborders.com*>. (Accessed June 2005).

23 The project recruits, trains and then employs someone to coordinate the project. The person receives a salary at the rate of 100 per cent for the first six months, then 70 per cent for the following three months, and finally 30 per cent for the last three months. The camp needs to cover the shortfall for the coordinators through money generated by the internet centre. The monthly salary for an ABP coordinator in Gaza at the time was US$350.

24 Known simply as 'Geneva', one of the (failed) negotiation attempts at the time, according to most of the refugees it was promoted by a section of the Palestinian elite, and therefore watered down to the extent that the right of return was to be sacrificed.

25 Two years later it was clear why Bachir's arguments had been important. Nahr al-Bared was heavily attacked. All the people, centres and projects mentioned in this book were forced to leave their belongings, buildings were destroyed, people killed and many refugees uprooted again. Bachir and his comrades argued for a coalition because, unlike these activists, a part of Lebanese society was very susceptible to the racist rhetoric and applauded rather than protested at the annihilation of the camp, even

while these horrors were taking place. This is why Bachir and his comrades argued for working together and building unity with local Lebanese groups.

26 Available from: <*http://www.mawared.org/*>. (Accessed January 2004).

27 *Al-Safir* daily newspaper, Beirut, 31 May 2000.

Chapter 5

1 *Beit Rima* is available from: <*http://www.beitreema.com. Remembering Jenin*> is no longer available (Last accessed 2003).

2 The internet was a tool for organising and mobilising rather than merely offering administration-related information. However, after an exciting start, its capacity to inspire and forge an organic link with student bodies mobilising grass-roots campaigns started to decline. It is not clear whether this had to do with the departure of people with key roles during this period of experimentation. One of the regrettable consequences was BZU's removal of the section *Complete Guide to Palestinian Websites* from its website.

3 The original website was available from: <*http://www.geocities.com/CapitolHill/9836/nakba.htm*>. (Accessed June 2002).

4 Available from:< *www.iamapalestinian.org*>. (Accessed June 2003).

5 Available from: <*http://www.adalah.org/eng*>.(Accessed February 2008).

6 *Maktoob* received the Best Information Portal award at the Middle East Economic Forum summit. In 1999 it had 100,000 members, in 2001 one million, in 2003 three million, and by mid-2006 4.5 million (source *Maktoob.com*). According to an Alexa report in May 2006 it was still one of the Arab websites most visited by Palestinians.

7 One of the first mentioned websites of Palestinians living outside was that by Khalid Madam-Bey. He was a software writer who interestingly enough designed the later very famous mIRC, the first widely-used multi-user/multilingual chat system that allowed people to communicate by downloading the IRC chat software.

8 Available in 2000 from: <*http://www.geocities.com/SouthBeach/lagoon/8522*>. (Accessed June 2001).

9 Available from: <*http://www.amin.org/pages/dkuttab*>.(Accessed June 2005).

10 A blog is set up to be used as a diary, but can be used for any purpose: local news, political commentary or food recipes.

11 2006 *Arabic Blogs: An Embodiment of Freedom of Expression*. In *Implacable Adversaries: Arab Governments and the Internet.* Open Arab Internet material available from :<*http://www.openarab.net*>. One of the examples confirming the potential threat was when blogger Alaa Abdul Fattah posted the picture of an officer who was enjoying oppressing demonstrators during a protest. The officer, notorious among activists

for torture in police stations, was uncovered and challenged by the blogger online.

12 Al-Bawaba was one of the first services to offer free and Arabic blog hosting at, <*http://blogs.albawaba.com/*>. The direct link between on-the-ground activism and political upheaval on one hand, and the increase in online activism on the other, became particularly important in Lebanon and Palestine after 2006. More on Arab blogs Available from: <*http://www.al-bab.com/arab/blogs.htm*>.

13 Palestine @ Information Society Data Set (2007); a joint project of the Advanced Network Research Group (University of Cambridge, GOVCOM.org, and The SecDev Group). Contributors and Analysts: Rafal Rohozinski, Richard Rogers, Deirdre Collings, Wassim Abdullah, Miriyam Aouragh, Sam Bahour, Erik Borra, Michael Dahan, Isabelle Daneels, Anat Ben-David, Reem Fada, Adam Hanieh, Safa' Madi, Koen Martens, Nora Lester Murad, Andrei Mogoutov, Jamil Rabah, Micheal Stevenson, Nart Vileneuve, Mohamed Waked, Marieke van Dijk, Ester Weltevrede.

14 The maps are too big for book-size pages. The maps and graphs I refer to are offered on: < *http://govcom.org/pisp_maps1.html*>

15 Of particular concern at the time was the *Jerusalem.ps* domain name; this URL needed protection because of its symbolic implications and its implicitly controversial nature – Jerusalem is also claimed by Israel as its capital. The domain name could have been bought by a pro-Israeli in order to prevent it from being used as a Palestinian website. (*Jerusalem.com* is an Israeli tourist website, and *Jerusalem.org* refers to the holy city as Israel's capital.)

16 See Appendix 2 for main scheme and sub-markers that were used to categorise and subsequently analyse the website.

17 To improve the coverage P@ISP also searched the major registries (RIPE, ARIN, APNIC) to see if there were any administrative, billing or technical contacts that listed Palestine, the West Bank or Gaza as their place of residence. This should have picked up the Palestinian non-*.ps*/non-Palestinian OPT IP-range registrants. Moreover, for possible non-*.ps* diaspora references we looked (through qualitative and quantitative analyses) at possible degrees of 'Palestinianess' via links to other Palestinian websites.

18 The complete 'Migration of .edu to .edu.ps: Three universities compared' is found at: < *http://govcom.org/pisp_maps1.html*>.

19 'Palestinian' websites are considered to be those made by Palestinians and/or clearly addressing Palestinians in Palestine or the diaspora. Web traffic and ranking tool *Alexa* was used to see how the listed websites were rated. Apart from these ethnographic sources, there were also valuable references online, such as the Birzeit University links mentioned

above and of *Passia* (<*http://www.passia.org/*>).

20 This was based on a selection of websites collected at the time. Appendix 2 shows how the basic website categorisation was further improved and made more specific during the P@ISP workshops in 2007, resulting in the seven categories and sub-markers.

21 This phenomenon - creating a site for the mere sake of having it without a specific policy to reach or influence an audience - would increase on the Web.2.0 blogosphere.

22 Available from: <*http://palestinechronicle.com*> (Accessed February 2008).

23 Available from: <*http://www.palestine-pmc.com*> (Accessed February 2008).

24 Available from: <www.*dying2live.com*> (Accessed June 2005). The responses are to be found via its feedback link: <www.*dying2live.com/feedback_text.htm*>.

25 The site started as <*www.rafah.vze.com*>, then became <*www.rafah.virtualactivism.net*>, and finally <*www.rafahtoday.org*>.

26 Available from: <*http://www.palestine-net.com/geography/kth.html*>. (Accessed June 2005).

27 Available from: <*http://www.al-bireh.org/*> and <*http://www.nablus.org/*>. (Accessed June 2005).

28 Available from: <*http://www.virtualpalestine.net*>. (Accessed June 2005).

29 Available from: <*http://www.gaza.net/*and*http://thechildrenofshatila.com*>. (Accessed June 2005).

30 He also added an English forum, but since his audience consisted predominantly of Arabs it had hardly any visitors.

31 Its URL was <*www.aoweiti.com*>, but the website is no longer active as Akram has left Lebanon.

32 As of 2008 it is no longer prohibited to make phone calls from Lebanon to the OPT; see at <*http://www.pita.ps/newweb/pdfs/connect3.pdf*>.

33 Available respectively from: <*www.ezzedeen.net*>; <*www.amrkhaled.net*>, <*www.arabs48.com*>, <*www.gazapress.com*>, these sites are in Arabic. (Accessed June 2005).

Chapter 6

1 'Lebanese young men seem seduced by the internet café'. Garine Tcholakian, *Daily Star*, 21 February 2004.

2 The term 'internet cafe' was the most commonly used during interviews. Some interviewees also spoke of 'cyber cafes' or 'net cafes', and the terms will be retained in the relevant quotations.

3 Although Lebanese law, until 2008, prohibited telephone connections between Lebanon and Israel (see Chapter Two), even landlines for domestic use are not allowed in Palestinian refugee camps, with only

a Lebanese-registered NGO in a camp being able to apply for special permission.

4 Refugee camps in Beirut were in due course influenced by the dominant presence of the Lebanese state – by Hezbollah in the south, or by Syria (then itself dominant) in the north.

5 'Lebanese young men seem seduced by the internet café'. Garine Tcholakian, *Daily Star*, 21 February 2004.

6 See 'Implacable Adversaries: Arab Governments and the Internet' for similar internet regulations. Available from: <*http://www.openarab.net/en/node/346*>. (Accessed February 2008).

7 The 'family room' referred to an area for (married) couples, or where parents with children could feel comfortable.

8 The Italian journalist Rafaelle Cirello was killed on 13 March 2002 near Manara Square, by Israeli snipers.

9 More information available from: <*http://www.unrwa.org/etemplate.php?id=253*>.

10 Although the introduction of the mobile phone was a major leap forward, reception quality in the camps is low and subscriptions were relatively expensive.

11 Fathi Mahmoud, 'Pumping an internet café in Al-Helwa camp'. *Al-Ahram*, 30 December 2004. Similar incidents were reported in Palestine, c.f. 'Unidentified gunmen pump cyber café in Jabaliya'. *Palestine Press*, n.d. Also: <*http://www.openarab.net/en/node/361*> and <*http://www.palpress.ps/arabic/index.php?maa=ReadStory&ChannelID=51462*>(A ccessed February 2008).

12 'Beyond the dating database'. Regina Lynn in *Wired*, 11 March 2005

13 For example, 3 stands for the Arabic letter *'ain*, 5 for *kha'*, 6 for *ta'*, 7 for *ha'*, etc. Existing signs were also adapted to make chatting or sms easier. such as 'w8' (*wait*), 'lol' (*laughing out loud*, but also used for *lots of love*), 'coz' (*because*), 'plz' (*please*), 'cu' (*see you*).

Appendix

1 Data from PCBS surveys for 1999 and 2004, analysed by Waked (2005).

2 I.e. as prepared and designed by P@ISP.

BIBLIOGRAPHY

Abu-Lughod, L. (2004) 'Return to half-ruins: memory, postmemory and living history in Palestine'. Paper presented at the staff seminar of the Amsterdam School for Social Science Research, 17 December 2004.

_____ and Sa'di, A. (eds) (2007). *Nakba: Palestine, 1948, and the Claims of Memory*. New York: Columbia University Press.

_____ Ginsburg, F.D. and Larkin, B. (eds.) (2002) *Media Worlds: Anthropology on New Terrain*. Berkeley, CA: University of California Press.

Abunimah, A. and Ibish, H. (2001) 'The US media and the New Intifada. In Carey, R. (ed.) *The New Intifada: Resisting Israel's Apartheid*. London and New York: Verso, pp. 233–58.

Abu-Sitta, Salman H. (2004) *Atlas of Palestine 1948*. London: Palestine Land Society.

Adams, P. (1997) 'Cyberspace and virtual places'. *Geographical Review*, Vol. 87, No. 2, pp. 155–71.

_____ (1998) 'Network topologies and virtual place'. *Annals of the Association of American Geographers*, Vol. 88, No. 1, pp. 88–106.

Ajial Center (2001) *International and Non-governmental Associations: Whose Services Include the Palestinian Refugees in Lebanon?* Beirut: Ajial Statistics and Documentation Office.

Alterman, J.B. (1998) *New Media, New Politics? From Satellite Television to the Internet in the Arab World*. Washington, DC: Washington Institute for Near East Policy.

Anderson B. (1991) *Imagined Communities: Reflections on the Origin and Spread of Nationalism*. London: Verso.

_____ (2001) 'Western nationalism and Eastern nationalism: is there a difference that matters?' *New Left Review*, Vol. 9, May/June, pp. 31–42.

_____ and Kligman, G. (1992) *Long-distance Nationalism: World Capitalism and the Rise of Identity Politics*. Berkeley, CA: Center for German and European Studies, University of California.

Anderson, J.W. (1999) 'Technology, media, and the next generation in the

Middle East'. Paper presented at the Middle East Institute, Columbia University, New York.

_____ (2001) 'New media in the Muslim world: the emerging public sphere'. *ISIM Review*, No. 5, p. 39.

Anderson, P. (2001) 'Scurrying towards Bethlehem'. *New Left Review*, Vol. 10, No. 10, pp. 5–30.

Andoni, G. (2001) 'A comparative study of Intifada 1987 and Intifada 2000'. In Carey (ed.) *The New Intifada*, pp. 209–18.

Aouragh, M. (2003) 'Cyber Intifada and Palestinian identity'. *ISIM Review*, No. 12, pp. 42–3.

_____ (2004) 'Palestine Online: Palestinian identity in cyberspace'. Paper presented at the 25th IAMCR Conference, American University in Cairo, 23–28 July.

_____ (2008a) *Palestine Online: Cyber Intifada and the Construction of a Virtual Community 2001–2005*. Unpublished PhD thesis, University of Amsterdam.

_____ (2009) 'Virtual Intifada: online activism and everyday resistance'. *Journal of Arab and Muslim Media Research*, Vol. 1, No. 2, pp. 109–30.

_____ (2009) 'Immobility and the Palestinian diaspora: crossing borders between virtual and territorial spaces'. In Husseini, J. and Signoles, A. (eds). Paris: Institut des Hautes Études.

_____ (forthcoming) 'Cyber Intifada: Palestinian and Lebanese activism and the use of Web 2.0'.

Appadurai, A. (1996) *Modernity at Large: Cultural Dimensions of Globalization*. Minneapolis, MN: University of Minnesota Press.

Armbrust, W. (ed.) (2000) *Mass Mediations: New Approaches to Popular Culture in the Middle East and Beyond*. Berkeley, CA: University of California Press.

Armbruster, Hedi and Lærke, Anna (2008) *Taking Sides: Ethics, Politics, and Fieldwork in Anthropology*. New York: Berghahn.

Artz, L., Macek, S. and Cloud, D.L. (eds.) (2006) *Marxism and Communication Studies: The Point Is to Change It*. New York: Peter Lang.

Aruri, N.H. (2001) *Palestinian Refugees: The Right of Return*. London: Pluto.

Baramki, G. (2010) *Peaceful Resistance: Building a Palestinian University under Occupation*. London: Pluto.

Baudrillard, J. (1994) *Simulacra and Simulation*. Ann Arbor, MI: University of Michigan Press.

Baumann, G. (1999) *The Multicultural Riddle: Rethinking National, Ethnic, and Religious Identities*. New York: Routledge.

_____ (2007) 'An ethics of duplicity: critiquing the concept of integration in times of globalization'. Paper presented at *Cool Passion: The Political Theology of Conviction* conference. Amsterdam: ASSR, University of Amsterdam.

Baumgarten, H. (2005) 'The three faces/phases, of Palestinian nationalism, 1948–2005'. *Journal of Palestine Studies*, Vol. 34, No. 4, pp. 25–48.

Becker, H.S. (1998) *Tricks of the Trade*. Chicago, IL: University of Chicago Press.

Beckles, C.A. (2001) 'Black liberation and the internet: a strategic analysis'. *Journal of Black Studies*, Vol. 31, No. 3, pp. 311–24.

Benschop, A. (2006) *Chronicle of a Political Murder Foretold: Internet and Jihad in the Netherlands*. Utrecht: FORUM, Instituut voor Multiculturele Ontwikkeling.

van den Bos, M. (2006) 'Hyperlinked Dutch-Iranian cyberspace'. *International Sociology*, Vol. 21, No. 1, pp. 83–99.

Brenner, R. (2003) 'Towards the precipice'. *London Review of Books*, Vol. 25, No. 3, pp. 15–22.

Brouwer, L. (2004) 'Het Amsterdams computer clubhuis: creatief met computers'. In de Haan, J. and Klumper, O. (eds) *In Beleid in Praktijk*. Amsterdam: Boom, pp. 141–57.

Bruckner, M. (2001) 'IslamiCity: creating an Islamic cybersociety'. *ISIM Review*, No. 8, p. 17.

Budeiri, M. (1997) 'The Palestinians: tensions between nationalist and religious identities'. In Jankowski, J.P. and Gershoni, I. (eds.) *Rethinking Nationalism in the Arab Middle East*. New York: Columbia University Press.

Bunt, G.R. (2000) *Virtually Islamic: Computer-Mediated Communication and Cyber Islamic Environments*. Cardiff: University of Wales Press.

_____ (2003) *Islam in the Digital Age*. New York: Pluto.

Burkhart, G.E. and Older, S. (2003) *The Information Revolution in the Middle East and North Africa*. Santa Monica, CA: RAND National Defence Research Institute. Available at <*http://www.rand.org/publications/MR/MR1653*>. (Last accessed 2006).

Calhoun, C.J. (1992) *Habermas and the Public Sphere*. Boston, MA: MIT Press.

Callinicos, A. (1989) *Against Postmodernism*. Cambridge: Polity.

_____ (1995) *Theories and Narratives: Reflections on the Philosophy of History*. Cambridge: Polity.

Camfield, D. (2007) 'The multitude and the kangaroo: a critique of Hardt and Negri's theory of immaterial labour'. *Historical Materialism*, Vol. 15, No. 2, pp. 21–52.

Carey, J.W. (2005) 'Historical pragmatism and the internet'. *New Media & Society*, Vol. 7, No. 4, pp. 443–55.

Castells, M. (1996) *The Rise of the Network Society*. Cambridge, MA: Blackwell.

_____ (1997) *The Power of Identity*. Malden, MA: Blackwell.

_____ (1998) *End of Millennium*. Malden, MA: Blackwell.

_____ (2001) *The Internet Galaxy: Reflections on the Internet, Business, and*

Society. Oxford and New York: Oxford University Press.

de Certeau, M. (1984) *The Practice of Everyday Life*. Berkeley, CA: University of California Press.

Chomsky, N. (1999) *Fateful Triangle: The United States, Israel, and the Palestinians*. Boston, MA: South End.

Cliff, T. (2000) *Marxism at the Millennium*. London: Bookmark.

Cvetkovich, A. and Kellner, D. (1997) *Articulating the Global and the Local: Globalization and Cultural Studies*. Boulder, CO: Westview.

Dahan, M. (2003) 'Between a rock and a hard place: the changing public sphere of Palestinian Israelis'. *Journal of Computer-Mediated Communications*, Vol. 8, No. 2.

Davis, M. (2006) *Planet of Slums*. London: Verso.

Dawson, L. (2003) *Networked Individualism and the Possibility of Virtual Diasporic Religious Communities: Seeking Conceptual Clarity*. Goteborg: Goteborg University.

Dor, D. (2004) *Intifada Hits the Headlines: How the Israeli Press Misreported the Outbreak of the Second Palestinian Uprising*. Bloomington, IN: Indiana University Press.

Downey, J. and Fenton, N. (2003) 'New media, counter-publicity and the public sphere'. *New Media and Society*, Vol. 5, No. 2, pp. 185–202.

Eagleton, T. (2004) *After Theory*. London: Penguin.

Eickelman, D. and Anderson, J. (eds) (2003a) *New Media in the Muslim World: The Emerging Public Sphere*. Bloomington, IN: Indiana University Press.

_____ (2003b) 'Redefining Muslim publics'. In Eickelman and Anderson (eds) *New Media in the Muslim World*, pp. 1–18.

Eickelman, D. and Salvatore, A. (2001) 'Public sphere and Muslim identities'. Paper presented at *Media, Religion, and the Public Sphere* conference. Amsterdam: ASSR-ISIM.

Ellis, D., Oldridge, R. and Vasconcelos, A. (2004) 'Community and virtual community'. *Annual Review of Information Science and Technology*, Vol. 38, pp. 145–86. Medford, NJ: Information Today.

Enteen, J. (2006) 'Spatial conceptions of URLs: Tamil Eelam networks on the world wide web'. *New Media & Society*, Vol. 8, No. 2, pp. 229–49.

Eriksen, T.H. (1993) *Ethnicity and Nationalism: Anthropological Perspectives*. New York: Pluto.

_____ (2006) *Nations in Cyberspace*. Ernest Gellner lecture, delivered at the ASEN conference, London School of Economics, 27 March.

Essed, P. and Nimako, K. (2006) 'Designs and (co)incidents: cultures of scholarship and public policy on immigrants/minorities in the Netherlands'. *International Journal of Comparative Sociology*, Vol. 47, No. 3/4, pp. 281–312.

Etzioni, A. and Etzioni, O. (1997) 'Communities: virtual vs. real. *Science*, Vol.

277. No. 5324, p. 295.

Evans, A. (2002) *This Virtual Life: Escapism and Simulation in Our Media World*. London: Fusion.

Eynon, R., Fry, J. and Schroeder, R. (2008) 'The ethics of internet research'. In Fielding, N.G., Lee, R.M. and Blank, G. (eds) *The Sage Handbook of Online Research Methods*. London: Sage, pp. 23–41.

Featherstone, M. and Lash, S. (1995) 'Globalization, modernity and the spatialization of social theory: an introduction', in Featherstone, M. (eds), Global Modernities, Sage, London, pp.1-14.

Feenberg, A. and Bakardjieva, M. (2004) 'Virtual community: no killer implication'. *New Media & Society*, Vol. 6, No. 1, pp. 37–43.

Fekete, L. (2006) 'Enlightened fundamentalism? Immigration, feminism and the 'right'. *Race & Class* 48, No. 2, pp. 1–22.

Fekete, L. (2009) *A Suitable Enemy: Racism, Migration and Islamophobia in Europe*. Sidmouth: Pluto.

Fenton, N. (2000) 'Problematics of postmodernism for feminist media studies'. *Media, Culture and Society*, Vol. 22, No. 6, pp. 723–41.

Ferguson, J. (1990) *The Anti-Politics Machine: 'Development,' Depoliticization, and Bureaucratic Power in Lesotho*. Cambridge: Cambridge University Press.

Forte, T. (2003a) 'Consuming projects in uncertain times: making selves in the Galilee. *Journal of Historical Sociology*, Vol. 16, No. 3, pp. 349–74.

_____ (2003b) 'Sifting people, sorting papers: academic practice and the notion of state security in Israel'. *Comparative Studies of South Asia, Africa and the Middle East*, Vol. 23, No. 1/2, pp. 215–23.

Franklin, M. (2004) *Postcolonial Politics, The Internet, and Everyday Life: Pacific Traversals Online*. London and New York: Routledge.

Giacaman, R., Abdullah, A., Abu Safieh, R. and Shamieh, L. (2002) *Schooling at Gunpoint: Palestinian Children's Learning Environment in War-like Conditions*. Ramallah: Institute of Community and Public Health, Birzeit University, at <*http://icph.birzeit.edu/Monograph.htm*>. (Last accessed 2005).

Gilroy, P. (1991) 'It ain't where you're from, it's where you're at: the dialectics of diasporic identification'. *Third Text*, Vol. 13, (Spring), pp. 3–16.

González, Roberto J. (2008) 'Human terrain: past, present and future applications'. *Anthropology Today*, Vol. 24, No. 1, pp. 21-6.

González-Quijano, Y. (2003) 'The birth of a media ecosystem: Lebanon in the internet age'. In Eickelman and Anderson (eds) *New Media in the Muslim World*, pp. 61–79.

Graham, S. 2001. Information Technologies and Reconfigurations of Urban Space. *International Journal of Urban and Regional Research*. Vol 25. No. 2, pp. 405–10.

Gramsci, A. (1978) *Selections from Political Writings 1921–1926*. London:

Lawrence & Wishart.

Gregory, D. (2004) *The Colonial Present: Afghanistan, Palestine, Iraq*. Oxford: Blackwell.

Griffiths, M. (2000) 'Does internet and computer "addiction" exist? Some case-study evidence'. *CyberPsychology & Behavior*, Vol. 3, pp. 211–18.

Guarnizo, L. and Smith, M.P. (1998) *Transnationalism from Below*. London: Transaction.

Habermas, J. (1992) 'Further reflections on the public sphere'. In Calhoun, C.J. (ed.) *Habermas and the Public Sphere*. Cambridge, MA: MIT Press.

HaCohen, Ran (2001) 'Say no to a Palestinian "state"'. At <*http://www.antiwar.com/hacohen/h111301.html*>. (Last accessed 2005).

Hafez, K. (ed.) (2001) *Mass Media, Politics, and Society in the Middle East*. New York: Hampton.

Hagopian, E.C., Aruri, N.H. and Abu Khalil, A. (1985) *Amal and the Palestinians: Understanding the Battle of the Camps*. Belmont, MA: Association of Arab-American University Graduates.

Hall, S. (1990) 'Cultural identity and diaspora'. In Rutherford, J. (ed.) *Identity: Community, Culture, Difference*. London: Lawrence & Wishart, pp. 222–37.

_____ (1992a) 'Cultural studies and its theoretical legacies'. In Grossberg, L., Nelson, C. and Treichler, P. *Cultural Studies*. New York and London: Routledge, pp. 277–94.

_____ (1992b) 'New ethnicities'. In Donald, J. and Rattansi, A. (eds) *Race, Culture and Difference*. London: Sage and Open University Press, pp. 252–59.

Halileh, S. and Giacaman, R. (2002) 'Distance learning: an educational survival strategy in war-like conditions at the Institute of Community and Public Health'. Available at <*http://icph.birzeit.edu/Monograph.htm*> (Last accessed 2005).

Hallward, P. (2004) 'Haitian inspiration'. *Radical Philosophy*, No. 123 (January–February). At <*http://www.radicalphilosophy.com/default.asp?channel_id=2187&editorial_id=14344*>.

Hammami, R. (1997) 'From immodesty to collaboration: Hamas, the women's movement, and national identity in the Intifada'. In Benin, J. and Stork, J. (eds) *Political Islam: Essays from the Middle East Report*. London: Tauris, pp. 194–210.

Hamzeh, M. (2001) 'Dahaysha diary: a view from the camp'. *Journal of Palestine Studies*, Vol. 30, No. 2, pp. 41–60.

Hannam, K., Sheller, M. and Urry, J. (2006) 'Mobilities, immobilities, and moorings'. *Mobilities*, Vol. 1, No. 1, pp. 1–22.

Hanafi, S. (2001) 'Reshaping geography: Palestinian community networks in Europe and the new media'. Paper presented at *The Second Mediterranean Social and Political Research Meeting*. Florence: European University Institute.

_____ (2005) 'Reshaping geography: Palestinian community networks in

Europe and the new media'. *Journal of Ethnic and Migration Studies*, Vol. 31, No. 3, pp. 581–98.

Hanieh, A. (1999) 'The www in Palestine: an informational and organizing tool'. *Middle East Report*, Vol. 41, No. 213, pp. 41-3.

_____ (2007) 'The dynamics of Palestinian networks on the internet: a study of online political discussions during the 2006 Palestinian Legislative Council elections. Paper for *Palestine Internet Society Project.*

Hannerz, U. (1980) *Exploring the City: Inquiries Toward an Urban Anthropology*. New York: Columbia University Press.

_____ (1998) 'Transnational research'. In Bernard, H.R. (ed.) *Handbook of Methods in Anthropology*. Walnut Creek, CA: Altamira.

Haraway, D. (1991) *Simians, Cyborgs and Women: The Reinvention of Nature*. New York: Routledge.

Hardt, M. and Negri, A. (2000) *Empire*. Cambridge, MA, and London: Harvard University Press.

_____ (2004) *Multitude: War and Democracy in the Age of Empire*. New York: Penguin.

Harvey, D. (1991) *The Condition of Postmodernity: An Enquiry into the Origins of Cultural Change.* Oxford: Wiley-Blackwell.

_____ (1993) 'From space to place and back again: reflections on the condition of postmodernity'. In Bird, J., Cutris, B., Putnam, T. and Tickner, T. (eds) *Mapping the Future: Local Cultures, Global Change*. London: Routledge, pp. 3–29.

Hassan, S.D. (2003) 'Nation validation: modern Palestinian literature and the politics of appeasement'. *Social Text*, Vol. 21, No. 275, pp. 7–23.

Hine, C. (2000) *Virtual Ethnography*. London: Sage.

Hroub, K. (2006) *Hamas: A Beginner's Guide*. London and Ann Arbor, MI: Pluto.

James, C.L.R. (1980) *The Black Jacobins: Toussaint L'Ouverture and the San Domingo Revolution*. London: Allison & Busby.

Jones, S.G. (1995) 'Understanding community in the information age'. In Jones (ed.) *Cybersociety: Computer-Mediated Communication and Community*. Thousand Oaks, CA: Sage, pp. 10–35.

_____ (1999) *Doing Internet Research: Critical Issues and Methods for Examining the Net*. Thousand Oaks , CA: Sage.

Kalir, B. (2006) *Christian Aliens in the Jewish State*. Unpublished PhD thesis, University of Amsterdam.

Kellner, D. (1998) 'Globalization and the postmodern turn'. In R. Axtmann (ed.) *Globalization and Europe*. London: Cassells. pp23–42.

_____ (2002) 'Theorizing globalization'. *Sociological Theory*, Vol. 20, No. 3 pp. 285–305.

Khalidi, R. (1997) *Palestinian Identity: The Construction of Modern National Consciousness*. New York: Columbia University Press.

Khalili, L. (2004) 'Grass-roots commemorations: remembering the land in the camps of Lebanon'. *Journal of Palestine Studies*, Vol. 34, No. 1, pp. 6–22.

Khawaja, M., Pedersen, J. and Randell, S. (2001) *Growing Fast: The Palestinian Population in the West Bank and Gaza Strip*. Oslo: FAFO

Khawaja, M. and Tiltnes, Å.A. (2002) *On the Margins: Migration and Living Conditions of Palestinian Camp Refugees in Jordan*. Oslo: FAFO

Khosravi, S. (2000) 'www.iranian.com an ethnographic approach to an online diaspora'. *ISIM Review* (newsletter), No. 6, pp. 13–14.

Kimmerling, B. (2000) 'The formation of Palestinian collective identities: the Ottoman and Mandatory periods'. *Middle Eastern Studies*, Vol. 36, No. 2, pp. 48–81.

_____(2003) *Politicide: Ariel Sharon's war against the Palestinians*. London: Verso.

_____ and Migdal, J.S. (1993) *Palestinians: The Making of a People*. New York: Free Press.

Kirchner, H. (2001) 'Internet in the Arab world: a step towards "Information Society?"' In Hafez (ed.) *Mass Media, Politics, and Society in the Middle East*. New Jersey: Hampton Press.

Kohan, N. (2005) 'Postmodernity, commodity fetishism and hegemony'. *International Socialism* , No. 105, pp. 139-58.

Koning, A. de, (2009) *Global Dreams, Class, Gender, and Public Space in Cosmopolitan Cairo*. Cairo: American University in Cairo Press.

Lægran, A.S. and Stewart J. (2003) 'Nerdy, trendy or healthy? Configuring the internet cafe'. *New Media & Society*, Vol. 5, No. 3, pp. 357–77.

Landon, S.N. (2009) *Education, Technology and Conflict: The Use and Perceptions of the Internet in Palestinian Higher Education*. Unpublished MSc dissertation, Oxford University.

Landzelius, K. (2002) 'Mapping the unfathomable frontiers of indigenous cyberspace: a survey of the expanding/contracting boundaries of going native on the net'. In Arvastson, G. (ed.) *IT Users and Producers in an Evolving Sociocultural Context*. Uppsala: Uppsala University Press, pp. 41–50.

Langlois, J.L. (2005) 'Celebrating Arabs'. *Journal of American Folklore*, Vol. 118, No. 468, pp. 219–36.

Larkin, B. (2002) 'The materiality of cinema theaters in Northern Nigeria'. In Abu-Lughod et al. (eds) *Media Worlds*, pp. 319–36.

Liff, S. and Lægran, A.S. (2003) 'Cybercafes: debating the meaning and significance of internet access in a cafe environment'. *New Media and Society*, Vol. 5, No. 3, pp. 307–12.

Liff, S. and Steward, F. (2003) 'Shaping e-access in the cybercafe: networks, boundaries and heterotopian innovation'. *New Media and Society*, Vol. 5, No. 3, pp. 313–34.

Locksley, G. (2000) 'An information technology strategy for the web economy in the West Bank and Gaza'. *Palestine-Israel Journal of Politics, Economics and Culture*, Vol. 7, No. 1/2, pp. 145–52.

Luyendijk, J. (2006) *Het zijn net mensen* . Uitgeverij Podium.

Madaville, P. (1999) 'Digital Islam: changing boundaries of religious knowledge?' *ISIM Review*, No. 2, p. 23.

Magpantay, E. (2003) *Measuring the Arab Region's Information Society*. Paper presented at the Fifth Annual Meeting on Telecommunication Development in the Arab Region. Beirut, Lebanon. 28–31 May. At: <*www.itu.int/ITU-D/ict/papers/2003/Measuring%20Arab%20States%20IS.ppt* >. (Last accessed 2005).

Mahmood, S. (2005) *Politics of Piety: The Islamic Revival and the Feminist Subject*. Princeton, NJ: Princeton University Press.

Mansell, R. (2004) 'Political economy, power and new media'. *New Media Society*, Vol. 6, No. 1, pp. 96–105.

Marcus, G.E. (1995) 'Ethnography in/of the world system: the emergence of multi-sited ethnography'. *Annual Review of Anthropology*, Vol. 24, pp. 95–117.

Masalha, N. (1992) *Expulsion of the Palestinians: The Concept of 'Transfer' in Zionist Political Thought, 1882–1948*. Washington, DC: Institute for Palestine Studies.

_____ (2003) *The Politics of Denial: Israel and the Palestinian Refugee Problem*. London: Pluto.

_____ (ed.) (2005) *Catastrophe Remembered: Palestine, Israel and the Internal Refugees. Essays in Memory of Edward W. Said (1935–2003)*. London: Zed Books.

Mazarella, W. (2007) 'The myth of the multitude: rethinking the crowd'. Paper presented at *Cool Passion: The Political Theology of Conviction*. Conference Amsterdam: Amsterdam School of Social Science Research, University of Amsterdam

McLaughlin, L. and Pickard, V. (2005) 'What is bottom-up about global internet governance?' *Global Media and Communication*, Vol. 1, No. 3, pp. 357–73.

McMillan, S.J. (2002) 'A four-part model of cyber-interactivity: some cyber-places are more interactive than others'. *New Media & Society*, Vol. 4, No. 2, p. 271-91.

Meyer, B. (2000) 'Modern mass media, religion, and the imagination of communities: different postcolonial trajectories in West Africa, Brazil, the Caribbean, and India'. Amsterdam: PIONIER Project.

_____ (2001) 'Religion, media, and the public sphere'. Paper presented at the ISIM and ASSR Conference, University of Amsterdam (.PIONIER Project).

_____ and Moors, A. (2006) *Religion, Media, and the Public Sphere*. Bloomington, IN: Indiana University Press.

Miller, D. and Slater, D. (2000) *The Internet: An Ethnographic Approach*. Oxford: Berg.

Miller, H. (1995) 'The presentation of self in electronic life: Goffman on the internet'. At <*http://www.ntu.ac.uk/soc/psych/miller/goffman.htm*>. (Last accessed 2002).

_____ and Mather, R. (1998) 'The presentation of self in www home pages'. Paper presented at IRISS '1998 Conference, Bristol.

Miladi, N. (2003) 'Mapping the Al-Jazeera phenomenon'. In Thussu, D.K. and Freedman, D. (eds) *War and the Media*. London: Sage.

Mitchell, T. (2003) 'The Middle East in the past and future of social science'. University of California International and Area Studies Digital Collection *MIT-IJMES* (1). At: <*http://web.mit.edu/cis/www/mitejmes/intro.htm*>. (Last accessed 2007).

Moors, A. (1995) *Women, Property and Islam: Palestinian Experiences, 1920-1990*. Cambridge: Cambridge University Press

_____ (2004) *Muslim Cultural Politics: What's Islam Got to Do With It?* Amsterdam: Vossius.

_____ Teeffelen, T. van, Abu Ghazaleh, I. and Kanaana, S. (1995) *Discourse and Palestine: Power, Text and Context*. Amsterdam: Het Spinhuis.

Morris, B. (1987) *The Birth of the Palestinian Refugee Problem, 1947–1949*. Cambridge: Cambridge University Press.

Nakhleh, K. and Zureik, E. (1980) *The Sociology of the Palestinians*. London: Croom Helm.

Narayan, K. (1993) 'How native is a "native" anthropologist?' *American Anthropologist* (new series) Vol. 95, No. 3, pp. 671–86.

Nunes, M. (2006) *Cyberspaces of Everyday Life*. Minneapolis, MN: University of Minnesota Press.

Oldenburg, R. (1999) *Great Good Place*. San Francisco, CA: Marlowe.

Open Arab Internet (2006) 'Arabic blogs: an embodiment of freedom of expression'. At: <*http://www.openarab.net/'en/reports/net2006/blogger.shtm*>. (Last Accessed 2007).

Pappé, I. (1988) *Britain and the Arab-Israeli Conflict, 1948–51*. Basingstoke: Macmillan, in association with St Antony's College, Oxford.

_____ (1992) *The Making of the Arab-Israeli Conflict, 1947–51*. London and New York: Tauris and St Martin's.

Parry, N. (1997) 'The past and future of information technology in Palestine: an introduction for the Palestinian NGO community'. Paper presented at the International NGO Meeting/European NGO Symposium on 'The Question of Palestine', United Nations.

_____ (1998) 'Permission to narrate'. *Middle East International*, No. 567 (January).

_____ (1999) 'Palestinian sites proliferate'. *Middle East International*, No. 593 (February).

Philo, G. and Berry, M. (2004) *Bad News from Israel.* Sterling, VA, and London: Pluto.
Plascov, A. (1981) *The Palestinian Refugees in Jordan 1948–1957.* London: Routledge.
Rheingold, H. (1991) *Virtual Reality.* New York: Summit Books.
_____ (1993) *The Virtual Community: Homesteading on the Electronic Frontier.* Reading, MA: Addison-Wesley.
_____ (1999) 'The new interactivism: a manifesto for the information age'. At: <*http://www.rheingold.com/*>. Last accessed 2002).
Rogers, R. (2002) 'The politics of webspace'. At: <*www.govcom.org/publications/*>. (Last accessed 2004).
Rose, J. (2004) *The Myths of Zionism.* London: Pluto.
Sa'di, A.H. (2002) 'Catastrophe, memory and identity'. *Israel Studies*, Vol. 7, No. 2, pp. 175–98.
Safieh, A. (1997) *Children of a Lesser God?* London: Palestinian General Delegation.
Said, E. (1979) *Orientalism.* New York: Vintage.
_____ (1984) 'Permission to narrate' . *Journal of Palestine Studies*, Vol. 13, No. 3, pp. 27–48.
_____ (1996) *Peace and its Discontents: Essays on Palestine in the Middle East Peace Process.* New York: Vintage.
_____ (1999) *Out of Place: A Memoir.* New York: Knopf.
_____ (2001a) 'America's last taboo'. In Carey (ed.) *The New Intifada*, pp. 259–68.
_____ (2001b) 'Palestinians under siege'. In Carey (ed.) *The New Intifada*, pp. 27-44.
_____ (2001c) *The End of the Peace Process: Oslo and After.* New York: Vintage.
Salibi, K. (1998) *A House of Many Mansions: The History of Lebanon Reconsidered.* London: Tauris.
Saloul, I. (2008) *Telling Memories: Al-Nakba in Palestinian Exilic Narratives.* Unpublished PhD thesis, University of Amsterdam.
Sartawi, T. (2003) *Profile of the Information Society in the Palestinian Authority.* United Nations Economic and Social Commission for Western Asia.
Sayigh, R. (1979) *Palestinians: From Peasants to Revolutionaries: A People's History.* London: Zed Books.
_____ 1993. *Too Many Enemies: The Palestinian Experience in Lebanon.* London: Zed Books.
Sayigh, Y. (1997) *Armed Struggle and the Search for State: The Palestinian National Movement, 1949–1993.* Oxford and New York: Clarendon.
Scheper-Hughes, N. (1992) *Death Without Weeping: The Violence of Everyday Life in Brazil.* Berkeley, CA: University of California Press.
Schulz, H.L. (1999) *The Reconstruction of Palestinian Nationalism: Between Revolution and Statehood.* Manchester: Manchester University Press.

Shaheen, J.G. (2001) *Reel Bad Arabs: How Hollywood Vilifies a People*. New York: Olive Branch.

Shiblak, A., and Rempel, T. 'Palestinian displacement: a case apart?' *Forced Migration Review*. Special issue on Palestinian refugees. No. 26 (August). University of Oxford.

Shlaim, A. (1995) *War and Peace in the Middle East: A Concise History*. Harmondsworth: Penguin.

_____ (1998) *The Politics of Partition: King Abdullah, the Zionists, and Palestine, 1921–1951*. New York: Oxford University Press.

Shohat, E. (1989) *Israeli Cinema: East/West and the Politics of Representation*. Austin, TX: University of Texas Press.

Soueif, A. (2001) 'Under the gun: a Palestinian journey'. In Carey (ed.) *The New Intifada*, pp. 45–68.

Sparks, C. (2007) *Development, Globalization and the Media*. London: Sage.

Stevenson, N. (1995) *Understanding Media Cultures: Social Theory and Mass Communication*.London:Sage.

Stockl, A. (2003) 'The internet, cyberspace and anthropology'. *Cambridge Anthropology*, Vol. 23, No. 3, pp. 67–78.

Strathern, M. (2000/2001) 'Virtual society? Get real! Abstraction or decontextualisation: an anthropological comment: or e for ethnography'. Vol. 22, No. 1, pp. 52–66.

Swedenburg, T. (1992) 'Seeing double: Palestinian/American histories of the Kufiya'. *Michigan Quarterly Review*, Vol. 31, No. 4, pp. 557–77.

Takkenberg, L. (1998) *The Status of Palestinian Refugees in International Law*. Oxford: Clarendon Press.

Tarazi, M. (2001) 'The Palestinian Status of Information Technology'. Unpublished.

Tawil-Souri, H. (2007) 'Move over Bangalore: here comes ... Palestine? Western funding and "internet development"' in the shrinking Palestinian state'. In Chakravartty, Paula and Zhao, Yuezhi (eds) *Global Communications: Toward a Transcultural Political Economy*. Boulder, CO: Rowman & Littlefield, pp. 263–84.

_____ (2008) 'Americanizing Palestine through internet development. In Goggin, Gerard and McLelland, Mark (eds) *Internationalizing Internet Studies*. London: Routledge, pp. 32–47.

Taylor, J. (1997) 'The emerging geographies of virtual worlds'. *Geographical Review*, Vol. 87, No. 2, pp. 172–92.

Terranova, T. (2004) *Network Culture: Politics for the Information Age*. Ann Arbor, MI, and London: Pluto.

Thelwall, M. 2008a. Quantitative comparisons of search engine results. *Journal of the American Society for Information Science and Technology*. Vol. 59. No. 11, pp. 1702–10.

_____ 2008b. How are social network sites embedded in the web? An exploratory link analysis. *Cybermetrics*. Vol. 12, No. 1, paper1.

Thompson, A. (2001) 'Nations, national identities and human agency: putting people back into nations'. *Sociological Review*, Vol. 49, No. 1, pp. 18–32.

Turkle, S. (1995) *Life on the Screen: Identity in the Age of the Internet.* New York: Simon & Schuster.

United Nations Development Programme (2003) *Programme of Assistance to the Palestinian People: Information and Communication Technology, United Nations Development Programme.* At: *<http://www.papp.undp.org/en/focusareas/ict/it.html>*. (Last accessed 2005).

Vertovec, S. (1999) 'Conceiving and researching transnationalism'. *Ethnic and Racial Studies*, Vol. 22, No. 2, pp. 447–62.

_____ (2001) 'Transnationalism and identity'. *Journal of Ethnic and Migration Studies*, Vol. 27, No. 4, pp. 573–83.

Waked, M. (2005) 'The maze of ICT indicators: the case of Palestine'. In Zureik, E. (ed.) *Information Society in Palestine: The Human Capital Dimension.* Report Submitted to the International Development Research Centre in Ottawa. Ottawa: International Development Research Centre.

Warner, M. (2002) 'Publics and counterpublics'. *Public Culture*, Vol. 14, No. 1, pp. 49–90.

Wayne, M. (2003) *Marxism and Media Studies: Key Concepts and Comparative Trends*. London: Pluto.

Wellman, B. (2004) 'The three ages of internet studies: ten, five and zero years ago'. *New Media & Society*, Vol. 6, No. 1, pp. 108-14.

_____ and Hampton, K. (1999) 'Living networked on and offline'. *Contemporary Sociology*, Vol. 28, No. 6, pp. 648–54.

_____ and Haythornthwaite, C. (2002) *The Internet in Everyday Life*. Oxford: Blackwell.

Wheeler, D. (2003) 'The internet and youth subculture in Kuwait'. *Journal of Computer-Mediated Communication*, Vol. 8, No. 2, pp. 148-63.

_____ (2006) 'Empowering publics: information technology and democratization in the Arab world – lessons from internet cafes and beyond'. Paper presented at the Annual Meeting of the International Studies Association, San Diego, CA.

Wilson, M.C. (1990) *King Abdullah, Britain and the Making of Jordan.* Cambridge: Cambridge University Press.

Wyatt, S. (2008) 'Technological determinism is dead: long live technological determinism'. In Hackett, E.J., Amsterdamska, O., Lynch, M. and Wajcman, J. (eds) *The Handbook of Science & Technology Studies*. Cambridge, MA: MIT Press, pp. 165–80.

Widyanto, L., & Griffiths, M. (2006). 'Internet addiction: A critical Review'. *International Journal of Mental Health and Addiction*. No. 4, pp. 31-51.

Zelaky, E., Eid, G. and Sami, S. (eds) (2006) *Implacable Adversaries: Arab Governments and the Internet*. Cairo: Arabic Network for Human Rights

Information.
Žižek, S. (1998) 'Cyberspace, or, how to traverse the fantasy in the age of the retreat of the big other'. *Public Culture*, Vol. 10, No. 3, pp. 483–513.
Zook, M. (2006) 'The geographies of the internet'. *Annual Review of Information Science and Technology*, Vol. 40, pp. 53–78.
Zureik, E. (1994) 'Palestinian refugees and peace'. *Journal of Palestine Studies*, Vol. 24, No. 1, pp. 5–17.
_____ (ed.) (2005) *Information Society in Palestine: The Human Capital Dimension, a Report Submitted to the International Development Research Centre in Ottawa*. Ottawa: International Development Research Centre.

News sources

Ascherman, Arik W. (2009) 'We never know what little act will tip the scales'. *Rabbis for Human Rights, and the Current Violence*, 12 January, at *<http://www.rhr.org.il>*. (Last, accessed February 2009).
Bahaa, Sherine (2003) 'Cyber Islam'. *Al-Ahram Weekly*, 27 February–5 March.
Bahour, Sam (1998) 'Telecommunications in Palestine: growing pains'. Unpublished.
_____ (2001) 'Palestinian private sector information technology policy study'. Ramallah: PalTrade.
_____ (2006) 'We can't go home again', at *<http://www.amin.org/look/amin/en.tpl?IdLanguage=1&IdPublication=7&NrArticle=37435&NrIssue=1&NrSection=3.%20Arab%20Media%20Internet%20Network>*. (Last accessed 9 September 2006).
Baroud, Ramzy (2002) 'The internet is not Occupied Territories'. *Arabia.com*, 7 August, at *<http://www.mafhoum.com/press3/108T44.html>*. (Last accessed 2003).
BBC News 20 November 2006. 'Egypt Arrests Another Blog Critic', At *<http://news.bbc.co.uk/2/hi/middle_east/6164798.stml>*.
Blanford, Nicholas (2003) 'Al-Aqsa cells being funded and guided from Ain al-Hilweh'. *The Daily Star* (Lebanon), 4 July.
Cisneros, Oscar (2001) 'Dot-ps: domain without a country', 1 December. At *<http://www.wired.com/politics/law/news/2001/01/41135>*.
Cohen, Catherine (2000a) 'Israel's supporters bombard the net for that feel-good fix'. *Ha'aretz*, 27 October.
_____ (2000b) 'Israeli web sites take on American disguise to fool cyber terrorists'. *Ha'aretz*, 10 November.
Cozens, Claire (2002) 'Israeli cable companies threaten to pull plug on CNN'. *The Guardian*, 2 August.
Clarke, Richard (2004) 'Nations using internet to spy'. Al-Jazeera English.
Dror, Yuval (2000a) 'Hackers disrupt NetVision service'. *Ha'aretz*, 25 October.
_____ (2000b) 'Crisis of Israeli internet sites intensifies'. *Ha'aretz*, 26 November.
El-Haddad, Laila (2003) 'Free Internet Palestine could have negative impact

on local ISPs'. *The Daily Star* (Lebanon), 16 December.

Fisk, Robert (2001) 'CNN caves in to Israel over its references to illegal settlements'. *The Independent*, 3 September.

_____ (2003) 'Web lets Palestinian children find world beyond refugee camp'. *The Independent*, 31 December.

The Guardian (2007) 'Egyptian blogger jailed for insulting Islam'. 22 February, at <*http://www.guardian.co.uk/technology/2007/feb/22/egypt.blogging*>.

Klein, Naomi (2002) 'Sharon's best weapon'. *In These Times*, 26 April, at <*http://www.inthesetimes.com/issue/26/13/feature2.shtml*>.

Lynn, Regina (2005) 'Beyond the dating database'. *Wired*, 11 March, at <*http://www.wired.com/culture/lifestyle/commentary/sexdrive/2005/03/66854*>.

Mahmoud, Fathi (2004) 'Pumping an internet café in Al-Helwa camp'. *Al-Ahram*, 30 December.

Mayton, Joseph (2006) 'Popular Egyptian blogger arrested'. *The Daily Star* (Egypt), 11 May.

McNeil K. (2002) 'The war on academic freedom'. *The Nation*, 25 November, at: <*http://www.thenation.com/doc/20021125/mcneil*>.

Monbiot, George (2005) 'Thanks to corporations, instead of democracy we get Baywatch'. *The Guardian*, 13 September.

Palestine Press News Agency (2006) 'Unidentified gunmen pump cyber cafe in Jabaliya', 10 September, at: <*http://www.palpress.ps/arabic/index.php?maa=ReadStory&ChannelID=51462*>.

Rohde, David (2007) 'Anthropologists help US Army in Afghanistan and Iraq'. *International Herald Tribune*, 4 August.

Rubinstein, Danny (2002) 'Survival strategy'. *Ha'aretz*, 5 February.

Saadi, Dania (2004) 'Lebanon tops Levant PC sales'. *The Daily Star* (Lebanon), 16 January.

Tcholakian, Garine (2004) 'Lebanese young men seem seduced by the internet cafe'. *The Daily Star* (Lebanon), 21 February.

Online sources

Committee to Protect Journalists, at:
www.cpj.org

UN Economic and Social Commission for Western Asia, at:
www.escwa.un.org/divisions/main.asp?division=ictd.

Initiative for an Open Arab Internet, at:
www.opennet.net

Information Warfare Monitor, at:
www.infowar-monitor.net/index.php.

International Data Corporation, at:
www.idc.com

International Telecommunication Union (World Telecommunication Report 2003), at:

www.itu.int/ITU-D/ict/publications/wtdr_03/
Middle East Internet Usage and Marketing Report, at:
www.internetworldstats.com/me/
United Nations Relief and Works Agency for Palestinian Refugees, at:
www.un.org/unrwa

INDEX